INNOVATION, ENTREPRENEURS AND REGIONAL DEVELOPMENT

This book is dedicated to the memory of the late Professor Al Shapero and to his wife Gitel.

INNOVATION, ENTREPRENEURS AND REGIONAL DEVELOPMENT

G. P. SWEENEY

Frances Pinter (Publishers), London

First published in 1987 by
Frances Pinter (Publishers) Limited
25 Floral Street, London WC2E 9DS

British Library Cataloguing in Publication Data
Sweeney, G. P.
Innovation, entrepreneurs and regional development.
1. Europe—Industries
338.94 HC240
ISBN 0-86187-647-4

Typeset by Joshua Associates Limited, Oxford
Printed by SRP Ltd, Exeter

Contents

List of Tables

List of Figures

Preface

Regional disparities in economic development have become a topic of increasing concern, and led to a re-orientation of the goals, instruments, substances and target groups of governmental action in many countries. To re-examine recent developments in regional innovation policies, their pre-conditions and effects, was the topic of a workshop of the Six Countries Programme on aspects of governmental policies towards technological innovation in industry. The Six Countries Programme is an informal club of governmental officials who have responsibility for innovation policy in their respective countries and scientists engaged in consultancy in innovation policy matters. The Six Countries Programme organises a Workshop on innovation policy matters twice a year with the purpose to discuss in an open atmosphere the aims, impacts and efficiency of innovation policies.

In November 1984, the Six Countries Programme held a Workshop on 'Innovation, entrepreneurship and regional development' in Limerick, Ireland. Mr Gerry Sweeney was in charge of organising the workshop and was subsequently commissioned to write a report which should not only summarize the papers and discussion of the Workshop but also present the state-of-the-art in this area. The result of that report and other work is this book.

Gerry Sweeney was formerly Assistant Director-General of the Irish Institute for Research and Standards and is now working as a consultant in the field of innovation management. He also serves as an advisor to the Commmission of the European Community and was the former Chairman of the Six Countries Programme.

His analysis focuses on the major determinants of regional economic growth and prosperity which are seen in the entrepreneurial vitality of a region, the regional innovation potential and the quality and intensiveness of information flow between firms. The role of the Six Countries Programme is to present a systemic view of recent developments and to suggest governmental action—when appropriate—in a systemic perspective, taking into account the interdependence of public and private action on all levels of an economy. The book contributes to the actual discussion by thoroughly analysing the role of small firms and their interaction with large ones, and by elaborating the role of technological knowledge as a source for regional innovation potentials.

Gerry Sweeney concludes his broad analysis with a systemic approach to the development of governmental policies to stimulate regional development.

Gerhard Braunling
Chairman, Six Countries Programme

Foreword

The original conception of this book lay in two projects. One was a study on 'Information networks designed to support technological innovation in less-favoured regions of the Community' carried out for the Commission of the European Communities. The other, initiated at about the same time, was to hold a Six Countries Programme Workshop on the topic 'Regional Innovation Policies and Programmes', in Limerick, Ireland, in November 1984.

It seemed that the two could be mutually reinforcing and that out of the knowledge and information accumulated a publication could be produced useful to both policy-makers and practitioners in the field. The specific orientation of the work for the Six Countries Programme was to set out a model system for a regional information programme, which would be the *sine qua non* of a regional innovation programme, and a first step which could be taken quickly whilst other programmes were being adopted or developed. This is set out in Chapter 9, but even though based on what was happening in several European countries (Chapter 8) and on more than twenty years of providing technical services to small firms, such a model programme had to be justified. Were the hypotheses correct? Undoubtedly from an information-seeking behaviour point of view (Chapters 5 and 6) they are. But were they from innovation, entrepreneurial and economic development viewpoints?

Hence, the first part of the book looks at various factors which appear to be much more critical to the support of economic growth than theories of monetarism, Keynesian-style demand or economies of scale. These seem now to be more barriers to growth than supports. In fact, entrepreneurial investment in innovation on which economic growth primarily depends is a very human and social process. In looking at the various factors which in practice seem to lead to entrepreneurship and innovation, one, the role of the customer, proved much stronger than originally envisaged. It seems to say that whether you are a firm or a regional economy you should never have as an initial or major customer a firm or a regional market which is not technically progressive. If you do, you will not compete internationally.

This is more of a social factor than an economic or technological one. Indeed, the justification for the kinds of social network-based services developing in Europe and the model system set out in Chapter 9, is that innovation, entrepreneurial investment and economic development do not happen unless there is a social environment of attitudes, of giving and receiving information and of stimulating creativity in others.

The role of the customer, and those of the educational system and information technology could each have been the ultimate focus of this book. They remain for another day.

This book in itself is part of the Six Countries Programme series of workshops and publications, and I am grateful to my colleagues in the Programme for the opportunity to write it. I am also very much indebted to D. G. XIII and D. G. XVI of the Commission of the European Communities for the opportunity to carry out work which is embodied in this publication. My thanks are also due to others who have stimulated further work on parts of this book.

Finally my thanks to Paula Mulhall who put together so many drafts, and to my wife Margaret who watched and suffered the long labour pains.

The dedication to the late Al Shapero and his wife Gitel is a small thanks for years of friendship, inspiration and information. He was one of the few people in the world who had a clear feel for the role of information and communication and the personal bonds in innovation, entrepreneurship and development. But then he had a real feel for people.

Gerry Sweeney

CHAPTER 1

Setting the Scene

A Less than National Phenomenon

Economic development is a less than national phenomenon—economic development, that is, in the sense of being able to generate and maintain economic prosperity from own resources. It happens in some places and not in others, in some localities at one corner of a country and not in any locality in another corner. The phenomenon can be observed everywhere. In every country one can see the differences between more prosperous and less prosperous regions, and in parts of the developed as well as the less developed world these differences can be striking. The regional problem is very real for many national governments but it also exists at a supranational level, as, for example, in the European Economic Community, and the main focus of this book is the regions of Europe and the EEC. The difference between the per capita income in 1982 of Denmark, 9,665 ECU, and Greece 3,861 ECU, and now of the latest member, Portugal, with 2,521 ECU, is very wide (*Eurostat Review*). OECD also has long been concerned with assistance to less-industrialised countries through its Technical Co-operation Division, less-industrialised and less-developed in terms of the nation-state members of OECD. Therein lies the illusion that there is such an entity as a national economy. The phrase 'less-industrialised country' or 'less-developed country' really means that a country has no regions able to generate growth from within themselves.

If one looks at the most prosperous state of the European Community, Denmark, one perceives differences in prosperity between the citizens of the capital, Copenhagen, and those of the island of Bornholm. Ireland shows considerable difference, and that at a lower level of prosperity, between Dublin and Mayo, a county in the west of the country. Probably the best-known contrast between two parts of any country is that between the north and south of Italy. The products, crafts and technologies of the north have international recognition and markets. The south languishes in a continuum of poverty, a labour pool for the north and beyond when times were good, but unable to generate its own means of survival in spite of national and EEC projects and aids.

What we see at the national level is the average of the growth and decline of the several parts of a country. The real economies are at a regional level, even quite small regions in land area. One prospers and another declines. One, like Paris, may have been prosperous for a long time, perhaps as far back as its known history. Another may have been prosperous and is now in decline, like Manchester in England. A region like North Rhine-Westphalia in West Germany has only very recently slipped from the top of its country's growth league to the bottom. Other regions have not known prosperity for several centuries, like parts of Ireland or Greece. Even Japan has its regional problems, and regions such as the northern island of Hokkaido are looking to the same kind of solutions to their problems as are states in the southern United States and countries such as Scotland and Ireland.

Past Policies and New Regions

Regional development policies of the past have tended to be focused on the problem regions, the clearly 'less-favoured regions', to use the terminology of the European Community. This term 'less-favoured region' has been used until relatively recently to describe regions which for the most part lie on the periphery of the European Community—Greece, Ireland, southern Italy, Scotland and parts of France. To the north lie other peripheral countries. Sweden has maintained a relatively high level of prosperity. Finland and Norway are prosperous and still making progress. Yet, under this average national surface the peripheral problems remain—northern Sweden, the country beyond Helsinki, northern Norway. To the west, Spain and Portugal have now added to the peripheral problems of the European Community. Yugoslavia shares many problems with Greece and the Mezzogiorno. Two small countries tucked into the EEC behave much as Denmark and Sweden: Switzerland remains very prosperous, Austria appears to have recovered from being an empire to being a prosperous country. Even the period of economic growth following the Second World War and persisting through the 1970s to a large extent bypassed these peripheral regions of the West and South. Some gained from tourism from the more prosperous regions but this, like dependence on an agricultural economy, does not produce enduring growth. It becomes susceptible to competition from more exotic regions, or regions which find that the cost of distance is eliminated. They are receiving a transfer of wealth from the self-generating regions. To these peripheral regions must now be added industrialised and relatively prosperous regions which since the early 1960s have entered into a state of decline. They are rapidly adopting characteristics of less-favoured regions particularly in their inability to generate economic growth from within themselves. Such regions exist in several EEC member states such as France or Belgium but the problem is at its most acute in the United Kingdom, the first country to become industrialised. These regions tend to be ones which have specialised in their industries and technologies—the north-west of England and north-east of France in textiles, the Ruhr and eastern France in steel and coal, the Midlands of England in car manufacture, and so on. These regions have declined, overtaken by later investment in newer technologies elsewhere in the world, and by the growth of new industries and technologies in other parts of their own or other countries. Shipbuilding has gone east, as has steel production. Plastics have replaced so much metal in so many products. Microelectronic components replace moving mechanical parts.

Information technology and the self-generated growth of the Pacific rim are bringing further and still unknown threats. The recession of the 1980s has revealed the weaknesses of yet more regions like North Rhine-Westphalia. Are these about to enter into a long-term decline or are they merely in recession? These new regional problems have at least raised questions as to the efficacy of the policies of the past. These past regional development policies and programmes have included:

- creation of employment by financial and fiscal incentives to large industrial corporations to establish branch plants, or to all sizes of industrial and other organisations to relocate;
- relocation of large government offices and establishments or military production or location of other state industries as in Italy;
- disincentives to location in more prosperous regions including through planning regulations;
- amelioration of living conditions such as by the 'Western dole' in Ireland, a weekly welfare payment to small holders on marginal land;
- improvement of agricultural productivity and protection of agriculture to increase the living standards of those remaining on the land;
- enhancement of employment opportunity, albeit in more advanced regions, by creating higher levels of education opportunity;
- protection and support of large industries which are in difficulty through technological change and competition from newly industrialising countries;
- funding by national governments and the EEC of infrastructure such as roads, telecommunications, water supply, and so on.

None of these measures has succeeded in laying the basis for self-generated growth. Some have indeed been counterproductive. The European Community and its agriculture policy have run into problems of large surpluses as the American government has previously done. Branch plants seem to have an ever decreasing half-life. Sweden has found that 'increasing unemployment has led to economically unsound levels of subsidies', the main explanation being that regional incentives were originally designed to influence mobile industry instead of non-mobile indigenous small and medium enterprises (Eriksson 1984).

Short-term job creation is not a sufficient objective, and prosperity dependent on job creation measures can prove to be very volatile.

Unfortunately, the confusion created by the concept of a national economy is at the root of the problem. Governments govern as though there were a unity instead of a mix of regional economies with very different capabilities to create wealth. A consequence is that, in the terminology of the European Community, regional policies have been focused on 'less-favoured regions', as problems which could be dealt with only from the centre, by some form of transfer from the centre, not from within the regions themselves.

The centre, the capital of the national economy, may well be the main or only truly self-maintaining prosperous region in a country. The measures may be well-intentioned in transferring wealth from the prosperous to the less prosperous in direct payments or through investment in infrastructure, employment in branch plants or branch government offices. But whilst the formulators of economic policy may wish to assist the regions, they instinctively do not wish to damage the economy of the centre and, perhaps even more, they wish to retain control from the centre. That is, after all, the function of the government of a national economy. Measures adopted for the country as a whole may negate impact of some regional policies since they tend to favour the prosperous rather than the less prosperous, those with their headquarters in the capital rather than those wholly based in the regions.

In some countries, the appearance of the capital as a region more prosperous than the rest of the country may be misleading. It may not be a self-generated prosperity. The national economy may be one which supplies commodities, primary produce for processing elsewhere, or it may be one which supplies finished products from foreign-owned branch plants, that is, it supplies relatively cheap labour. In such a primary supply economy, the capital prospers like any middleman prospers, and the policies formulated tend to have the bias of the middleman—improve productivity and keep costs down rather than invest in new products and new technologies, assist trade in exports of primary materials and produce and imports of manufactured goods rather than support indigenous production. Prosperity depends on the price competition in prosperous markets between alternative suppliers of primary produce and labour. Where these become uncompetitive, then the capital also declines. No part of the country has a self-generating economy.

Extremely few of the policies of the past have aimed at the fundamental need for regions to create economic activities from within themselves. The failure of most policies is attributable to the fact that neither income redistribution nor development of the physical infrastructure nor employment distribution are key factors in economic growth.

Innovation, Information and Entrepreneurs

Economic growth and prosperity are essentially dependent on the creation of new economic activities to replace declining economic activities such as the coal, steel and other industries of Europe. New economic activities are also needed to absorb the manpower resources released by economic activities such as agriculture as these increase their productivity or to absorb the manpower released by large firms as these concentrate and rationalise. New economic activities come into existence essentially through the foundation of new firms by entrepreneurs. Entrepreneurs base their new firms on some innovative idea. Most often it is a relatively small innovation, an incremental improvement on what was in the market before, but not always. It may be a major innovation such as the Apple computer. It may even be, and often has been, an imitation of some innovation in a much more advanced region. But as the British White Paper on regional industrial development (Department of Industry, 1983) states, 'Self-generating growth requires a high rate of innovation and new firm formation'.

Entrepreneurial vitality is the key characteristic of a region which generates its prosperity from within itself. It is the entrepreneurs who possess and utilise the five great forces which Jane Jacobs (1984) sees as originating in 'import-replacing cities'—markets, jobs, technology, transplants and capital—and who thus bring wealth not merely to these city regions but also to other regions.

Entrepreneurial vitality, examined further in Chapters 2 and 3, does not grow anywhere. It exists, as we shall see, only in those places which have an information-rich environment. There are several components in the creation of this information rich environment:

- the education and training system in a region;
- the quality and intensiveness of the information flows between firms and entrepreneurs and their friends;
- the cycle time between need and delivery of information for decision-making;
- the technical culture and progressiveness which determine the innovative potential of a region.

This information-rich environment is becoming even more critical to entrepreneurial vitality, as the industrial economy evolves into the information economy. In this economy, competitiveness will be determined by the information component of the end-product and by the quality and efficiency of the information-intensive functions of the producing firm. Furthermore, information technology will be a key and pervasive technology comparable to the energy technologies of the industrial age. Information technology is bringing new dimensions not only to jobs and the nature of jobs but also to innovation and the opportunities for new economic activities.

In this book, an attempt is made to bring together four concepts:

- Self-generated and maintained economic wealth is a local or regional phenomenon, not national.
- This self-generated wealth is a product of the entrepreneurial vitality in a region, and entrepreneurial vitality is nourished in an information-rich environment which gives a strong innovation potential.
- The need for this information-richness is intensifying as the industrial economy evolves into the information economy.
- Economic development is perhaps more a social phenomenon than a technological or political or financial one.

None of these concepts is new but only the concept of the information economy has a reasonably wide acceptance. The others are as yet accepted by only a few. Only the French have formulated a policy for information-richness in the regions. Only the Danes appear, as they always do, to have got on with the job of creating this environment without bothering with the fuss of a policy. Other countries in Europe are taking tentative steps, tentative because still confused with past ideologies or economic theories, or still unable to get off the hook of past policies.

Nevertheless, amongst these new initiatives are ones which acknowledge the humanity of entrepreneurs and the kind of environment in which they prosper and innovate. Some of these are described later in this book but first the elements which seem to make up an entrepreneurial culture are examined and the way in which information is actually transmitted both in general and in specific cases is described. From these an attempt is made to characterise or classify regions according to their entrepreneurial and innovation potentials and their information-richness. Matching these various characteristics with the types of initiative being undertaken enables one to outline a model infrastructure to support and stimulate self-generated growth or renewal in regions which lack the capability for these, whether currently apparently prosperous or not. It is an information infrastructure, because 'whatever approach is chosen, the present rapid and intensive technological developments demand that regional policy promote not only their translation into economic activities but also access and receptivity to relevant knowledge' (Boeckhout *et al.* 1984), otherwise the gaps will enlarge and yet more problem regions will emerge.

References

Boeckhout, I. J. *et al*. (1984). 'Innovation profiles and regional policy in The Netherlands'. Six Countries Workshop, Limerick.

Department of Industry: *Regional industrial development*. London, HMSO.

Eriksson, A. (1984). 'Regional policy in Sweden—from job creation to regional development'. Six Countries Workshop, Limerick.

Eurostat Review (1974–83). Luxembourg, Office for Official Publications for the European Communities.

Jacobs, Jane (1984). *Cities and the wealth of nations: principles of economic life*. Toronto, Random House.

CHAPTER 2

Entrepreneurial Vitality and Information

Dynamism in a national economy is strongly correlated to the size of the small-firms sector in that economy and to the buoyancy of this sector in terms of a high birth rate and as the seed bed of fast-growth firms (EAG 1978). That is, it is related to the entrepreneurial vitality in that economy. Amongst the major economies, it has been said (EAG 1978) that those which showed the strongest growth up to the recession, Japan, France and West Germny, had the stronger small-firm sectors, but only Japan has shown real continuing growth in this sector. Employment in Japanese small firms increased from 70 per cent of total industrial employment in 1975 to 74 per cent in 1981 (MITI 1984). This buoyancy is the evidence of the entrepreneurial vitality, the ability to generate new economic activities through the foundation of new firms. They replace the older economic activities of older firms. A few grow fast and big and thereby create large numbers of new jobs, replacing the big losses in whole sectors of older industry and agriculture. Many of the firms which die are new or relatively new firms, but that is an aspect of a try, try again behaviour which characterises the entrepreneur and the small-firm sector.

Innovation

This correlation stems from the role of the entrepreneur in economic development. 'It is the dynamic competition among entrepreneurs, primarily in terms of industrial innovation, which forms the basis of economic development. Thus the emphasis is on the supply side' (Freeman *et al.* 1982). The emphasis is also on the entrepreneur rather than on innovation. Innovation is not *per se* the foundation of economic growth. It has no existence without the entrepreneur. It is also an extremely varied phenomenon. It has been defined (OECD 1978) as comprising those technical, industrial, commercial or other steps which lead to the successful marketing of new manufactured products and/or to the commercial use of technically new processes or equipment. Memory tells me that an earlier OECD definition went something like this: 'The application of scientific or technological knowledge for the first time with commercial success.' It can take many forms, as another OECD document (1982) on innovation in SMEs showed:

- a familiar product manufactured from new materials;
- a fresh combination of existing products to give improved performance;
- adaptation of an existing product to meet new demands;
- a new product utilised to perform a new function;
- a new process either to make a new or modified product or to lower production costs.

As the Director-General of the British CBI has said (Beckett 1986):

> Innovation is not just about new ideas, welcome though these may be. It is also about minor improvements to products, range extensions, slight differences which can make considerable differences, and also unsuspected spin-offs. Innovation in fact takes many forms and the search for new, or existing, needs applies to all functions—research, production, distribution, advertising, salesmanship.

Yet the concept of innovation as something science-based and distinct from the entrepreneur continues to haunt the literature and the thinking of many in industrial policy administration. On the one hand, there are demands for more investment in 'science' and academic research on the grounds that this investment will lead directly to innovation which will lead directly to economic growth. In spite of all that is said, there is no linear relationship between science and innovation, if only because there needs to be an entrepreneur. These do not often come out of research even where the conditions are most favourable. Of 243 Palo Alto start-ups, Cooper (1972) found only six who were spin-offs from Stanford University. The route from research and university to a successful product is very circuitous. At the same time, possibly arising from the same beliefs, industrial and technology policies of many countries continue to focus on the same new technology-based firms (NTBFs) and high technology innovation as the sole road out of the recession. They neglect the role which new firms can play in the much more numerous other technologies and sectors. In one estimate (Niederwemmer 1980) of the 16,000 new industrial firms founded annually in the Federal Republic of Germany, 800 could be regarded as innovative in the narrower and 3,500 in the wider sense, but all contribute to the economic vitality of the country. In the United States, high technology has provided less than 3 per cent of the new jobs created since the beginning of the 1970s (*The Economist* 1984). Fast-food operations may have created more. Long-leap and major innovations, new and high technology, although directly responsible for only a relatively small proportion of new jobs, are, however, the initiators of new growth. They become the best technical practices. Adoption of new technology as the current best practice can revitalise an industry, as, for example, the clothing industry of the New

England states. After a long decline this sector now seems to be undergoing a rebirth aided by its adoption of new technology and more flexible response to the market. Nevertheless, the key element in economic growth remains the entrepreneur. The entrepreneur, by founding his firm, introduces a change into the market, and observation of this led Shapero (1977) to the conclusion that the real innovation was the founding of the firm. The means by which the firm creates new wealth and replaces declining economic activities is secondary. To Jane Jacobs (1985), creating new wealth by meeting a market need through imitation of an innovation elsewhere is the very stuff of economic growth. Thus, economic growth is entrepreneur-led and the small-firm sector is the major source of entrepreneurs.

The evidence for this role of small firms has been provided by studies of its role as a source of new employment, carried out in the last decade. Small and young firms have been shown to be the major source of new employment. This role in job creation is a consequence of their role in innovation.

> Very frequently, innovations close to the market are carried out by small and medium size companies. Companies in these size categories are characterised by a particularly high degree of flexibility. This flexibility allows them to utilise quickly and at low cost new technical possibilities for conversion into marketable innovations (Niederwemmer 1980).

'It is worth noting that evidence exists from several European countries that in general "innovativeness" is associated with employment generation. Piatier (1981) for example found that innovation was associated with employment gains in 59% of innovative firms and in employment loss in only 5%. For non-innovative firms the employment gains and losses were 26% and 14%' (Rothwell 1985). Entrepreneurs through their small firms are not only the source of a disproportionately large number of innovations, relative to large firms, they are also more successful in long-leap innovations. Large firms, whilst producing a majority of their own incremental innovations, have a high dependency on external inventors and small firms, even for process innovations. Smaller firms are also more efficient, producing more innovations per unit of expenditure than large firms, and they produce them more quickly. This role of the smaller firm in economic development and the characteristics of entrepreneurs I have examined in more detail elsewhere (Sweeney 1985). The achievements of smaller firms are even more remarkable when consideration is taken of the increasing dominance of the large firm and the overall decline of the small-firms sector in most developed countries. They occupy a smaller sector of the economy, yet still play the role of injecting vitality into an economy.

Localisation of Entrepreneurial Vitality

The correlation between entrepreneurial vitality and economic prosperity is equally, if not more strongly evident, at the regional level as at the national (EAG 1978). Indeed, 'economic development is a less than national phenomenon. It does not happen in general; it happens to specific people in specific places', it occurs in some localities and not in others (Shapero 1977). In the United Kingdom, there is a good correlation between the level of income per head and the proportion of small establishments by region (Gudgin 1978). In the United States, the regions with the highest rate of growth in new and small enterprises have the highest growth in income.

> Small firms appear to breed other small firms in an organic fashion so that their role in the process of growth and decline in manufacturing employment is cumulative, either upwards or downwards. Birth rates are highest in areas where there are already large concentrations of small firms and in areas where economic growth is most rapid (EAG 1978).

And regions with the lowest rate of foundation of new firms also have the lowest employment growth. There is similar evidence elsewhere of this relationship between prosperity and a large small-firm population as in the textile industry of Tuscany with its highly paid work-force (Macrae 1982).

Jane Jacobs (1984) has focused on the vigorous cities which continue to be creative in replacing imports as the self-generating economies which create the wealth on which the rest of the world depends. She refers to the citizens of Tokyo in tiny workshops, building up their skills in making import-replacing cycles, cluster upon cluster of workshops, intertrading in components and the tools to make components. The skills led to replacement of other and more sophisticated imports and so to today, without being inventors, the Japanese have become technological leaders in the string of cities from Tokyo to Osaka. But this, of course, is nothing new. Venice, a village on a marsh which became a trading port, evolved to being an import-replacing city. It imported, imitated and developed its skills to a yet higher level. It once imported the work of the Byzantine glass-makers, but eventually Venetian glass was the coveted ware. Jacobs quotes Sabel (1982) on the source of wealth of northern Italy. He was 'amazed at the small size of these innovative and highly successful firms, most of which employ from 5 to 50 workers, a few as many as 100, and a very few 250 or more', in the aggregate 'specialising in virtually every phase of the production of textiles, automatic machines, machine tools, automobiles, buses and agricultural equipment'. Sabel was impressed by the sophistication and quality of the work being done in production of ceramics, shoes, plastic furniture, motorcycles, woodcutting machinery, metal-cutting machinery, ceramics machinery. He reports the ease with which new enterprises have formed through breakaway of workers from older enterprises, and the amazing economies of scale that are obtained not, as has been conventionally assumed, within the framework of huge organisations but rather through large symbiotic collections of little enterprises.

> The innovative capacity of this type of firm depends on its flexible use of technology; its close relations with other, similarly innovative firms in the same and adjacent sectors; and above all on the close collaboration of workers with different kinds of expertise. These firms practice boldly and spontaneously the fusion of conception and execution, abstract and practical knowledge, that only a few exceptional giant firms . . . have so far been able to achieve on a grand scale.

In fact this fusion on a grand scale is what has been happening for centuries without giant firms in wealth-creating cities.

This ferment of entrepreneurial activity is observable in the large population of small firms in a prosperous region, in the high birth and death rates, in the spin-offs and breakaways and in the continuous pursuit of a new project, a new product, by the younger of these firms in their pursuit of survival.

Malecki (1981) has called the process of 'creation of new economic activities through the foundation of new firms', 'a circular and cumulative process'. It is a process of one bit leading to another, building on yet another, spreading laterally and increasing in volume of output and of input.

A Social Phenomenon

It is also a very human process and a process deeply dependent on the society in which it happens. Areas which have a strong small industry sector tend to renew themselves (Shapero 1972). Founders of new firms tend to have worked previously in small firms or in small divisions of large firms (Cooper 1973). New firms are also founded mostly by people who have a parent or parents who owned their own business or were self-employed, perhaps as farmers. Hence, Bearse (1981) found that people from the country were more likely to found new firms than people from the city—even in the United States.

These social linkages are further reinforced by other characteristics. New businesses in more than 90 per cent of cases are founded in the same sector as the founder's previous industrial experience (Cooper 1973; Susbauer 1972) and 80 per cent of the products or services are related to those of his previous employment (Cooper 1973; Lamont 1972). Two-thirds of new entrepreneurs set up in their own locality—even in the United States (Boswell 1973). 'The origins of small firms are highly localised. Small business founders, or at least the majority of them, are not footloose but find the inspiration and the means to set up their firms only in or near their own community' (EAG 1978). Localities with a diversity of technology and industry have not only a higher vitality but a more continuing vitality (Shapero and Sokol 1982). 'Transfer between sectors is probably one of the forms of innovation that can have a rapid and significant effect on economic growth rates' (Piatier 1981). 'Where variety and diversity abound, there is a higher likelihood for achieving meaningful associations of items not previously associated, one definition of creativity' (Shapero 1977), as a comparative study of Manchester and Birmingham demonstrated (Jacobs 1969). In the nineteenth century, Manchester appeared to be the paragon of industrial structure and infrastructure. Its core business of cotton manufacture was based on natural resources of ports and water, and led to the development of textile engineering, chemicals, dyeing, printing and related service industries. In contrast, Birmingham showed a messy industrial structure. It had no specialisation and a lot of very small businesses, characteristics which gave Birmingham 'certain dynamic qualities', 'a capacity to create new work from their existing work'. Manchester, with the neat structured appearance of a company town, has declined. Birmingham, too, has more recently suffered as it specialised more and more in the car industry.

A Local Culture

What emerges from the foregoing is that investment to support entrepreneurs and small firms has the potential to be much more productive than other forms of investment in economic development or job creation. The role of the small firm is being recognised by many governments, but few measures recognise how local a phenomenon is the entrepreneur and how local is the environment which is necessary for his vitality.

Creation of such an environment is an intangible. 'It is easier to lobby for existing jobs for known persons in known firms than to argue for creation of new jobs in new firms for unknown persons' (Lindbeck 1981). Hence, so much money has been spent on propping up ailing industries and, when these have failed, yet more money is spent on branch plants of national or foreign industries. It is not only easier but also much more of a vote catcher to be able to open the new plant 'which I ensured was brought to you to give you jobs again'. Who opens the backyard start-up of the entrepreneur? Who gets the credit for his new plant? There are no votes.

Nevertheless, 'to attain the desired characteristics of diversity, innovativeness and resilience that have been identified with a dynamic (regional) economy implies a multiplicity of companies and, by inference, the kind of industrial ecology or environment that facilitates the formation of the next company and the next company in answer to opportunities or problems' (Shapero 1977).

Brophy (1982), drawing on several studies gave as a key factor in the founding of a new business 'a local culture conducive to the formation of new small firms by technological entrepreneurs'. Keynes (1936) was also sharply aware of how essential was the 'atmosphere'.

> Most, probably, of our decisions to do something positive the full consequences of which will be drawn out over many days to come can only be taken as a result of animal spirits—of a spontaneous urge to action rather than inaction ... Thus if the animal spirits are dimmed and the spontaneous optimism falters ... enterprise will fade and die. This means not only that slumps and depressions are exaggerated in degree, but that economic prosperity is excessively dependent on a political and social atmosphere which is congenial to the average businessman.

Bouvier (1984) suggested quickly relegating accepted ideas and theories to second place, so that one can take an ecological approach like that of the good gardener.

The Six Countries Programme has also focused (Gaudin 1985) on the creation of an environment in its statement of the three principles on which technological innovative policy and programmes should be founded and which should permeate other policy formulation:

- Creation of a technical culture, a cultural environment, and a cultural awareness within each individual, of traditional skills and an aesthetic appreciation wedded to an understanding of technology; that is, provision of an environment favourable to innovation and of the skills and creativity to generate innovation. This is dealt with later in more detail.
- Direct support to the entrepreneur. Studies of the innovation process have demonstrated that innovation measures should be aimed to provide direct support to entrepreneurs and innovative firms rather than indirect measures or support of projects. The support system in information, advice and services, technical, managerial and financial, should be sympathetic and responsive to the needs of the entrepreneur/innovator and must be easy to approach and therefore local. The orientation of the support system must be the success of the entrepreneur and not job maintenance, job creation, high technology or other objectives which might in fact inhibit the entrepreneur and his innovation.
- Removal of obstacles to the entrepreneur and innovation. Innovative entrepreneurial endeavour can only thrive in a climate of optimism

> and opportunity—the removal of regulatory, procedural, fiscal and other obstacles to entrepreneurial innovation should be taken hand-in-hand with development of policies and attitudes within the administration which cross administrative divisions. Unintended effects, such as self-cancelling measures of different departments or ministries, can thus be avoided.

It is a systemic approach rather than a mechanistic one, one which endeavours to develop the total system as a system. There are others, however, who have focused on specifics as the means to self-generated growth. Science administrators have tended to focus attention on research and a relationship between research and innovation as being a key element in this national or local environment. Others focus on the need for capital, skilled labour, or other resources in the locality. The Charpie report (CTAB 1967) was not at all sure.

> Cities and regions appear to vary markedly with respect to successful generation of new technologically based enterprises ... important factors exist which go beyond such indices as the total number of scientists or the total R & D expenditures or the availability of capital.

Deutermann (1966) investigated why two cities, Philadelphia and Boston, apparently with comparable infrastructure, exhibited such strong differences in entrepreneurial vitality. Shapero (1983), intrigued by the ubiquitous presence of venture capital firms in urban centres which were also endowed with universities, research laboratories, etc., but with different levels of entrepreneurial vitality, investigated the venture capital firms. Deutermann found a sympathetic responsiveness in the universities and banks of Boston which was absent in Philadelphia. Shapero 'inadvertently' found an openness to give information in the venture capital firms in the entrepreneurial cities, absent in the cities with low entrepreneurial vitality. Furthermore, 'technologically based firms within Philadelphia seemed to have less contact with suburban firms than their counterparts in Boston' (Freedman 1983). The factors seem to be social in the sense that they contain interactions between people, attitudes, and communication of information. The infrastructure is supportive in one area and not in another. There is a willingness to give freely of advice and information in areas with entrepreneurial vitality, entrepreneurs talk to one another, large firms buy from small and there are myriads of networks of personal contact.

Schell (1983) found that

> three different studies using three different levels of analysis and substantially different sources of information tentatively conclude that entrepreneurship is a phenomenon due less to size of a community or metropolitan area and perhaps more to regional location and other

factors not directly related to size. Pennings (1982) for instance found the most important predictors of organisational birth frequencies to include (1) occupational and industrial differentiation, (2) the proportion of immigrants, (3) the size of the industry the new firm is entering, (4) the availability of venture capital and (5) to a lesser extent the presence of universities. Bruno and Tyebjee (1982) list additional features, thought to be significantly related to entrepreneurial activity—(1) presence of experienced entrepreneurs and incubator organisations, (2) skilled labour force, (3) accessibility of suppliers, (4) accessibility of customers and new markets, (5) favourable government policies, (6) availability of land and facilities, (7) accessibility of transportation, (8) receptive population, (9) availability of supporting services and (10) attractive living conditions.

Storey attempted to classify British regions by a range of factors associated with high levels of entrepreneurship (Table 2.1).

Table 2.1 Factors associated with high levels of entrepreneurship

Factors	High entrepreneurship	Index
Size of incubator firm	Small firms	% of small firms % employment in small firms % employment in large firms
Occupational experience	Managerial experience	% of population in managerial groupings
Education	High levels	% with degrees
Access to capital	Easy access	Savings per head % house owning
Entry into industry	Low entry barriers	% of population in low-entry barrier industries
Markets	Wealthy local markets	Regional income distribution

Boeckhout *et al.* (1984) have pointed out that

recent enquiries have shown that private companies differ widely in their propensity to innovate. On the one hand, the differences spring from the regional production structure, that is, the characteristics of the economic activities located in the region and the relations between them. On the other hand, they spring from the regional production

> environment, by which is understood the combination of external circumstances influencing the location and performance of private companies in a region.

He and his colleagues at The Netherlands Economic Institute have developed the notion of a 'regional innovation profile, by which is understood the combination of a region's strong and weak points when it comes to expanding and renovating ... by creating new economic activities or adapting existing ones to changing market conditions'. They drew up lists of indicators under the two headings, 'production structure' and 'production environment' (Table 2.2). The objective was to identify a large number of indicators of the strong and weak points of regions 'with respect to their ability to respond to new technological developments'. Putting values for each indicator for each region appear to narrow the profiles whilst showing considerable differences between regions. 'Most regions offer fewer or more (specific) possibilities that might lead to renovation.' The technique pointed to specialisation rather than diversity, perhaps because the focus was on new technology rather than on new technology pervading a mix of all industries. Quantification of many of the factors involved, for example, social relationships, is difficult.

Table 2.2 Selected indications of production structure and production environment

Production structure	Production environment
Location of (technologically) promising economic activity — number of employees — number of establishments	Presence of knowledge centres Educational level of professional accessibility — national gravity point/ road/aeroplane) — international gravity points (road)
Creation and survival change of establishments	— water — communication infrastructure
Location of large companies with R & D activities	Availability of industrial accommodation — industrial sites — industrial buildings
Location of SME companies' R & D activities — number of establishments	— business centres — offices Agglomeration advantages
Licence applications	Attractiveness of residential environment
Use of government instruments for innovation	Institutional and policy framework

In presenting a dynamic model of the entrepreneurial/economic development process, Schell (1983) summarises that the 'model places a great deal of importance on the community power structure as a major factor in creating a supportive climate for entrepreneurship in a community. It emphasises qualitative more than quantitative variables.' The presence of a critical mass of entrepreneurs and institutions involved in the gestation of new hard and soft technologies and an active, supportive venture capital community are important factors. Important also are the cultural traditions of relevant groups affecting the atmosphere for entrepreneurship.

The 'Cambridge Phenomenon' (Segal Quince 1985) illustrates a number of these factors. Segal Quince plotted the relationship of the high-tech firms and of firms servicing them. Taking 1960 as a starting point, their 'family tree' chart showed that, as of 1984, 355 businesses had been founded, of which 330 survived. Of these 244 had parent–child relationships. The rest were firms which had moved into the area or were founded by Cambridge graduates or by previous employees of local high-tech firms but who had had experience elsewhere before returning to Cambridge to set up business. Furthermore, there has been an unusually high incidence of movement of key highly trained people between these firms around Cambridge. These people also have sometimes had experience elsewhere before returning again to Cambridge. The process is cumulative, therefore, not only in growth of 'families' but also in the informal networks of highly skilled labour strengthening the interconnections between firms.

Segal Quince placed considerable emphasis on the roles of King's College, Cambridge, and Barclays Bank, Cambridge, in providing encouragement and support to the high-tech firms. King's College was both a large landowner and a technologically-orientated institution anxious to promote high-tech start-ups amongst its own and other Cambridge graduates. Barclays Bank occupied a special position in Cambridge, and the senior local director, the latest of several generations in the Cambridge bank, assigned virtually the whole of the time of the Bank's district business advisory service to the new high-tech companies.

The Cambridge phenomenon confirms (Figure 2.1) the cumulative growth to which EAG referred but also a point made by Shapero (1977). This was that the technical company formation process in a community begins slowly with a very small number of firms founded in a first phase, followed by a period of accumulation and incubation, followed in turn by a third phase of accelerated and sustained growth. It also confirms that a local culture which nurtures entrepreneurial vitality is a culture in which there is a rich diversity and openness in information flow, a supportive giving of information. This information flow makes the start-up of a new venture feasible to the extent that entrepreneurship seems to reflect

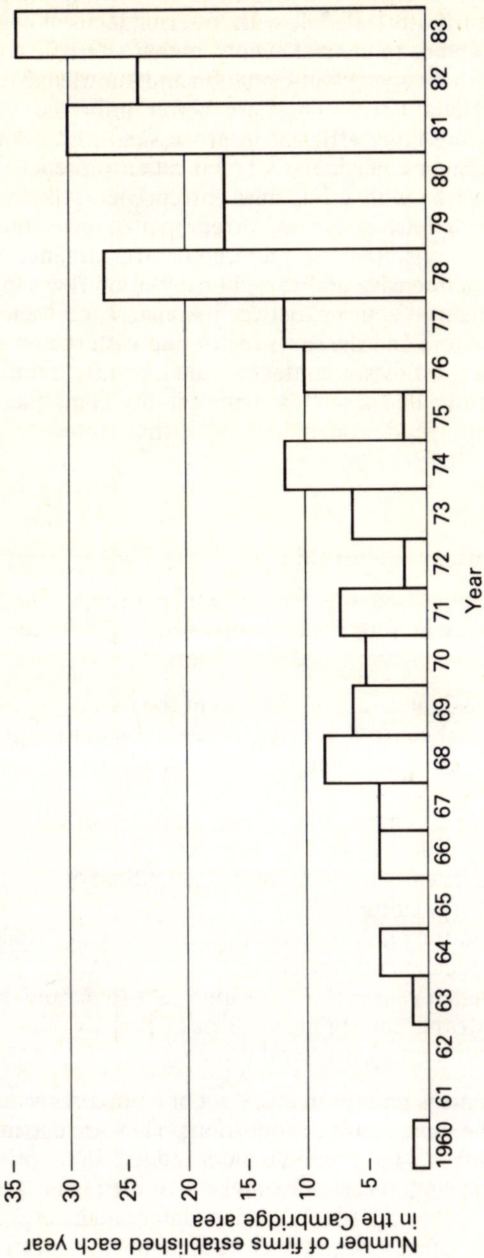

Figure 2.1 Date of establishment of survey firms.
Source: Segal Quince (1985).

superior information (Seeman and Evans 1962). Entrepreneurs themselves are major contributors. People with 'internal locus of control', the belief in their own ability to control events, a characteristic common in entrepreneurs, more actively seek information and knowledge relevant to their situation (Valecha 1972). They are better informed (Wolk and DuCette 1974) and are more efficient in processing information (Dean 1983). New entrepreneurs, particularly technical entrepreneurs, quickly form informal networks with other new entrepreneurs in the locality. Before founding their business, new entrepreneurs have intensive informal contacts with consultants in research centres, finance and other businesses. There are intensive and varied information flows in localities with high entrepreneurial activity, between suppliers, customers, entrepreneurs in other sectors and the same sector and with the service infrastructure. All these flows, contacts and bonds reinforce the entrepreneurial culture and strengthen the vitality. This factor of the generously open information networks was that noted by Charpie, Deutermann and Shapero.

The Decline of Entrepreneurship

Shapero (1977) summarised the factors which promote and support entrepreneurial vitality in 'four major elements that go into the company formation process':

- An apparent disposition to act on the part of the nascent entrepreneur, 'the internal locus of control' or belief in one's ability to control events (Rotter 1966); a personal characteristic which seems common to successful entrepreneurs (Sweeney 1985).
- The act of forming a company, of setting up a new business, has been made credible by role models, by the example of others, such as colleagues, former employers, parents, neighbours; a local entrepreneurial small-firm culture.
- The availability to the entrepreneur of resources which make the act economically and technically feasible.
- Some displacement event which precipitates the action, something which happens to the entrepreneur to push him to take control of events himself by founding his own business.

Each of these elements is present in every act of company formation, but not necessarily in the same relative proportions. They are partially substitutable for each other. To these he later added in a private note 'knowledge—general and specific' to make five elements. This briefly referred to the 'stock of knowledge' described later and incorporating the diversity of industries, technologies and occupations in a locality.

Whilst locus of control and displacement are personal elements, the other three are elements belonging to the external environment. Each of these—entrepreneurial culture, availability of technical and financial resources and knowledge—has been in a process of decline in its availability to the entrepreneur in many regions and developed countries. This process of decline has been under way since the beginning of the twentieth century. The overriding cause has been the growing domination by large bureaucratic organisations in all sectors of economies—manufacturing, distribution, finance and other services. This domination has reduced the small-firm population and entrepreneurial culture of most countries. It has had particular impact on peripheral regions and industrially declining regions and has brought the threat of decline to other regions. It represents the other side of the coin to entrepreneurial vitality.

In regions dominated by large firms there is a lower level of entrepreneurial vitality. The rate of foundation of new firms is much lower and therefore the ability to generate new economic activities is much weaker.

Beesley (1955) found a clear contrast between south-west Birmingham, dominated by small component manufacturers, and the north-west, dominated by large assembly plants. The entry rate of new establishments was 70 per cent higher in the former than in the latter. Gudgin (1978) showed that in the East Midlands of England, Lincolnshire and Derbyshire, whose main towns were dominated by large heavy engineering firms, had lower rates of new-firm foundation than Leicestershire, Nottinghamshire and Northamptonshire. Schell (1983) quotes a local entrepreneur as saying that the problems of Forsyth County were due firstly to the presence of R. J. Reynolds Industries: its high wages, outstanding benefits and dominance in community decisions acted as a deterrent to new companies.

It is worth, therefore, looking at the effects of a large-firm culture and the dominance of large firms. They have had a depressing effect on entrepreneurial vitality in many regions of Europe and the United States and in a most complex manner have raised many barriers to new-firm entry. It may also be that this dominance is a watershed between the industrial and the information economies. The distinct trend in divesting of non-compatible businesses by conglomerates has seemed to be one indicator of an emerging information economy, albeit that mega-takeovers are reaching a near-mania in 1986.

Domination of Large Bureaucracies

Porat (1978) who carried out a major analysis of the information sector of the American economy was led by his analysis to conclude that 'an information economy is largely bureaucratic in nature; decisions are made and power is wielded not by many independent firms competing for a market, but by relatively insulated public and private bureaucracies'. In fact, what he identified was the structure of the industrial economy in a late, perhaps final phase.

In the industrial economy, productive growth was achieved primarily through economies of scale and mass-production technology allied with organisation. As the industrial economy has evolved through the twentieth century, American production technology and scientific management techniques have increasingly dominated European industry and business organisation (Pavitt 1979).

Economies of scale and organisation to achieve these through division of labour were based on the opportunities presented by new production technology and perception of the market. A relatively low-income population required a lower price if their range of purchasing and repurchasing was to be extended. To achieve this lower price and reach a wider market a greater volume of products had to be produced at lower cost. For the producers of these goods to achieve the lower price, they, too, bought materials and capital goods on a price preferential basis. Gradually markets become dominated by price. Products had to be standardised, since diversity increased costs. Quality in its several aspects was sacrificed. It was a necessary trade-off against cost. Ever larger volumes of the same product required mass markets. To develop these over wider geographical areas required mass advertising and mass distribution. Inevitably, markets for products having quality and embodying traditional but costly skills became depressed. Regional suppliers of these markets could not compete against price manipulation in local markets or reach remote markets to survive.

Organisation therefore became critical to success in management of the complex interrelationships of production and distribution and control of the inputs of labour and capital. Scientific management evolved of which the fundamental principle was the division of labour. In the production process, each job was broken down into the smallest discrete element. This allowed the manufacturer to employ unskilled or semiskilled labour and, with minimum cost in training, to become highly efficient in performance of simple predetermined repetitive tasks. No single worker could see how his task fitted into the total process or had responsibility for the process or product.

The inputs of skills, technology and experience, once provided by the craftsman and his supervisor, had to be replaced. To do this, to design the product, to specify and monitor the tasks in the production process and to gather, analyse and present information for decision-making, a bureaucracy was required. This bureaucracy had also to control all the other tasks of the organisation in development, marketing, distribution and finance and to process information for these tasks. The same scientific management principles were applied to the bureaucracy as an information-processing system as to the production system. It was broken down into specialised tasks so as to achieve economies of scale in information-processing activities (Arrow 1974). A hierarchical structure and centralised decision-making were imperative since few, other than those at the top of the hierarchy, could see or claim to see the entire process.

The bureaucracies came increasingly under the control of professional managers (Bannock 1976). Short-term profitability became the primary objective, and decision-making was increasingly based on quantitative information rather than qualitative. Risk was eschewed, and takeover became a prime means of expansion rather than direct investment in new products and new markets (Utton 1971). Takeover was used to minimise competition, to protect market share, and to provide security through integration of suppliers and distributors. Rationalisation and concentration went well beyond that required for efficient economies of scale in production technology (Bulloch 1979). Conglomeration developed to ensure continuing profitability. The needs of the bureaucracy became paramount, not the needs of the market. The diseconomies of scale are considerable, and in most mass-production industries, efficient technology is available to supply relatively small regional markets. Innovation becomes difficult.

> The temptation to reject new concepts grows, rigidity sets in and change is resisted because it threatens the hierarchy of power and prestige on which the firm's system of control is built ... Executives tend to select growth opportunities by using elegant planning and decision-making techniques that favour precision over insight and judgement based on experience. The use of quantitative decision-making procedures limits a firm's ability to act on necessarily qualitative speculation about future markets and technologies (Lewis 1982).

This view corroborates Porat's perception of insulated bureaucracies and underlines the cause–effect relationship between the dominantly bureaucratic structure of society and the decline in innovative and entrepreneurial vitality. These developments, whilst originating in manufacturing industry, have not been confined to it. Concentration in large bureaucratic organisations is self-reinforcing. One sector responds to concentration in another sector (Bannock 1976). Professional management techniques are similar in all sectors. Hence the service sector, including government, has become even more dominated by large bureaucracies than the manufacturing sector (ABT 1982).

Concentration in large organisations, particularly in manufacturing, has also been reinforced by government policies and actions. Industries in decline have been rationalised. Other industries have been rationalised and even nationalised in the belief that international competitiveness could be restored through achievement of larger economies of scale. Government procurement policies as well as fiscal aids tend to be orientated to the needs of large firms. Regional policies favouring branch plant operations of large firms have led to further growth of both national and international large corporations, increasing their overall dominance of economies.

Effects of Domination

The single most important effect of this domination has been the decline in entrepreneurial vitality. The number of smaller firms has declined in most Western economies. New entrepreneurial ventures have failed to compensate for the mortality of existing ventures, and the flexibility of economies, sectors of economies and regions within economies to respond to change has also declined. The current recession has its origins in the decline in product innovation which started in the mid-1960s (OECD 1979). The cumulative process of entrepreneurial decline necessarily leads to decline in innovative new products and inevitably the downward cumulative process leads to recession. The barriers to entrepreneurial vitality can be summarised as follows:

- New entrepreneurs find much greater difficulty in obtaining finance. Increased taxation to raise revenue for investment by the state and savings invested in pension funds and large banks restricted the supply of private capital once formerly available. The size of a new venture at start-up has as a consequence declined in the last hundred years (Dahmen 1970; Firn and Swales 1978).
- Large bureaucratic organisations cannot respond to new entrepreneurs with flexibility and risk-taking; since decision-making is subject to bureaucratic procedures and quantitative assessment, they prefer to deal with other large bureaucracies.
- Costs of financing are higher for smaller firms and new entrepreneurs. Finance is much more difficult for them to obtain, yet the losses of large firms probably exceed those of small firms.
- Domination of markets by large production and distributive organisations competing on the basis of price makes market entry more difficult for new products from new and smaller entrepreneurs.
- Information is more restricted since bureaucracies treat information as the source of power and domination.
- Information-providing organisations, research institutes, universities, consultants, and other suppliers of information have developed to meet the needs of large organisations including both in specialist manpower and in development of new technology.

As a result new venture foundation has been increasingly restricted to sectors which need only small start-up capital and small size at start-up.

In many regions a further result of the domination of large bureaucracies, of markets dominated by the price factor and of division of labour, has been the decline in technical culture, creative use of technology and/or the lack of development of a modern technical culture. This is a complex issue influenced by several factors:

- decline in traditional crafts and skills in the face of cheaper standard product domination of mass markets;
- narrowing of technical skills, the ability to see the total process, through the division of labour and lack of responsibility for the technical processes within a large organisation;
- impoverishment of information flows and contacts due to the concentration of these in core regions.

Concentration of Information

Information-intensive contact is a major reason for the growth of large conurbations (Bannon 1977) and this growth is further reinforced where there is centralised government, such as in the United Kingdom, France, Greece and Ireland. Headquarters of large organisations congregate in such centres because of the proximity to one another. 'Numerous communication studies have revealed both the higher level of face-to-face contact maintained by senior office staff, and also that most contact sources are within half an hour's travelling time of one another' (Mandeville 1983). Indeed indexes of 'contact potential' have been developed to determine the business implications of communication and information variations between urban centres (Tornquist 1970).

Close proximity allows for intensive communication with the decision-making functions of government, supplier and customer organisations and with suppliers of services. Decision-making can be more closely influenced and more speedily obtained. The cycle time for information exchange is within the time permitted for efficient decision-making and the centre becomes autonomous in information exchange (Kendrick 1983).

The desire for autonomy in information exchange is a powerful driving force. In search of it, large bureaucracies internalise much of their information activities and tend to locate these within close proximity to the central headquarters. Research, development, design, marketing and financial functions are within 'half an hour's travelling time'. The effect is self-reinforcing. Research institutes, universities, consultancy firms, libraries, professional and trade associations, information services, newspapers, etc., all concentrate in the core or dominant centres, since their major market lies within close proximity. More highly qualified and higher-calibre staff are therefore also more concentrated in these areas. Not only is the information-intensive contact reinforced, but the stock of knowledge of the centre which feeds this contact is enormously strengthened.

Impoverishment of Regions

The concentration in central core regions of decision-making by these large organisations and of information-intensive contact has had a specific effect on the more peripheral regions and on industrially declining regions remote from the centres. For example in Ireland, 'the majority of these (jobs) were highly skilled and in contact intensive industries with little alternative to a Dublin based location, thereby re-inforcing the "primacy" and relative dominance of the capital city region' (Bannon 1982). Even when located in the regions, information-intensive organisations such as universities and research institutes tend to be linked more strongly to the informal networks of the centre than of their own region, just as those of less-developed countries are linked more to the international networks rather than any national ones (Crane 1974).

In their growth as major conurbations, the core regions have become markets for all goods and services. Proximity to these large and prosperous markets has therefore been essential to entrepreneurial development (Thompson 1965). They have formed also the major labour markets and in particular the more-skilled manpower. Migration from the regions to these centres has been a strong feature of the post-war economic boom. This migration has been both of those in search of jobs and of those seeking to create their own employment, whether as self-employed in the narrower sense or in setting up a business. As a result, regions have been depleted of more skilled and more entrepreneurial economically active inhabitants and thus their 'stock of knowledge' has been impoverished. This of itself is a critical factor but has been reinforced by other effects of domination and concentration.

With the concentration of decision-making of suppliers of resources—government, finance, materials, equipment, expertise, and information—in core or dominant regions, potential and existing entrepreneurs in more distant regions suffer a number of disadvantages in the availability of resources and efficient access to them. Communication with suppliers of resources is costly and time-consuming both in the search for the appropriate resource and in developing a response or input from the resource.

It is not merely that the suppliers are at a distance but they are organised to supply the richer more concentrated market of the centre and the large more dominant enterprises of the centre. Supply of resources outside of this centre is more costly. Economies of scale cannot apply in serving a dispersed and smaller customer. Furthermore, the suppliers of these resources tend themselves to be large and bureaucratic in structure, a factor which inhibits dealings with all small firms and entrepreneurs but is exacerbated by problems of distance and the lower level of awareness of the regional entrepreneur in using the resources. Inevitably, decision-making by the regional entrepreneur occupies a longer cycle time than that necessary for efficient management and adaptation to change or new opportunity. Start-up, survival and growth are thus further inhibited in regions remote from the centres.

This remoteness inhibits also the diffusion of technology. Entrepreneurs in the regions have poorer access to and involvement in informal networks of information flow, whether these are of a professional, industrial or social character. The major informal networks are spatially located in the dominant centres. Awareness of new developments in technology, equipment and markets is therefore much slower in reaching remoter regions. Smaller enterprises in remoter regions are highly dependent in access to information on the representative or salesman of the supplier of technical resources (EPA 1958; Murray *et al.* 1973). This dependence extends wider than the particular remit of the salesman. He is used as a source of information generally on the sector, on developments affecting it and on resources to solve specific problems. However, his major objective is to sell equipment, materials, etc., and in countries such as Ireland or Greece he represents an agency of the major supplier rather than the supplier himself. Inappropriate technology in equipment and materials which are being superseded is often provided. Service back-up is difficult and costly. Less-favoured regions tend therefore to be at the end of the chain of diffusion of technology, a position which stems from their remoteness from informal networks and lack of autonomy in information.

Creativity, inventiveness and identification of new opportunity are not nourished when, firstly, there is a weak stock of knowledge and, secondly, when the informal flows of information are both weak and lacking in progressiveness or state-of-the-art. The stock of knowledge needs to be continuously enriched with awareness and understanding of new business techniques, materials, equipment, and market trends. Information flowing through the network stimulates interaction with the stock of knowledge and leads to generation of ideas for expansion, new products and new opportunity. Implementation of the ideas requires further skills and information which may be easy to obtain in a dominant centre through recruitment, courses, consultancy and person-to-person contact, but difficult in a region.

Information and the Technically Progressive Firm

Localities having high entrepreneurial vitality have characteristics similar to those of technically progressive firms, openness in giving as well as taking information, continuing effort in their own search for information and good internal communication flows. The vitality once initiated becomes self-reinforcing and -sustaining. The skills and knowledge of each unit are continuously exposed to new inputs from information flows, which have quality and a wide diversity. There is more immediate and responsive contact for information required for decision-making. An apparent independent self-support in information exchange is developed by the locality, and it becomes self-sustaining in economic development.

Excellence in the search for information, that is in maintaining a high-quality stock of knowledge, in ensuring rich information flows and in having information capability for efficient decision-making, has been shown in a wide range of studies to be the characteristic distinguishing successful technically progressive and innovative firms from the unsuccessful. A technically progressive firm is one which is early in the adoption of the best current practice and in the application of science, technology and management techniques.

The technically progressive firm has been described as possessing a terrain of knowledge which it must continuously nourish, extend and change in order to absorb technical progress and use it to advantage (Hertay and Leroy 1974). Carter and Williams (1957), in a seminal study, reported that the distinguishing characteristics of the technically progressive firm, confirmed and complemented by later studies such as Allen (1977) and SAPPHO (SPRU 1972; Rothwell *et al.* 1974 were as follows:

- There is a deliberately organised inward flow of high-quality information through journals, personal contact with scientists, visits overseas to exhibitions and conferences and other sources. This information is scrutinised for new ideas, better techniques and practices and better standards of performance; identified knowledge is willingly brought from outside, including through licensing and joint ventures.
- High-calibre staff are recruited for all managerial and professional levels; effective programmes for updating or training in new techniques are in force. This is not only another aspect of knowledge acquisition but the deliberate acquiring of the capability to identify and evaluate new information of relevance to the firm.
- Staff have a better understanding of user requirements, through close contact with users, good market research, publicity, user education and after-sales service.
- There is direct personal contact with external expertise, such as with a

research institute, of specific relevance to the particular technical development or problem.

- There is good internal communication and co-ordination which draws on all the expertise available in formulating policies and actions. Good use is made of the best managerial techniques, especially of internal management information systems for control and for provision of information for decision-making. The firm has a good financial control system.
- Top management is of high quality with speedy and effective decision-making procedures and with time to assess new policy and forward strategy by use of good middle management for daily operations.
- Management is open in providing information to others through papers to conferences, visits to the firms, etc.

As one economist has said, 'in a world where a firm is obliged to make unique and crucial decisions to optimise and to innovate, the making of such decisions puts a premium on information; its acquisition, storage and utilisation become a major business activity' (Lamberton 1972). The progressive and innovative firm is essentially a learning system (Schon 1973) sensitively reaching out through a variety of formal and informal systems and networks to sources of information which may change or impinge on its activities. It is an active participant in these networks, giving as well as taking.

Clearly the progressive firm is one which in a self-reinforcing way is continuously building up its stock of knowledge, exposing itself to information flows and new ideas and ensuring that it has or can obtain information within the time required for effective decision-making and response to opportunity. It also has a critical influence on its own environment by being an active participant in information networks and by its 'buy' rather 'make' policies. It thus exerts a technology pull on its suppliers and diffuses the 'best technical practice'.

The propensity to adopt is the dominating characteristic of technically progressive firms and of prosperous economies. Their openness and search for information and willingness to buy in innovation and technology developed elsewhere lead to early identification of new knowledge and technology and its early and rapid adoption. Such companies and economies are active not in being major innovators but in being first to adopt innovation and new techniques. They are distinguished by their high-level of use of the best current technical practice, the first users of innovation. This is a characteristic independent of the level of research activity within a company or an economy (Sweeney 1975). This propensity to adopt new knowledge more rapidly than other countries has been identified as the major factor in the growth of economies such as Germany and Japan (Holm 1973; Dennison 1967).

Types of Information

When we analyse the above characteristics of a technically progressive firm we find that they correspond to the characteristics of regions with high entrepreneurial vitality and self-generated growth. They are information characteristics and they are concerned with three types of information: stock of knowledge; nutrient information; logistic information.

The stock of knowledge is that knowledge possessed by the entrepreneur and by the locality in which he sets up business. It is made up of both culture and the expertise and skills available to him. It is the terrain of knowledge of the technically progressive firm which is constantly being further extended and enriched.

The core of the stock of knowledge is the skills of the entrepreneur himself, acquired through education and training in earlier years and experience since. He usually sets up business around these skills, and he does this for the most part in his native locality and predominantly in the same industry and product sector as his previous employment. He is therefore highly dependent on the stock of knowledge of his region or locality. Technical entrepreneurs and entrepreneurs using new technology are no different in this regard (Udell 1982). However, where there is a more diverse stock of knowledge at the start-up of a firm it is more likely to survive and grow—for example, when a firm is founded by three or four partners with a mix of skills in technology, marketing, finance and production (Hoad 1964; Roberts 1983).

The stock of knowledge can also be considered as the technical culture of a region. It embraces the traditions of a region in its crafts, skills and technology and also in its aesthetic culture or faculty. This faculty finds expression both in the appreciation of the well-designed, well-made product and in the marriage of technology and design to produce a creative or innovative product. Where the tradition is maintained but renewed and reinforced with new techniques and technology, then the potential for innovation and creativity is enhanced.

Nutrient information (Shapero 1985), as the term implies, is that information which nourishes the stock of knowledge of the entrepreneur and leads to creativity. It creates an awareness of new developments in technologies, techniques and markets and thus leads to new ides for innovation. It consists of attendance at conferences, courses and exhibitions, talking with suppliers, customers and fellow entrepreneurs, all the informal reading, meeting and talking of everyday life, and of browsing and finding by chance. Chance is the source of many innovative ideas. The wealth of the nutrient information flow to which an entrepreneur is exposed is pre-eminently dependent on the wealth of the stock of knowledge of his locality, a wealth in quality and diversity. Localities which have a multi-technology and multi-sectoral industrial structure, particularly amongst its small and medium enterprises (SMEs), have higher entrepreneurial vitality than those with a predominant technology or sector.

Logistic information (Shapero 1985) is that information which is required for decision-making in managing the business and for the implementation of an idea. The question is known but not the content of the answer. It has been postulated that the cycle time between demand for the information, that is the identification of the problem and the defining of the question, and the supply of the information is the determining factor in the efficiency and effectiveness of decision-making (Kendrick 1983). If the cycle time exceeds that within which a decision must be made to seize an opportunity or to solve a problem, the business may not grow or may not survive. It is therefore a vital factor in the management of any entrepreneurial venture. The cycle time relates to internally generated as well as to externally generated information therefore and includes management information. Most new firms fail for management rather than technical reasons (Merrett Cyriax Assocs. 1972). 'Inadequate financial planning accounts for most new product and venture failures' (Udell 1982). The externally generated information is primarily from local sources. Where there is autonomy in information supply and the half-hour information-contact potential, the supply of logistic information can be efficient. The cycle time and the quality of the decision are therefore dependent on the stock of knowledge of the locality, either in supplying the information or in directing to an efficient source of supply.

Technical Culture

The concept of technical culture (Hubert and Moatbi 1984), referred to earlier as being part of the stock of knowledge of a region or locality, is one which will have increasing significance as the industrial economy merges into the information economy. Introduced by Thierry Gaudin in France some time in the 1970s, it is perhaps a philosophical concept with all the greyness of a philosophical concept. Nevertheless, it was incorporated into the French Ninth Plan (1984–8), such had been its success in promoting new thinking and new initiatives to support the innovative process.

The concept grew from the realisation that innovation in the past had stemmed from a single culture that was both aesthetic and technical. The great cathedrals of Europe, for example, were not the brainchild of an artist without technology or a technologist without art. Da Vinci was representative of his age, albeit a genius. Gaudin saw that if Europe was to attain prosperity again it must return to a unitary culture. Innovation in the future would be a product of a mix of design, taste, the aesthetically pleasing, and of technologies of materials and shaping of materials, pervaded by the new technologies of biotechnology and information technology. The divisions between culture and technology, as well as between technologies, were becoming a barrier to innovation, since 'Industrial action has to reconcile technical, economic and aesthetic needs' (Lang 1983).

The industrial mass-production society brought about a division between the arts and technology. Culture came to be associated solely with the humanities, literature, music, art—and pure science. It was and is a snobbish culture. Technology and industry are considered to be somehow at a lower level, tedious, dirty and certainly not creative activities. Perhaps even worse, technologies became separated. The specialisation of the industrial mass-production society had ramifications right through society. As Massingham said in his introduction to *Lark Rise to Candleford*, a classic description of the end of English rural culture, 'what suffered most [from industrialisation and proletarianisation] was that inborn aesthetic faculty, once the possession of all countrymen' and the possession also of many others.

This destruction of the aesthetic faculty by the mass-production society and its mass-media culture has come about also through a debasing and loss of traditional skills. Aubert and Gaudin (1978) have referred to the contempt of the Eskimo son for the old-fashioned skills of the father. Seamus Murphy, the Irish sculptor, says: 'It is a sad thing to see that happen to any craftsman: the very thing that sustained him in his young years, and his father before him, becoming a subject of ridicule with the new generation.' Yet traditional skills are as essential to new technology as they were to past technologies. Explaining why Philips bought into Grundig, a Vice President of Philips said 'Grundig has an image of high quality and don't forget that the company is based in a part of Germany where mechanical arts and skills have been important for centuries' (Fox 1982). Cornwell, in discusssing 'Stuttgart: Germany's job creation machine' (1986), states that the city 'has profited considerably from an extraordinary ability to blend academe and industry'. He thereby reveals what has become the strong British tradition to identify academics with culture and as something separate from the technical innovation which makes Stuttgart prosperous. Nevertheless, he quotes the president of the Chamber of Commerce and director of the Bach Academy.

> A lot of intelligence used to be channelled into philosophy and science (in the nineteenth century) but the next generation went into industry. This intellectual curiosity and imagination turned into technological innovation. I run a company and have several patents to my name. I know my cultural background has helped a lot with my job.

The alienation between technology and culture has been reinforced by an education system which has organised itself to associate culture and creativity with the humanities and 'pure' sciences. Technology, the creation and application of 'know-how' has been increasingly associated with all that is anti-social or at best a 'vulgar' art. Technologists are not only given no education in the humanities and arts but are also taught their specialisation in a narrow way. Having a specialist understanding rather than a polyvalent one, their innovative capability is constrained since creativity is essentially dependent on bringing together concepts from differing arts and technologies.

Society, influenced in attitude by the education system, including its lack of understanding of technology, has in effect ostracised technology, industry, and industrial culture from its culture.

Western Europe therefore needs to recreate its technical culture through revitalising its many diverse regional cultures and through an education and training system which gives a polyvalent understanding of art and technology to all its specialists, whether they be in humanities or technologies. Europe needs a policy of diversity for its regions rather than the standardisation for which the European Commission seems to strive. Northern Italy has pre-eminently shown how the traditional culture married to excellent engineering can give world leadership in textiles, furniture and household and office fittings and equipment. But it is a regional, not a national, culture.

The Regional Problem

The major problem confronting the regions of Europe, peripheral, declining, and in recession, can be simply expressed. How can the quality and diversity of the technical culture and the stock of knowledge be nourished, the flow of nutrient information be made open and diverse and the cycle time of logistic information supply so reduced that the region can support an innovative and entrepreneurial vitality equivalent to that of a technically progressive firm or a technically progressive or innovative region? The problem of regions which do not have self-generated growth may be exacerbated by the evolution of the information economy. This emerging economy appears to be reducing some of the barriers but it is also creating a yet higher need for knowledge and information.

The Information Sector

The role of information in economic development has accelerated in the last two to three decades. There is now considerable evidence indicating the emergence of information-based economies in the developed countries of Europe (OECD 1979), in the United States (Porat 1977), Japan, Australia (Tucker 1977), and in more recently industrialising countries such as Singapore (Jussawala and Cheah 1983). Wealth creation in a modern economy is shifting from the production-technology-dominated materials and energy-intensive industries of the industrial economy to industries whose central activities are information processing, and whose main capital inputs are information and knowledge. Their competitiveness is dependent on the information component of the end-product.

Technically progressive and successfully innovative firms are active in their quest for information. Their success has been shown to be attributable to their continuing search for and openness to information in order to deal with an increasingly complex and more rapidly changing environment. As a result, they are changing in structure and organisation. Their main objective is the pursuit of knowledge, not profit (Shackle 1982). They are learning systems (Schon 1973). They are structured around their information-intensive functions rather than round their production function, and their main activities have become enquiring, communicating and deciding (Marschak 1968). Their information systems have become central to the basic business and information has become the crucial resource to be managed (Tricker 1982). Information activities are no longer support activities. Competitiveness is determined by the quality and cost of the information and knowledge component of the end-products (Parker 1981). The main capital inputs are no longer lands, buildings and equipment but information and knowledge (Lamberton 1972). These changes at the microeconomic level of the firm are inevitably having a macroeconomic effect.

The perception of this change at the macroeconomic level led to the identification of a knowledge sector in the American economy by Machlup (1962). He identified this sector as the one providing the main source of growth in employment rather than the service sector. Porat (1977) developed a definitional framework which he used to carry out a more in-depth analysis of the American economy and which has been used for comparative studies of member states by OECD (1979) and elsewhere. These confirmed and continued Machlup's original findings—the information sector, as now termed, is the main source of employment and growth in a modern economy. They also confirmed Marschak's thesis that the main activities of a modern economy are enquiring, communicating (including evaluating) and deciding (1968). They masked, however, the fact that much of the employment was in large bureaucracies which, although heavily engaged in information processing, were still primarily in pursuit of profits not knowledge. These bureaucracies were for the most part neither innovative nor entrepreneurial as has been indicated in such studies as those of Lewis (1982) and Peters and Waterman (1982).

The information sector began to adopt its strong growth curve in the 1950s in most countries. Its initial impetus was the need for information to control expanding large national and multinational businesses and the complexities in their administration and external environment (Hughes and Sasson, 1980). However, in more recent years there has been a discernible trend in national and international markets towards information-intensive products, a new market culture and environment, and this is leading to change in industrial organisation.

Information-Intensive Markets

Mass production generated unprecendented wealth and new standards of living and opportunity for the peoples of the industrialised West. Their industries served not only their own markets but also the markets of less-developed, colonial and former colonial countries. These were largely sources of raw materials rather than competitors. The last twenty years have seen a radical change and it is in the changes in markets, both international and domestic, that one can discern the needs of the future.

The developing world is in process of transition. Some, the newly industrialising countries, having brought in mass-production technology, often more up to date than that in use in the countries of origin, are able to outsell the West in the very products on which the West based its growth. They are now markets for technology, equipment and systems, custom-designed to meet particular needs and for other products which embody technical excellence, quality and skills.

Domestic markets in the West, and indeed in the rest of the world, are becoming more discerning. Increased standards of living have given the ability to choose. Increased standards of education have created a new level not only of taste but of awareness. The consumer is increasingly wanting products suited to his particular tastes, needs or wants. He is demanding more creativity, more diversity and better performance and quality in his purchases (Dept of Trade 1983). 'Design is tending to become one of the vital factors in innovation' (Piatier 1981). *Business Week* (1983), the corporation magazine, has been increasingly talking of fragmented markets and forecasting 'every market breaking into smaller and smaller units, with unique products aimed at defined segments'. Price is no longer a dominant factor, as has been demonstrated in, for example, a study of the buying of tractors by British farmers (Rothwell 1983). 'Entrepreneurial activity is not focused on competing on the basis of price' (Pavitt 1979). Communications, transport and the higher added value of an information-intensive product diminish the need to be close to dominant centres. 'Its main competitive advantage is not geographical proximity to a richer expanding market but its ability to respond to international threats and opportunities emerging from changing tastes, technology, relative prices and competition' (Pavitt 1979).

The significant factor in the market change is that the knowledge-, information- and skills-intensive component will increasingly determine competitiveness. This component consists of design, technological excellence, performance in use, and close matching to user needs. The users themselves are becoming more information-intensive. The customers are more aware and demand more information to increase their awareness. They seek value for money and therefore more information on which to base their choice.

> The trend towards a more mature customer suggests a shift from image oriented adverts towards information oriented adverts. With the aid of more information, and the maturity to make use of it, consumers will shop with greater self-assurance. This greater self-assurance will accelerate the concern for quality, demands for reliability and good customer service (Ogilvy 1984).

Consumers are reacting against a production-orientated manufacturing system and seeking a manufacturing system orientated to servicing their needs. Servicing these needs involves a process of virtually continuous innovation and creativity to meet constantly changing and developing needs and to produce diverse and more customised products. 'The dominant activity moves from investment in productive capacity to investment in R & D and in other activities necessary for product innovation and related process change' (Pavitt 1979).

A Molecular Economy

Hence pursuit of knowledge and information becomes the dominant central activity of the firm, but in a new organisational structure. Flexibility, rapid response to change, diversity in production, require smaller units of organisation.

> In the era of human capital, an era that all industrialised countries are entering, high volume standardised production will to a great extent be replaced by flexible system production, in which integrated teams of workers identify and solve problems. This new organisation of work necessarily will be more collaborative, participating and egalitarian than is high volume standardised production, for the simple reason that initiative, responsibility and discretion must be so much more widely exercised within it. Since its success depends on quickly identifying and responding to opportunities in its rapidly changing environment, the flexible enterprise cannot afford rigidly hierarchical chains of command (Reich 1983).

The entrepreneurial organisation of the information economy would therefore seem to be one structured at the level of the small unit of organisation, a small unit in itself or a large organisation broken down into such small units. Japan appears to be leading this trend. Quality circles were a first step in this direction—the Japanese name for them being 'small group activities'. Kyoto Ceramic has broken into small virtually autonomous units integrating all functions within their product specialisation. Toyota sees itself breaking into smaller units each with a high level of information activities to produce customised vehicles. The trend is observable elsewhere. Firms in Italy producing information technology and at the forefront in internal diffusion and use of the technology, are demonstrating a 'centrifugal force' at work (Lamborghini and Antonelli 1979), decentralising into small units, each with autonomy in decision-making and integrating their research, design and marketing functions. This decentralisation is being reinforced by desire for a higher-quality lifestyle and work-style. 'The widening of both work and life-style choices will be among the many big growth small scale industries, on sub-contracting to which larger firms will increasingly rely' (Macrae 1976).

> When *Small is Beautiful* appeared in 1973, it was viewed in some circles as yet another attack on big business ... It ridiculed the conventional wisdom at the time, which held that the bigger a plant—or even a company—the more efficient it was likely to be ... But in a growing number of industries the death knell is tolling for a philosophy that has dominated manufacturing since the days of Henry Ford ... in a lot of industries we've discovered that small is beautiful (*Business Week* 1984).

A further impact of these changes is that 'barriers to entry to a market by new small firms are diminished and the larger company anxious to retain market share and leadership relies for much of its input and indeed product range on buying from smaller specialised companies which are leading in specific areas' (Sweeney 1981).

Present indicators are therefore that the information economy will be a 'molecular' economy composed of small units of production and service, each being information-intensive in its internal functions and organised around these but also being heavily dependent on and interconnected with external information and networks. It will be an economy with high entrepreneurial vitality. Information technology will be the nervous system of this economy, accelerating the trend to decentralisation, and supporting the increasing dependence on external information.

Externalising of Information Processing

Internalisation of information processing has been until recently reinforced by informaton technology. In its early stages, computer technology was a technology which could be adopted only by large organisations due to cost and to the character of the technology as a central technology. This centralising effect was reinforced by the use of telecommunication networks to transmit data to the central computer and provide improved control over dispersed operations by central decision-making (Hughes and Sasson 1980). It strengthened the hierarchical centralised structure (Antonelli 1981). The market demand for more innovative, higher quality and more diverse products and services is creating a counterpressure in favour of more decentralisation and for externalisation of information activities.

The evidence of technically progressive firms and of localities with high entrepreneurial vitality points to high dependence on external information which will tend to grow as market and competitive trends towards information-intensive products and services develop. As information and knowledge become the main capital inputs to economically productive enterprise, so will manufacturing and service business intensify the search for and purchase of information and knowledge from external sources.

The analyses of the information sectors in developed economies bear out this point. Information is now a traded good as well as a private good (ITAP 1983). There has been a remarkable growth in all types of information-providing industries—in technical, financial, managerial and marketing consultancy, in databanks and databases, in 'information brokers', in publishing and semi-publishing and in information-dissemination industries based on new information technology. The extraordinary development of Reuters is one example, as is the realisation by Sears Roebuck that its future development is as an information provider rather than a department store.

The quaternary information sector is now analogous to the primary sector and part of the secondary sector. External know-how and processed data and information are readily bought as necessary inputs to the final product. They are bought as if they were materials for further processing or as components for assembly into the final products. The potential for more liberal access to information is thus enhanced. It becomes more available on the market.

Impact of Information Technology

The impact of information technology in accelerating the evolution towards an information economy derives from it being the integration into one technology of the previously separate telecommunications, computing and control technologies, and the ability which it will have to transmit through one channel information in all modes—data, text, sound and vision. It will provide abundant, varied and versatile modes of gathering, storing, processing and transmitting information.

Since information can be gathered, stored, processed and accessed at the point at which it is generated, and stored, processed or accessed at any other point regardless of geographical distance, the technology provides for any decision-making point to be fully informed. The technology is distance independent. Appropriately developed, it will allow the small unit, however remote, the same power of information and knowledge as the larger organisation. For this reason, it is itself a major influence in the decentralisation of larger organisations which have intensively adopted it internally. Equally, it can provide the means, the total nervous network system, to create an economy equal in vitality in all its parts to the core centre.

The technology and the services which it makes feasible cannot be considered independently, and it was for this reason that Nora and Minc (1978) coined the term '*telematique*', indicating that it was not merely the technology but the information it carried which is the driving force of 'l'informatisation de la société'. The energy and other technologies of the industrial society extended man's muscle power and manipulative skills. Telematics, a word coined by the French to embrace all the above elements, extends man's intellectual skills. Only his imagination will limit its applications.

A significant factor in the impact of information technology lies in its incorporation in manufacturing processes and the evolution of 'flexible manufacturing'. A flexible manufacturing system is one in which computer-controlled and robotic equipment carries out the manufacturing processes. The equipment itself is flexible in its ability to adjust to different sizes and shapes of components to be machined or processed. It is fed by databanks which provide the various parameters for the specific item.

It can thus produce small batches to meet the diverse and customised needs of the market, and do this at 'mass-production prices'. Above all, it frees the organisation to devote itself to its information-intensive activities including those concerned with the production process itself.

At one time it appeared that the potential of information technology lay in providing logistic information, in reducing the cycle time of information exchange and in improving the quality of the information and the ultimate business decision-making. Now it seems that its major impact will be in the richness and interactivity of person-to-person communication which it makes possible, and in that combination of nutrient and logistic information supply which person-to-person contact gives.

What Kind of Regions?

This chapter has set out a number of hypotheses and issues. It remains to ask what kind of regions have prosperity and the ability to maintain a cumulative pattern of growth through the creation of new economic activities? What distinguishes the prosperous from the non-prosperous? What has led some regions into decline and prevented others from achieving prosperity in modern times? Is the analogy between a technically progressive firm and a prosperous region the correct one, and, therefore, are the quality of the stock of knowledge and the nutrient information flows and the autonomy of the logistic information the critical factors? In other words, is it the information-richness allied with entrepreneurial potential which gives a region or locality its self-generated growth and vice versa?

If one could set out a classification of regions according to a set of characteristics which were related to their information and entrepreneurial characteristics, governments might then be able to adopt programmes which would be more effective in promoting growth and overcoming disparities than programmes pursued to date.

From the empirical studies referred to in this chapter and the thrust of the discussion, there are a number of characteristics which seem to merit investigation in regard to the information-richness and -poverty and the entrepreneurial potential:

- The size of the small firm sector and the tradition of self-employment, and conversely the dominance of large firms in an economy; these would appear to determine the entrepreneurial potential of a region or locality.
- The mix and diversity of technologies, sectors of industry and therefore occupations in a region; these affect the stock of knowledge in a region but more particularly they affect the nutrient flow of information. The mix leads to identification of opportunities and to creativity.
- The education system, concentration of research or other knowledge institutes also have a strong bearing on the stock of knowledge and nutrient flow of information. The education system is, however, probably the more important, since, as has been mentioned, the presence of research of itself is not an essential characteristic of 'technical progressiveness'.
- The concentration of decision-making determines the autonomy of a region and those within it since it determines the cycle time of logistic information. The 'half-hour information-contact potential' determines not only the accessibility of information but also the obtaining of an input from another's decision. Without this, the making of a decision extends beyond the cycle item for initiative-taking and entrepreneurial seizing of an opportunity.

References

ABT Forschung (1982). *An overall view of employment in small and medium sized enterprises in the EEC*. Report prepared for the Commission of the European Communities, Bonn, September.

Allen, T. J. (1977). *Managing the flow of technology*. Cambridge, MA, MIT Press.

Antonelli, C. (1981). *Transborder data flows and international business—a pilot study*. Paris, OECD (DSTI/ICCP/81.16).

Arrow, K. J. (1974). *The limits of organisation*. New York, Norton.

Aubert, J.-E. and Gaudin, T. (1978). 'Innovation and unemployment: towards a cultural reading.' Six Countries Workshop, Paris.

Bannock, G. (1976). *The small business in Britain and Germany*. Aldershot, Wilton House Publications.

Bannock, G. (1983). *The economics of small firms: return from the wilderness*. Oxford, Blackwell.

Bannon, M. J. (1977). *Service type employment and regional development*. NESC Report no. 28, Dublin.

Bannon, M. J. (1982). 'Urban growth and regional policy'. Ann. Conf., Regional Studies Assoc. Dublin.

Bearse, P. J. (1981). *A study of entrepreneurship by region and SMSA size*. Philadelphia, Public/Private Ventures.

Beckett, T. (1986). 'An essential feature of company operation' in Gardiner, P. and Rothwell, R., *Innovation, a study of the problems and benefits of product innovation*. London, The Design Council.

Beesley, M. (1965). 'The birth and death of industrial establishments: the experience of the West Midlands conurbation', *Jnl. Ind. Econ*., 4.

Boeckhout, I. J. *et al*. (1984). 'Innovation profiles and regional policy in the Netherlands'. Six Countries Workshop, Limerick.

Boswell, J. (1973). *The rise and fall of small firms*. London, Allen & Unwin.

Bouvier, F. (1984). 'Setting up technological networks: theory and practice'. Six Countries Workshop, Limerick.

Brophy, D. J. (1982). 'Venture capital research' in Kent, C. A. *et al*., *Encyclopedia of entrepreneurship*. Englewood Cliffs, NJ, Prentice-Hall.

Bruno, A. V. and Tyebjee, T. T. (1982). 'The environment of entrepreneurship' in Kent, C. A., *et al*., *Encyclopedia of entrepreneurship*, Englewood Cliffs, NJ, Prentice-Hall.

Bulloch, J. F. (1979). 'The vital role of small scale enterprises in job creation and business development'. 6th. Intl. Symp. on Small Business, Berlin.

Business Week (1983). 'Marketing: the new priority: a splintered mass market forces companies to target their products', 21 November.

Business Week (1984). 'Small is beautiful now in manufacturing', 22 October.

Carter, C. F. and Williams, B. R. (1957). *Industry and technical progress*. Oxford University Press.

Cooper, A. C. (1972). 'Incubator organisations and technical entrepreneurship' in Cooper, A. C. and Komives, J. L., eds, *Technical entrepreneurship: a symposium*. Milwaukee, Center for Venture Management.

Cooper, A. C. (1973). 'Technical entrepreneurship: what do we know?', *Res. and Dev. Management*, 3, February.

Cornwell, R. 'Stuttgart: Germany's job creation machine', *Financial Times*, 20 March.

Crane, D. (1984). *An inter-organisational approach to the development of indigenous technological capabilities: some reflections on the literature*. Paris, OECD, Development Centre (Industry and Technology Occasional Paper, no. 3).

CTAB (Commerce Technical Advisory Board) (1967). *Technological innovation: its environment and management*. Washington, DC, Dept of Commerce (Charpie Report).

Dahmen, E. (1970). *Entrepreneurial activity and the development of Swedish industry*. Homewood, IL, Irwin.

Dennison, E. F. (1967). *Why growth rates differ: postwar experience in nine Western countries*. Washington, DC, The Brookings Institution.

Dean, B. V. (1983). 'A network method in the management of innovative start-ups' in Hornaday, J. L., *et al.*, *Frontiers in Entrepreneurship Research*. Wellesley, MA, Babson College.

Dept of Trade (1982). *U.K. Standards, quality and international competitiveness*. London, HMSO (Cmnd 8621).

Deutermann, E. P. (1966). 'Seeking science based industry', *Fed. Res. Bank of Philadelphia Business Review*, May, 3–10.

EAG (Economists Advisory Group) (1978). *Small firms in cities: a review of recent research*. Shell U.K. Ltd.

Economist (1984). 'Fast fries or high tech', 16 June, 12.

EPA (European Productivity Agency) (1958). *Technical information and the smaller firm*. Paris, OECD.

Firn, J. R. and Swales, J. K. (1978). 'The formation of new manufacturing establishments in the central Clydeside and West Midlands conurbations, 1963–1972', *Regional Studies*, 12, 199–213.

Fox, B. (1982). 'Has European industry a future?', *New Scientist*, 7 January, 16–18.

Freedman, A. E. (1983). 'New Technology based firms: critical location factors' in Hornaday, J. L., *et al.*, *Frontiers in Entrepreneurial Research*. Wellesley, MA, Babson College.

Freeman, C., Clark, J. and Suete, L. (1982). *Unemployment and technical innovation*. London, Frances Pinter.

Gaudin, Th. (1985). 'Definition of innovation policies' in Sweeney, G. P., ed., *Innovation policies: an international perspective*. London, Frances Pinter.

Gudgin, G. (1978). *Industrial location processes and regional employment growth*. Saxon House, Farnborough.

Hertay, P. and Leroy, G. (1974). 'Increasing innovation potential of firms by management of resources and of information', *R & D Management*, 4(2), February, 113–14.

Hoad, W. and Rosko, P. (1964). *Management factors contributing to the success or failure of new small manufacturers*. Ann Arbor, University of Michigan, 1964.

Holm, K. (1973). *Innovation*. Milan, The International Institute for the Management of Technology.

Hubert, P. and Moatbi, J. P. (1984). 'Technological culture and success in industry'. Six Countries Programme.

Hughes, P. and Sasson, R. (1980). 'The usage of international networks in Europe' in *Policy implications of data network developments in the OECD area*. Paris, OECD.

ITAP (Information Technology Advisory Panel) (1983). *Making a business of information: a survey of new opportunities*. London, HMSO.

Jacobs, J. (1969). *The economy of cities*. New York, Random House.

Jacobs, Jane (1984). *Cities and the wealth of nations: principles of economic life*. Toronto, Random House.

Jussawalla, M. and Cheah, C.-W. (1983). 'Towards an information economy: the case of Singapore', *Inf. Econ. and Policy*, 1(2), 161–76.

Kendrick, J. G. (1983). 'Cycle times of informaton', *The Information Society*, 2(2), 97–106.

Keynes, J. M. (1936). *The general theory of employment, interest and money*. New York, Harcourt Brace.

Lamberton, D.McL. (1972). 'Information and profit' in *Uncertainty and expectations in economics: essays in honour of G. L. S. Shackle*. Oxford, Blackwell.

Lamborghini, B. and Antonelli, C. (1979). 'The impact of electronics on industrial structures and firms' strategies'. OECD Special Session on impact of microelectronics on productivity and employment, November.

Lamont, L. M. (1972). 'The role of marketing in technical entrepreneurship' in Cooper, A. C. and Komives, J. L., eds, *Technical entrepreneurship: a symposium*. Milwaukee, WI, Center for Venture Management, 1972.

Lang, J. (1983). 'Minister of creation', *Design*, November, 58–9.

Lewis, J. D. (1982). 'Technology, enterprise and American economic growth', *Science*, 215, 5 March, 1204–11.

Lindbeck, A. (1981). 'Can the rich countries adapt? Need and difficulties', *OECD Observer*, January, 6–9.

Machlup, F. (1962). *The production and distribution of knowledge*. Princeton, Princeton University Press.

Macrae, N. (1976). 'The coming entrepreneurial revolution: a survey', *The Economist*, 25 December, 41–65.

Macrae, N. (1982). 'Intrapreneurial now', *The Economist*, 17 April, 47–52.

Malecki, E. J. (1981). 'Science, technology and regional economic development: review and prospects', *Res. Policy*, 10, 312–34.

Mandeville, T. (1983). 'The spatial effects of information technology', *Futures*, February, 65–72.

Marschak, J. (1968). 'The economics of enquiring, communicating and deciding', *Am. Econ. Rev*., 58(2), 1–8.

Massingham, H. J. (1973). 'Introduction' to Thompson, F., *Lark Rise to Candleford*. Harmondsworth, Penguin Books.

Merrett Cyriax Assocs (1972). *Dynamics of small firms. Research Report no. 12. Committee of Enquiry on Small Firms*. London, HMSO.

MITI (1984). White paper on small and medium enterprises in Japan. Small and Medium Enterprise Agency.

Murray, F., O'Brolchain, D. and Sweeney, G. P. (1973). *A survey of scientific and technical information in Ireland*. Dublin, IIRS, 2 vols.

Murphy, S. (1966). *Stone mad*. London, Routledge & Kegan Paul.

Niederwemmer, U. (1980). 'Management support of innovative company founders'. Six Countries Workshop, Limerick.

Nora, S. and Minc, A. (1978). *L'Informatisation de la société: raport à M. Le President de la Republique*. Paris, La Documentation Française.

OECD (1978). *Policies for the stimulation of industrial innovation. Analytical Report*. Paris, Vol. 1.

OECD (1979). *Report on the economic analysis of information activities and the role of electronics and telecommunication technologies*. Paris.

OECD (1980). *Technical change and economic policy*. Paris.

OECD (1982). *Innovation in small and medium firms*. Paris.

Ogilvy, J. A. (1984). *Social issues and trends: the maturation of America*. Stanford Res. Inst., Res. Rept. no. 697.

Parker, E. B. (1981). 'Information services and economic growth', *The Information Society*, 1(1), 71–8.

Pavitt, K. (1979). 'Technical innovation and industrial development', *Futures*, December, 458–70.

Pennings, J. M. (1982). 'Organisational birth frequencies: an empirical investigation', *Administrative Science Qtly*., 27, 120–44.

Peters, T. J. and Waterman, R. H. (1982). *In search of excellence*. New York, Harper & Row.

Piatier, A. (1981). *Barriers to innovation in European Community countries*. Brussels, C.E.C.

Porat, M. U. (1978). 'Communication policy in an information economy' in Robinson, G. O., ed., *Communications for tomorrow*. New York, Praeger.

Porat, M. U. (1977). *The information economy*. Washington, DC, US Dept of Commerce, 9 vols.

Reich, R. B. (1983). *The next American frontier*. New York, Times Books.

Roberts, E. B. (1983). 'Business planning in the start-up high technology enterprise' in Hornaday, J. L., *et al*., *Frontiers of Entrepreneurship Research*, Wellesley, MA, Babson College.

Rothwell, R., *et al*. (1974). 'SAPPHO updated—project SAPPHO phase II', *Res. Policy*, 3, 258–91.

Rothwell, R. (1983). 'Design matters more than price', *Design*, January.

Rothwell, R. (1985). 'Venture finance, small firms and public policy in the U.K.', *Research Policy*, 14, 253–65.

Rotter, J. B. (1966). 'Generalised expectancies for internal versus external control of reinforcement'. Psychological Monographs, 80.

Sabel, C. F. (1982). 'Italy's high technology cottage industry', *Transatlantic Perspectives*, December.

Schell, D. W. (1983). 'Entrepreneurial activity: a comparison of three North Carolina communities' in Hornaday, J. L. *et al*., *Frontiers in entrepreneurship*. Wellesley, MA, Babson College, 495–507.

Schon, D. A. (1973). *Beyond the stable state: public and private learning in a changing society*. Harmondsworth, Penguin Books.

Seeman, M. and Evans, J. W. (1962). 'Alienation and learning in a hospital setting', *American Sociological Review*, 27.

Segal Quince and Partners (1985). *The Cambridge phenomenon*. Cambridge.

Shackle, G. L. S. (1972). *Expectation, enterprise and profit*. Oxford, Blackwell.

Shapero, A. (1972). 'The process of technical company formation in a local area' in Cooper, A. C. and Komives, J. L., eds, *Technical entrepreneurship: a symposium*. Milwaukee, Center for Venture Management.

Shapero, A. (1977). *The role of entrepreneurship in economic development at the less than national level*. Washington, DC, Dept of Commerce.

Shapero, A. (1983). *The role of the financial institutions of a community in the formation, effectiveness and expansion of innovating companies*. Washington, DC, Small Business Administration.

Shapero, A. (1985). *Managing professional people: understanding creative performance*. New York, The Free Press.

Shapero, A. and Sokol, L. (1982). 'The social dimensions of entrepreneurship' in Kent, C. A., *et al.*, *Encyclopedia of entrepreneurship.* Englewood Cliffs, NJ, Prentice-Hall.

SPRU (Science Policy Research Unit), Univ. of Sussex (1972). *Success and failure in industrial innovation: Report on Project SAPPHO*. London, Centre for the Study of Industrial Innovation.

Storey, D. J. (1982). *Entrepreneurship and the new firm*. London, Croom Helm.

Susbauer, J. C. (1972). 'The technical entrepreneurship process in Austin, Texas' in Cooper, A. C. and Komives, J., eds, *Technical entrepreneurship: a symposium*. Milwaukee, Center for Venture Management.

Sweeney, G. P. (1975). 'The pursuit of knowledge', *The Inf. Scientist*, 9(2) June, 51–6.

Sweeney, G. P. (1981). *New entrepreneurship and the smaller firm*. Dublin, IIRS for Six Countries Programme.

Sweeney, G. P. (1985). 'Entrepreneur-led innovation' in Sweeney, G. P., *Innovation policies: an international perspective*. London, Frances Pinter.

Thompson, W. (1965). *A preface to urban economics*. Baltimore, Johns Hopkins University Press.

Tornquist, G. (1970). *Contact systems and regional development*.Lund Studies, Series B (35).

Tricker, R. I. (1982). 'How to plan information strategy', *Management Today*, September, 62ff.

Tucker, K. A., ed. (1977). *The service sector of the Australian economy*. London, Croom Helm.

Udell G. (1982). 'Elaboration on entrepreneurs and innovation', in Kent, C. A., *et al.*, *Encyclopedia of entrepreneurship*. Englewood Cliffs, NJ, Prentice-Hall.

Utton, M. (1971). 'The effects of mergers on concentration in U.K. manufacturing, 1954–65', *Jnl. Ind. Econ.*

Valecha, G. K. (1972). 'Construct validation of internal–external locus of reinforcement related to work-related variables', Proc. 80th Annual Convention, American Psychological Assocn., 7.

Wolk, S. and DuCette, J. (1974). 'International performance and incidental learning as a function of personality and task dimensions', *Jnl. of Personality and Social Psychology*, 29.

CHAPTER 3

Entrepreneurial Potential

Separation of entrepreneurial and innovation potential can be difficult, particularly since investigation of the sectoral distribution of small firms involves the same statistical data. Hence, this chapter consists first of a country-by-country presentation of data on industrial structure by size and sector, with some data on specific regions. The second part of the chapter discusses the relative entrepreneurial potentials in Europe. Chapter 4 discusses the influence of sectoral distribution together with a number of other factors influencing innovation potential.

Examination of statistical data on industrial structure is a difficult task, since they are not in fact easy to obtain for comparison of entrepreneurial and innovative vitality at regional, national and European Community levels. Data on small-firm deaths and births are virtually impossible to obtain. This problem of the lack of data relevant to such regional analysis has been referred to by others investigating regional economic performance, for example Boeckhout and Molle (1982). Other factors which cloud interpretation are, firstly, that administrative regions are often much larger than a natural entity such as a city and its immediate environs and, secondly, that there have been shifts in population across regional boundaries and within regions. In most European countries what effect these factors may have on longer-term ability to create new economic wealth in central more dominant regions cannot be seen without more specific data.

In presenting the various tables of data, one is presenting circumstantial evidence, indicators of the factors which characterise regions, rather than substantiating them in detail. Nevertheless the data, taken in conjunction with the empirical data, do seem to provide sufficient evidence on which to lay the foundation for a classification or systematic differentiation of regions.

Countries, regions and localities with a strong small-firm sector and a high vitality in this sector tend to have a higher level of prosperity. They also tend to have the capacity to renew and reinforce this prosperity over the long term, and to have a resilience in meeting technological, market and economic change. Yet there are regions with substantial employment in small firms which are not prospering.

On the other hand, areas and regions dominated by large enterprises seem to lack the resilience to renew themselves which a large small-firm sector gives. They find difficulty in developing that 'circular and cumulative' pattern of growth (Malecki 1981) which is based on the ability of the local economy to generate new firms and activities as economic and technological conditions change. Areas dominated by large firms tend to be ones with specialisation in a technology or with industries controlled from outside the region. Their rise and decline is associated with the product cycle and the rise and decline of a cycle of innovation and with this the redistribution of production in the international division of labour. At the core of their problem lies the inability to spawn new firms. They have no entrepreneurial culture, which would incubate new firms. The size of the small-firm sector and relative dominance by large firms are important indicators of the entrepreneurial potential for new manufacturing firms. Entrepreneurial potential is also related to the numbers of self-employed and some attempt has been made to include data on these.

Belgium

Belgium has a relatively high population density. In the decade 1971–82 there was a modest increase in population of 200,000. Flanders increased by 252,000, Wallonia by 52,000, and Brussels declined by 90,000. These three regions are gradually becoming more autonomous in management of their regional economies.

Between 1974 and 1982, there was a 4.9 per cent decline in total employment but manufacturing industry employment declined by 28 per cent. Belgium has tended to have a higher unemployment rate than the rest of Europe. Unemployment is highest in Wallonia. 64 per cent of manufacturing industry is located in Flanders, which tends to have the more modern manufacturing sectors such as electronics. The declining steel industry is concentrated in Wallonia, with mining in Flanders. Generally, manufacturing and construction have declined substantially in numbers employed since 1974. Employment in the public services grew by 25 per cent from 1974 to 1982. Belgium also has the highest number of American companies in Europe: over 1,000 have some activity, using the country as a base for European operations with either headquarters or manufacturing or both established there.

The size distribution of manufacturing industry tends towards concentration in larger establishments, but there has been some evidence of deconcentration since 1972, small and intermediate firms increasing their employment share (Table 3.1).

Using different measures, another analysis showed that SMEs increased their share of employment in the private sector from one-third in 1975 to 37 per cent in 1980. In absolute terms, they increased their

Table 3.1 Belgium: change in distribution of manufacturing employment by firm size, 1972–8

Firm size	Employment (1972) (%)	Employment (1978) (%)
10–49	17.9	19.5
50–99	11.0	11.1
100–199	15.5	13.4
200–499	17.7	20.4
500–1,000	12.9	11.0
1,000+	25.1	24.6

Source: ABT (1982).

employment by 2 per cent whereas large enterprises cut their employment by 15 per cent. The number of SMEs grew by 9 per cent while large firms declined by 18 per cent (*Progress* 1983).

The pattern of sectoral distribution of industry (Table 3.2) was that small firms were concentrated in the more traditional sectors such as leather, clothing and footwear, timber and wooden furniture. Large firms dominated in industries, such as production and preliminary processing of metals, electrical engineering, motor vehicles and transport equipment. Smaller firms were stronger in mechanical engineering and metal products. Much of the growth in Flanders has been in foreign-owned firms, of which Flanders has the highest proportion in Europe.

The overall impression is therefore that self-generated growth has been weak. The economy has been dominated by large firms and their decline has been compensated for mainly by new foreign firms and employment in the services sector as well as by early retirement and a high rate of unemployment. Small firms, even though they have shown a small increase, tend to be concentrated in lower technological sectors, but with a good proportion in engineering. The entrepreneurial potential in the industrial sector appears stronger than in some countries with some 30 per cent of employment in firms of less than 100 and 40 per cent in firms of less than 200 employees.

Denmark

Denmark, a decentralised country, has little in the way of raw materials, apart from its agricultural produce. Thus it has a bare minimum of heavy basic industry, and of this a large proportion is concentrated in Copenhagen. There are few firms engaged in mass production of standard

Table 3.2 Belgium: distribution of employment by firm size—1978

Sector	Firm size						
	10–49	50–99	100–199	200–499	500–999	1,000+	Percentage of total mfg
Production and preliminary processing of metals	0.8	1.3	2.2	4.4	1.9	89.4	
Manufacture of non-metallic materials	20.0	11.1	6.8	26.9	20.6	14.7	24.5
Chemicals	6.9	5.3	10.0	31.7	16.8	29.3	
Man-made fibres	3.5	4.6	0.0	24.9	67.1	0.0	
Manufacture of metal articles	22.5	14.4	14.6	15.4	14.9	18.1	
Mechanical eng.	13.4	14.1	12.8	22.6	13.1	24.0	35
Electrical eng.	5.5	1.3	5.3	10.3	16.3	61.3	
Motor vehicles	7.0	4.7	3.3	12.4	18.4	54.3	
Other means of transport	7.3	3.3	6.9	19.1	6.2	57.2	
Instrument eng.	24.2	3.6	19.3	37.7	15.2	0.0	
Food, drink, tobacco	22.6	10.9	20.0	25.1	9.4	11.9	
Textiles	18.6	18.0	16.2	28.7	14.6	3.8	
Leather	41.8	18.8	6.0	33.4	0.0	0.0	
Clothing & footwear	35.4	16.3	19.2	19.0	10.1	0.0	40.4
Timber & wooden furniture	42.6	20.3	17.1	13.4	3.6	3.0	
Paper & printing	19.6	15.0	17.2	25.0	23.1	0.0	
Rubber & plastics	18.2	16.4	25.9	18.6	11.3	9.5	
Other manuf.	38.2	24.7	18.7	14.6	3.8	0.0	
Building & construction	30.0	14.4	17.7	24.9	7.0	5.7	

Source: ABT (1982).

goods. On the contrary, Danish industry is extremely diversified with many enterprises concentrating on products of high value-added content and reputation for quality. No region is dominated by a single technology or large plant.

Copenhagen dominates the rest of the country with over a quarter of industrial firms being located in the municipal area or the surrounding counties. Not surprisingly, industries such as paper, printing and publishing and chemicals show an even higher percentage in the Copenhagen area, but, for industries such as food, based on agricultural produce, and craft industries such as textiles or furniture, the regional spread is much more marked (Table 3.3). Metal fabrication and machinery and equipment sectors are important in all parts of the country.

The engineering sector in fact is the largest, with a third of firms and some 40 per cent of total employment. It has also the largest number of firms and employment amongst firms with less than 100 employees (Table 3.4), but the firms in this sector do tend to be larger than in most other sectors. Food is the next most important sector. Table 3.3 illustrates also the areas with some specialisation, such as Ringkobing in textiles and clothing.

There are significant numbers of small firms in all parts of the country (Tables 3.5 and 3.6) and in all sectors (Table 3.7). Denmark has more than 50 per cent of manufacturing employment in firms of less than 200 employees. It has also the highest per capita income in the EEC, and although there has been some decline in the recession it is not as marked as in some countries. In fact some regions of the country have shown increases. Denmark has also shown a good increase in exports.

Denmark appears to have a well-balanced industrial structure, with a good proportion of employment in firms of under 50 and over 500 employees. The engineering sector is strong and does not include a large car industry. As in other sectors, there is much more specialised small-scale production than mass production. There is a good entrepreneurial potential in the industrial sector in Denmark, significantly more so than in other member states of the EEC. The potential has been realised in a small-firm sector which is competitive internationally and not merely a supplier to its home market.

France

France is a heavily centralised country in terms of government and population, but with a recent tendency to delegate some decision-making to regional councils. The Île de France has nearly one-fifth of the population and one-quarter of GDP. The population movement since 1954 has shown a continuing concentration around Paris and a redistribution to the West and South-West from the North and East. As in other countries,

Table 3.3 Denmark: numbers employed by industry analysed by sector and by region, 1982 (thousands)

Region	Food	Textiles clothing leather	Wood & furniture	Paper printing publishing	Chemicals rubber & plastics	Non-metallic mineral products	Basic metal ind.	Metal fabrication & machinery	Other	Total
Copenhagen	6.6	1.0	0.1	8.7	3.3	1.6	—	11.4	0.4	33.3
Copenhagen County	7.0	0.7	0.7	3.6	9.6	2.1	0.9	21.2	0.8	46.8
Frederiksberg Municipality and County	1.7	0.2	0.3	1.4	3.5	1.9	2.0	9.3	0.2	20.6
Roskilde	1.5	—	1.2	0.5	2.0	0.6	0.1	1.8	0.1	8.0
West Zealand	3.7	0.6	0.6	1.4	1.9	0.6	0.2	6.3	0.3	15.6
Storstrøm	4.6	0.6	0.9	1.7	1.1	1.7	0.1	6.9	—	17.6
Bornholm	1.3	—	—	0.2	—	0.4	—	0.4	—	2.3
Fyn	6.6	2.3	2.0	2.5	2.4	0.6	0.5	17.9	0.5	35.2
South Jutland	3.3	2.3	0.8	0.9	0.2	0.6	—	12.2	0.1	20.6
Ribe	4.4	0.8	1.9	0.5	1.9	0.6	0.3	3.7	2.1	16.3
Vejle	7.8	2.8	1.7	2.5	3.2	1.2	0.2	9.6	0.6	29.6
Ringkøbing	4.1	10.1	3.2	0.8	0.9	0.4	0.5	6.4	—	26.6
Århus	8.5	3.9	2.9	5.4	2.2	1.1	0.3	14.4	0.5	39.2
Viborg	3.9	2.0	2.5	0.9	0.6	0.8	0.4	7.0	0.1	18.2
North Jutland	9.4	1.5	1.2	1.7	1.2	3.1	0.4	14.2	0.2	33.1
Total	74.6	28.8	20.2	32.8	34.2	17.3	6.3	142.7	5.7	363.0

Source: Danish National Industrial Statistics.

Table 3.4 Denmark: distribution of firms and employment by size, 1980

Number of persons employed	Percentage of manufacturing firms	Percentage of manufacturing employment
6–9	19.1	2.4
10–19	30.7	7.5
20–49	27.3	14.8
50–99	11.5	14.0
100–199	6.5	16.0
200–499	3.6	18.9
500 or more	1.4	26.4
Total	100.0	100.0

Source: Danish National Industrial Statistics.

Table 3.5 Denmark: number of firms analysed by region and by size of firm for manufacturing industry, 1982

Region	6–9	10–19	20–49	50–99	100–199	200–499	500+
Copenhagen & Frederiksberg Municipalities	117	190	112	36	21	11	17
Copenhagen County	113	256	196	82	44	32	13
Frederiksberg County	57	102	81	31	20	12	2
Roskilde	46	57	50	18	8	6	1
West Zealand	51	86	82	53	16	16	2
Storstrøm	55	74	76	26	21	13	5
Bornholm	12	16	13	9	4	2	—
Fyn	109	186	181	69	40	21	9
South Jutland	63	99	78	35	13	10	4
Ribej	47	80	78	44	19	9	4
Vejle	89	145	141	54	46	23	6
Ringkøbing	90	204	222	83	33	9	3
Århus	117	243	179	98	39	34	9
Viborg	64	97	115	51	26	11	1
North Jutland	107	152	153	56	45	21	9
Total	1,137	1,987	1,757	745	395	230	85

Table 3.6 Denmark: numbers employed by size of firm and by region for manufacturing industry

Region	Employees by size of firm	
	6–49	50+
Copenhagen and Frederiksberg Municipalities	6,836	29,183
Copenhagen County	10,443	34,642
Frederiksberg County	4,260	11,889
Roskilde	2,667	5,244
West Zealand	4,081	11,679
Storstrøm	3,796	13,626
Bornholm	641	1,799
Fyn	8,761	26,238
South Jutland	4,340	16,164
Ribe	3,864	12,369
Vejle	7,007	22,175
Ringkøbing	10,525	15,910
Århus	9,674	28,861
Viborg	5,397	12,902
North Jutland	7,703	24,969
Total	89,995	267,650

Source: Danish National Industrial Statistics.

Table 3.7 Denmark: employment in small firms by sector, 1982

Sector	0–4	5–9	10–19	20–49	50–99
Food, drink & tobacco	3,509	3,033	3,967	5,490	7,379
Textiles, clothing & leather	1,523	1,658	3,538	6,993	4,854
Wood & furniture	1,565	2,004	3,396	5,558	3,009
Paper, printing & publishing	2,518	3,133	3,414	4,017	4,877
Chemicals, rubber & plastics	712	1,141	1,836	3,988	3,481
Non-metallic mineral products	756	751	1,467	1,533	1,852
Basic metal industries	64	109	219	554	691
Metal fab. & machinery	6,132	6,924	9,854	16,159	13,679
Other industry	649	531	614	996	563
Total	17,428	19,284	28,305	45,288	40,385

Source: Federation of Danish Industries.

urban centres have declined and areas peripheral to large conurbations have grown. Equally, industry is concentrated in the Île de France.

The size distribution of French industry conforms to the pattern of most European countries. There is a bias towards larger industry, with a continuing trend to establishments of more than 1,000 employees between 1972 and 1978. Transport equipment, office machinery, and motor vehicles show the heaviest concentration with mechanical and instrument engineering sectors having a more balanced distribution. Electrical engineering lies between the two (Table 3.8). Small firms tend to be more heavily represented in the traditional industries and in these sectors there was a trend towards deconcentration between 1972 and 1978.

Table 3.8 France: manufacturing employment by sector by firm size, 1978 (per cent)

Industry sector	Firm size					
	10–49	50–99	100–199	200–499	500–999	1,000+
Coke ovens	9.4	6.2	5.8	17.2	19.1	42.3
Nuclear fuels	3.3	1.6	10.1	28.6	40.7	15.7
Production & prelim, processing of metals	2.4	2.4	4.3	14.4	17.3	59.3
Non-metallic mineral products	19.5	12.5	15.1	20.5	14.9	17.4
Chemicals	5.2	8.1	13.9	27.6	15.0	30.3
Man-made fibres	0.8	0.8	4.0	7.2	42.9	44.4
Metal articles	21.5	14.3	15.7	21.4	14.7	12.4
Mechanical engng.	13.8	13.1	14.4	30.6	14.3	13.8
Office machinery, data processing	2.7	3.6	5.3	7.9	6.3	74.1
Electrical engng.	7.8	4.3	6.5	17.0	23.2	41.2
Transport equipment	2.1	2.5	2.5	8.6	10.1	74.1
Motor vehicles	3.6	3.6	3.8	8.8	14.9	65.2
Instrument engng.	19.3	13.6	18.5	28.1	11.3	9.0
Food, drink & tobacco	19.0	16.2	14.4	28.5	11.0	11.0
Textiles	15.9	14.2	22.3	27.7	12.0	7.9
Leather	40.5	21.1	21.2	12.4	4.7	0.0
Clothing & footwear	20.2	15.5	19.2	32.6	9.7	2.8
Timber & furniture	35.8	15.5	20.2	18.2	6.9	3.4
Paper & printing	18.7	14.1	20.1	24.6	13.5	9.0
Rubber & plastics	10.6	9.2	14.2	16.8	14.1	35.1

Source: ABT (1982).

The relative proportions of numbers employed by large and small industries varies widely across the country (Table 3.9). There is almost a 30 per cent gap between the share of employment held by large enterprises in the North-East (Lorraine with 82.7 per cent) and that in the Mediterranean regions (Languedoc-Roussillon with 52.8 per cent).

The regions of industrial decline tend to be the ones with the lowest percentage of employment in firms of less than 100 employees, such as Lorraine with 16 per cent, and Nord-Pas de Calais, 21 per cent.

The employment share of large enterprises reached a maximum in 1975; since then large enterprises have been responsible to varying

Table 3.9 France: employment share of large establishments by region (large establishments having more than 100 employees)

Region	Employment share of large establishment (%)	Ratio of business start-ups to bankruptcies 1984 and 1985 (averages)
Île de France	60.2	4.2
Champagne-Ardenne	71.0	3.1
Picardie	75.1	3.0
Haute-Normandie	79.7	3.0
Centre	71.2	3.2
Basse-Normandie	70.0	4.4
Bourgogne	76.6	3.3
Nord-Pas de Calais	78.8	3.1
Lorraine	83.8	2.7
Alsace	80.0	2.7
Franche-Comté	75.5	4.0
Bretagne	67.9	3.9
Poitou-Charentes	68.4	5.3
Aquitaine	63.8	4.1
Midi-Pyrénées	57.6	4.0
Limousin	56.2	3.5
Rhône-Alpes	62.9	3.9
Auvergne	65.1	3.9
Languedoc-Roussillon	71.5	4.7
Provence-Alpes-Côte d'Azur	53.2	4.1
Corsica	57.2	5.3
France	68.3	—

Source: INSEE (1982); Marsh (1986).

degrees for regional declines in employment. Prior to 1973, employment creation by large firms was three times greater than that by small firms. It ranged between nothing in the North, Lorraine and Île de France and 10–15 per cent in the West. Since 1973, small firms have made a small but positive contribution to employment, moving from a 1 per cent decline to a growth of 3 per cent. The major declines have been attributed to the large enterprises. The regions most affected by the decline were largely in the North and North-East—Nord-Pas de Calais, -10.3 per cent; Lorraine, -11.4 per cent; Champagne-Ardenne, -8.3 per cent; Haute-Normandie, -7.2 per cent; Picardie, -6.6 per cent; Rhône-Alpes, -6.3 per cent (INSEE 1982).

The ratio of business start-ups to bankruptcies does not follow exactly the regional distribution of industry. There is some correlation with entrepreneurial vitality. The industrially declining regions of the North-East have all relatively low scores, whereas the West and South have scores above 4.0, except Brittany at 3.9. Only three regions with 70 per cent of employment in larger enterprises have a ratio of more than 4. Of ten regions with less than 70 per cent in large enterprises, six have a ratio higher than 4 and three have 3.9.

The sectoral distribution of French industry shows that France has a particularly strong engineering sector, metal products and electrical and transport equipment accounting for 43 per cent of employment (Table 3.10). Of these sectors 26.6 per cent are located in the Île de France. Rhône-Alpes has a strong electrical engineering industry around Grenoble, based originally on the hydroelectric power developments in the region and now spawning an electronics and data-processing industry. This region has 14 per cent of the metal products and electrical industry sector. Its chemicals sector has 15.3 per cent of the national employment in this sector, and was based originally on the hydroelectric power generation of rivers feeding the Rhône from the Alps. Lyons is mainly responsible for the region's strong textile sector, in employment terms second in size and having 13.6 per cent of the sector's national employment.

The Île de France has the largest proportion of the food, chemicals, paper and printing, minerals, as well as the metal products and electrical, transport equipment and 'other' sectors. It lies third in the other two sectors. From the data available on industrial structure *per se*, the entrepreneurial potential in France tends to be good in the Île de France, weak in the traditionally industrialised North and East and stronger in the South. Overall, the 31.7 per cent of employment in firms of less than 100 employees gives France a relatively strong industrial entrepreneurial culture. The regional differences are, however, wide. One of the regions with a higher employment rating in smaller firms is the Midi-Pyrénées.

Table 3.10 France: industrial employment by sector and region, 1977 (thousands)

Region	Ferrous & non-ferrous metals	Minerals	Chemicals	Metal products electrical	Transport equipment	Food	Textiles	Paper & printing	Other
Île de France	20	41	94	431	211	78	89	119	93
Champagne-Ardenne	11	10	4	62	8	23	31	8	19
Picardie	10	15	17	69	24	25	29	9	28
Haute-Normandie	5	9	20	69	36	19	22	14	16
Centre	2	15	15	91	28	23	27	14	37
Basse-Normandie	10	4	3	38	24	24	11	5	14
Bourgogne	9	12	9	69	10	17	17	6	24
Nord-Pas de Calais	49	36	21	107	41	46	121	24	23
Lorraine	77	17	11	61	11	25	42	12	26
Alsace	4	15	10	64	22	21	33	14	16
Franche-Comté	2	5	6	61	52	11	11	4	23
Pays de la Loire	6	12	6	81	43	39	52	11	40
Bretagne	1	12	3	39	32	41	15	8	19
Poitou-Charentes	1	10	5	32	16	19	17	9	20
Aquitaine	2	12	13	38	22	27	30	14	29
Midi-Pyrénées	7	11	10	36	21	21	38	7	16
Limousin	1	7	1	17	7	7	12	6	9
Rhône-Alpes	22	27	51	238	51	45	101	31	66
Auvergne	5	6	6	33	11	15	13	6	46
Languedoc-Roussillon	6	10	6	19	1	15	15	4	10
Provence-Alpes-Côte d'Azur-Corsica	12	18	21	45	43	36	18	14	19
France	262	303	334	1,701	713	577	744	341	592

Source: *Eurostat Review* 1982.

The Midi-Pyrénées, on the periphery of France and, until 1986, of the EEC, was given closer examination in the Six Countries Workshop (Bouvier 1984). It is the largest of the 22 French regions, 8.3 per cent of the area of France, but it lies ninth in population with a population density of 51 per square km, half the French national average. The population is heavily concentrated in the Toulouse region. The First World War had dramatic long-term effects in the development of hydraulic power to meet the demands of textile, chemical and other industries and in the birth of an aircraft manufacturing plant which eventually was to become Aerospatiale. The textile industry is the largest employer, mainly in small firms, and employing only one-quarter as many people as in 1896. The industry is concentrated in southern Tarn, east Ariège and Toulouse. This is followed by Aerospatiale, with 22,000 employees. Aerospatiale has led to the development of advanced technological activities with a large network of widely dispersed subcontractors.

The Midi-Pyrénées in fact consists of several distinct regions. It contains eight *départements*. Haute-Garonne, which contains Toulouse, has six out of the ten largest firms, and in 1979 had 37.7 per cent of industrial salaries, 41.3 per cent of industrial value added and the majority of industries producing consumer goods. The Tarn and the Hautes-Pyrénées employ respectively only 21.3 per cent and 10.2 per cent of industrial employees. No other *département* reaches 8 per cent. The agricultural sector, with 390,000 employees, is still very much larger than the industrial sector, with 167,000, but it has not led to the development of agriculture-based industries. The high technology engineering of Toulouse has bypassed it.

Hence, the Midi-Pyrénées still presents the large agricultural employment of a developing region or country but with the contrast of having also a major and technologically advanced urban centre, Toulouse, weakly linked to the rest of the region. The entrepreneurial potential appears strong, but it is in industrial terms largely concentrated around Toulouse and in one sector outside Toulouse. This thus confirms how local is self-generated growth.

Federal Republic of Germany

The Federal Republic of Germany consists of 10 *Länder* which have considerable autonomy. The population pattern follows this decentralisation with major conurbations in most *Länder*, the largest being in the Rhine-Ruhr. Manufacturing industry is concentrated in the *Länder* of North-Rhine Westphalia, Bavaria, Baden-Württemberg, Lower Saxony, Hesse and Saarland.

In 1981, 52.5 per cent of enterprises in manufacturing were in the group employing less than 50, 42.5 per cent were medium-sized (50–500 employees) and only 5 per cent employed more than 500. However, only 9 per cent of the work-force were employed in small industries, 40 per cent in medium-sized and 51 per cent in large. Large enterprises accounted for more than half of total industrial output.

Table 3.11 gives some indication of the proportion of employment in firms of under 500 employees in different sectors of industry. In the primary industries category only the woodworking sector has a majority of employment (63.9 per cent) in firms of less than 500. In the capital goods industries, there is heavy concentration in large firms: in office and data-processing machinery, 83.3 per cent are employed in firms of more than 500; in vehicles, 78.3 per cent; in aerospace, 90.3 per cent. Precision engineering and metal products are less concentrated. The consumer goods industries are also less concentrated, showing the usual pattern that smaller firms tend to be in the more traditional industries. Only ceramics (44.6 per cent) and glass (43.9 per cent) have less than 50 per cent of employment in firms of less than 500. Of 11 subsectors, in this group, seven have more than 70 per cent employment in smaller firms.

Table 3.11 West Germany: SMEs (less than 500 employees) as percentage of plants and employees

	Percentage of plants	Percentage of employees
Primary industries and manufacturing industries (oil, processing, chemical and paper industries, foundries, etc.)	94.8	35.6
Capital goods industries	92.7	40.0
of which:		
Forged and die cast products	93.9	64.2
Constructional steel	98.3	81.6
Precision mechanics	96.4	56.9
Metal products	96.0	69.0
Consumer goods	97.4	77.0
of which:		
Musical instruments, toys, etc.	98.3	84.9
Wood processing	98.4	84.8
Clothes industry	99.1	92.0
Food, drink, tobacco	96.7	70.7

Source: *Stat. Bundesamt Jahrbuch*, 1983.

The structure of German industry is, however, biased towards the larger size of plant and firm, a concentration which it shares with the United Kingdom. The concentration in plant size is heavier than in the United Kingdom (Table 3.12) but the latter has a heavier concentration

Table 3.12 Numbers of firms in the UK and FRG by employment categories

Firm size	10–49	50–99	100–199	200–499	500–999	1,000+
Percentage of total UK	16.3	11.3	11.3	19.3	11.1	31.6
Percentage of total FRG	15.6	9.9	10.8	15.9	10.8	36.9

of ownership in conglomerates. The regional distribution of plants by size (Table 3.13) shows a heavy concentration of large plants in North Rhine-Westphalia, with Bavaria and Baden-Württemberg at a lower level but still concentrated. The latter two have more small firms and were the only two *Länder* to exhibit any growth in 1982. North Rhine-Westphalia, dominated by heavy industry, large plants and very large enterprises, has moved from the top of the growth league to the bottom. However, all regions have shown a steady decline in employees and hours worked since 1970 in manufacturing industry. In 1970 there were 8.887 million employees in manufacturing industry who worked 12.531 billion hours. In 1979, the figures were 7.608 million employees and 9.253 billion working hours (*Stat. Bundesamt Jahrbuch* 1983).

The sectoral distribution of German industry is shown in Table 3.14. The capital goods industries sector consists of machine, road vehicle and aircraft manufacture, shipbuilding, electrical engineering and office machinery and data-processing equipment industries. The engineering industry generally occupies a significantly large segment of German industry. Electrical engineering has almost 10 per cent of industrial output, and employs a wide range of new technologies. As in France and Belgium, the data-processing industry is highly concentrated.

North Rhine-Westphalia dominates in all sectors except in the stone, ceramics and glass industries, and in electrical and precision engineering, in which it lies second (Table 3.15). The chemical industry employs over half a million in West Germany, 80 per cent of whom are employed in three firms. Each of these has its main plants and headquarters in North Rhine-Westphalia. In engineering and constructional steel and electrical and precision engineering, Baden-Württemberg and Bavaria are second and third. The three hold 23.6, 22.5 and 17.8 per cent respectively of the engineering and constructional steel sector, and 23.4, 25.4 and 22.4 per cent of the electrical and precision engineering sector. As a proportion of total employment, the engineering and constructional steel sector has 26 per cent of employment in North Rhine-Westphalia, 33.4 per cent in Baden-Württemberg and 27.8 per cent in Bavaria. The electrical and

Table 3.13 Plants in mining and manufacturing industries by size and region, 1982

	1–49	50–99	100–199	200–499	500–999	1,000+	Total
Schleswig-Holstein	990	294	200	109	35	21	1,449
Hamburg	502	172	92	85	34	29	914
Lower Saxony	2,676	893	523	383	120	84	4,679
Bremen	194	76	49	27	20	16	382
North Rhine-Westphalia	5,070	2,552	1,668	1,152	396	317	11,155
Hesse	2,159	786	483	335	118	96	3,977
Rheinland-Pfalz	1,594	576	321	237	67	40	2,835
Baden-Württemberg	5,252	2,084	1,272	891	280	172	9,951
Bavaria	5,625	1,798	1,174	802	256	176	9,831
Saarland	294	110	69	57	28	29	587
Berlin (West)	594	262	133	83	25	30	1,127
FRG	24,950	9,603	5,984	4,161	1,379	1,010	47,087

Table 3.14 West Germany: plants employing more than 20 persons and employment in manufacturing industry, 1982

	Plants	Numbers employed (000s)
Primary industries and manufacturing industries	9,456	1,448
Capital goods	18,389	3,656
Consumer goods	14,403	1,418
Food, drink and tobacco	4,653	472
Total	46,901	6,994

precision engineering sector holds 17 per cent in North Rhine-Westphalia, 24.8 per cent in Baden-Württemberg and 23 per cent in Bavaria. Engineering is more significant in both Baden-Württemberg and Bavaria than in North Rhine-Westphalia.

Baden-Württemberg is the largest state of the Federal Republic in terms of both land area and population, and each of these accounts for about one-seventh of the total for the Federal Republic. It has had an above average population growth of 40 per cent in 30 years, caused by immigration of refugees, displaced persons and foreigners such as Turks, Italians, Yugoslavs. The latter form one-tenth of the population. Since 1970 the state has had the highest growth rate in Germany, the GDP quadrupling in that time. The main centres of economic activity lie in the middle Neckar, around Stuttgart, and Rhine-Neckar areas, one-sixth of the land area contributing 40 per cent of total GDP.

Manufacturing industry had a very strong growth since the 1950s until 1973, when it declined. The decline came to a halt in 1978, but manufacturing employment in 1980 was still 165,000 lower than in 1970. The sectors hardest hit were the consumer goods industries, particularly the textile and clothing industries, employment in which decreased by one-third. The capital goods sector, with 62 per cent of all employees and 55 per cent of turnover, has maintained its position, especially in terms of international trade with exports of machinery, cars and electrotechnical goods.

Baden-Württemberg is a little less concentrated than the German average (Tables 3.16–3.19). Small firms of under 50 employees have more than 20 per cent of employment in the timber, quarrying, clothing, wood-processing and printing industries.

Table 3.15 West Germany: employment by selected *Länder* and sectors (thousands)

	FRG	Schleswig-Holstein	North Rhine-Westphalia	Hesse	Rheinland-Pfalz	Baden-Württemberg	Bavaria
Chemical industry & oil refining	607.9	14.0	218.0	95.4	70.6	66.7	67.6
Plastics, rubber & asbestos	333.6	7.9	77.8	43.3	24.0	66.9	52.4
Stone, sand, clay ceramics & glass	337.5	9.5	77.1	25.2	33.3	43.7	98.0
Non-ferrous metals	678.5	6.7	355.6	37.6	22.8	79.9	58.8
Engineering & constructional steel	2,463.5	73.8	581.9	225.1	111.8	554.2	438.5
Electrical & precision engineering & metal products	1,616.7	41.5	377.8	137.0	50.7	410.6	362.4
Wood, paper & printing	804.2	26.8	211.6	67.0	44.8	166.1	169.3
Leather, textiles & clothing	654.2	7.6	157.4	46.5	39.0	155.7	178.9
Food, drink & tobacco	771.6	32.5	163.6	51.1	39.0	102.2	148.6

Source: *Statistisches Jahrbuch*, 1983.

Table 3.16 Baden-Württemberg: employment by sectors and size of firm, 1982

Selected subsectors	Total employment	Employment in firms of size				
		1–19	20–49	50–99	100–499	500+
Chemical industry	63,827	202	2,614	4,903	17,301	38,807
Constructional steel	20,240	55	3,078	3,873	6,073	7,161
Machine engineering	252,650	601	16,901	22,319	89,217	123,612
Vehicles	210,818	677	8,805	7,341	23,069	170,926
Electrical equipment	228,293	423	7,191	12,521	55,161	152,997
Precision engineering, optics, watches, clocks	58,358	456	6,696	5,835	18,327	27,044
Metal products	61,030	366	6,357	7,634	26,089	20,584
Musical instruments, toys, jewellery, etc.	22,155	228	4,838	3,655	9,297	4,137
Office and data-processing machines	17,852	65	204	568	3,431	13,584
Timber and sawmills	9,660	3,946	2,599	1,108	NA	NA
Wood processing	45,134	386	8,865	8,013	20,144	7,726
Paper and board	20,787	NA	2,581	2,834	13,785	NA
Printing	34,773	300	6,752	6,221	14,896	6,604
Plastics manufacturing	38,851	460	5,061	8,271	16,186	8,873
Textiles	85,999	1,587	9,635	12,670	39,752	22,355
Clothing	29,766	670	6,429	7,119	11,133	4,415
Food and drink	55,795	1,067	9,101	NA	24,517	NA
Total manufacturing of which:	1,413,842	15,223	127,397	144,981	446,985	679,256
Manufacture of basic products	167,530	7,102	16,142	16,552	48,316	79,418
Manufacture of capital goods	884,393	2,945	54,856	65,022	237,074	524,496
Manufacture of consumer goods	304,254	4,054	47,158	53,015	136,466	63,561
Food, drink and tobacco	57,665	1,122	9,241	10,392	25,129	11,781

Source: Statistisches Landesamt Baden-Württemberg (1982).

Table 3.17 Baden-Württemberg: number of firms (local units) by size and sector, 1982

Selected subsectors	Total no. of firms	Employment in firms of size				
		1–19	20–49	50–99	100–499	500+
Chemical industry	274	16	82	69	79	28
Constructional steel	192	5	92	56	31	8
Machine engineering	1,411	48	509	320	427	107
Vehicles	575	45	273	108	106	43
Electrical equipment	770	31	220	179	243	97
Precision engineering, optics, watches, clocks	440	34	212	83	92	19
Metal products	482	25	196	108	132	21
Musical instruments, toys, jewellery, etc.	265	15	151	53	42	4
Office and data- processing machines	40	6	6	8	15	5
Timber and sawmills	554	440	89	16	8	1
Word processing	521	29	270	117	98	7
Paper and board	200	13	81	41	63	2
Printing	402	19	215	91	71	6
Plastics manufacturing	397	32	154	116	84	11
Textiles	836	122	298	188	201	27
Clothing	428	46	200	105	70	7
Food and drink	637	77	280	144	124	12
Total manufacturing						
of which:	9,938	1,289	3,954	2,082	2,161	452
Manufacture of basic products	1,746	699	528	233	228	58
Manufacture of capital goods	4,261	215	1,682	932	1,124	308
Manufacture of consumer goods	3,279	293	1,460	771	682	73
Food, drink and tobacco	652	82	284	146	127	13

Source: Statistisches Landesamt Baden-Württemberg (1982).

Table 3.18 Baden-Württemberg: distribution of manufacturing employment and firm numbers by firm size, 1982

Firm size	1–19	20–49	50–99	100–499	500+	Total
1. Number of firms	1,289	3,954	2,082	2,161	452	9,938
% of total number of firms	13.0	39.8	20.9	21.7	4.5	100
Cumulative total % of firms	13.0	52.8	73.7	95.4	100	
2. Employment	15,223	127,397	144,981	446,985	679,256	1,413,842
% of total employment	1.1	9.0	10.3	31.6	48.0	100
Cumulative total of employment	1.1	10.1	20.4	52.0	100	

German industrial structure is biased towards the large firm. The engineering sector is large and, for example, in Baden-Württemberg is very large. Baden-Württemberg has enjoyed a very strong growth in the last 30 years and is one of only two German *Länder* to enjoy recent growth. Baden-Württemberg has more smaller firms, but in manufacturing industry these tend to be more medium-sized than small.

The entrepreneurial potential as demonstrated by the data on industry structure is not strong in the Federal Republic of Germany. In Baden-Württemberg, one of the more prosperous regions, it is stronger than in most other *Länder*. The engineering sector is strong in West Germany and even stronger in Baden-Württemberg. The main losses in employment seem to have been in larger firms and plants and in Baden-Württemberg this seems to have been in the larger textile and clothing firms.

Greece

Greece is another heavily centralised country both in government administration and in population. Greater Athens contains one-third of the total population. Apart from the other main centre, Thessaloniki, the population is fairly evenly spread throughout the country, and is predominantly rural, with employment mainly in agriculture and small industry.

Inevitably, industry is concentrated in the two main conurbations, Athens and Thessaloniki. The headquarters of multi-plant companies and of Greek subsidiaries of foreign firms are located in Athens. Thessaloniki is the principal centre of heavy industry. The most common form of industrial organisation is a family unit of less than five members engaged

Table 3.19 Baden-Württemberg: sectoral distribution of manufacturing firms and manufacturing employment, 1982, and share of each sector held by firms of under 50 employees

Selected subsectors	All firms		Firms under 50 employees	
	Percentage of total no.	Percentage of employment	Percentage of no. in sector	Percentage employment in sector
Chemical industry	2.8	4.5	35.8	4.4
Constructional steel	1.9	1.1	50.8	15.5
Machine engineering	14.2	17.9	39.5	6.9
Vehicles	5.8	14.9	55.3	8.4
Electrical equipment	7.5	16.1	32.6	3.3
Precision engineering, optics, watches, clocks	4.4	4.1	55.9	12.3
Metal products	4.9	4.3	45.9	11.0
Musical instruments, toys, jewellery, etc.	2.7	1.6	NA	NA
Office and data-processing machines	0.4	1.3	30.0	1.5
Timber and sawmills	5.6	0.7	95.5	67.8
Wood processing	5.2	3.2	57.4	20.5
Paper and board	2.0	1.5	42.3	NA
Printing	4.1	2.5	58.2	20.3
Plastics manufacturing	4.0	2.7	46.9	14.2
Textiles	8.4	6.1	50.2	13.0
Clothing	4.3	2.1	57.5	23.8
Food and drink	6.4	3.9	56.0	18.2
Total manufacturing	100	100		
of which				
Manufacture of basic products	17.6	11.8		
Manufacture of capital goods	42.9	62.6		
Manufacture of consumer goods	33.0	21.5		
Food, drinks and tobacco	6.6	4.1		

in traditional craft-based activities such as clothing, footwear, woodworking and metalworking. Productivity varies with demand without recourse to creation of new jobs. The most significant aspect of the size distribution of Greek industry is that a firm of over 50 employees is a large firm (Tables 3.20 and 3.21). The concentration of larger plants in the Athens region can also be seen. 35.5 per cent of firms with over 50 employees are in Athens, 17.5 per cent in the Greater Athens area and 23.7 per cent in Macedonia (Thessaloniki); 41.2 per cent of employment in these firms is in Athens, 20.8 per cent in Greater Athens and 20 per cent in Macedonia.

Table 3.20 Greece: numbers employed in industry by size of firm and region, 1978 (thousands)

Region	All firms		No. of employees			
	No. of employees	(%)	0–4	5–9	10–49	49+
Athens	282	42	71	35	64	111
Central Greece less Athens	92	14	16	5	15	56
Macedonia	149	22	44	16	35	54
Peloponese	52	8	17	4	9	21
Thessally	38	6	12	4	7	15
Crete	18	3	10	2	3	3
Epirus	10	1	5	1	2	2
Thrace	12	2	5	1	2	3
Aegean Islands	14	2	7	2	2	3
Ionian Islands	5	1	4	1	0	1

Source EOMMEX, Greece (1984).

Between 1963 and 1978, there was some shift towards the larger firms, as Tables 3.22 and 3.23 show, but it was not in any way a major structural shift. Greek industry is weak in the more technologically based engineering sectors. The change over the period 1963–78 in numbers and size of firms (Table 3.22) showed some development of these sectors, but the percentage of gross domestic product originated by these sectors declined between 1975 and 1979 (Table 3.23). Food and textiles were the most important industries and showed a small increase in percentage of GDP between 1975 and 1979.

Looking at two smaller regions in Greece, within which the survey reported in Chapter 6 was carried out—Magnesia, which lies in Thessaly, and Phthiotis in Central Greece—there were some differences from the

Table 3.21 Greece: number of firms in industry by size and region, 1978

Region	All firms	0–4	5–9	10–49	50+
Athens	47,282	37,937	5,457	3,346	542
Rest of Central Greece	11,549	9,805	734	743	267
Macedonia	29,629	24,945	2,538	1,783	363
Peloponese	11,246	10,045	618	451	132
Thessally	8,150	7,144	585	331	90
Crete	6,757	6,239	342	157	19
Epirus	3,246	2,936	195	100	15
Thrace	3,498	3,152	212	107	27
Aegean Islands	5,248	4,874	260	96	18
Ionian Islands	2,332	2,214	89	24	5
Greece	128,937	109,291	11,030	7,138	1,478

Source: EOMMEX, Greece (1984).

Table 3.22 Greece: percentage change in number of firms in industry by size of firm and by sector, 1963–78

Sector	All firms	0–4	5–9	10–49	50+
Food	−14.3	−16.6	−7.4	+8.9	+52.0
Beverages	−37.5	−14.1	−1.6	+52.6	+100.0
Tobacco	−51.5	−40.6	−58.0	−62.7	−42.0
Textiles	+13.0	+10.6	+11.0	+13.9	+59.6
Clothing & footwear	−38.0	−43.8	+35.3	+140.0	+355.5
Wood and cork	—	—	+10.5	−4.7	+50.0
Furniture	+47.6	+48.7	−20.5	+99.5	+107.0
Paper	+37.0	+72.4	−1.1	−8.1	+107.0
Printing	+47.3	+56.3	+37.4	+20.0	+2.5
Leather, furs, etc.	+114.7	+136.8	+82.9	+33.5	−29.4
Rubber & plastics	+157.8	+165.8	+149.5	+119.4	+204.0
Chemicals	+23.2	−5.9	+65.7	+64.8	+160.0
Oil, coal & derivatives	+66.2	+9.5	+133.3	+138.4	+175.0
Non-metallic minerals	+10.2	+1.0	+4.2	+13.6	+73.3
Metallurgical industries	+126.9	+50.0	—	+150.0	+271.0
Metal mfr.	+18.9	+18.2	+10.1	+57.2	+59.3
Machinery mfr.	+96.4	+124.2	+46.8	+24.8	+25.0
Electrical	+54.3	+168.0	+91.9	+79.0	+175.0
Transport equipment	+103.2	+108.0	+68.7	+62.0	+14.9
Other mfr. industry	+27.5	+25.4	+39.5	+63.0	+100.0
Total all industry	+5.5	+1.8	+22.4	+41.4	+72.9

Source: EOMMEX, Greece (1984).

Table 3.23 GDP of Greek manufacturing industry, 1975 and 1979

Sector	1975 (%)	1979 (%)
Total	100.0	100.0
Food, beverages, tobacco	17.4	18.7
Textiles	17.3	17.7
Chemicals	13.2	11.3
Metals, engineering, electrical	11.0	10.8
Clothing, footwear	8.9	9.2
Non-metallic minerals	6.7	8.2
Transport equipment	6.1	6.3
Wood, cork, furniture	6.1	5.8
Basic metal industries	5.9	5.2
Paper, printing	4.5	4.6
Other	2.9	2.2

Source: General Directorate of National Accounting.

Table 3.24 Greece: number of firms in industry by size and sector, 1978

Sector	All firms	0–4	5–9	10–49	50+
Food	19,311	16,289	1,837	957	228
Beverages	1,901	1,533	189	145	36
Tobacco	131	38	13	38	42
Textiles	5,049	3,272	787	709	281
Clothing, footwear	21,926	18,915	1,548	1,258	205
Wood and cork	12,365	11,352	707	282	24
Furniture	10,778	9,598	770	383	27
Paper	444	238	84	93	29
Printing	2,848	2,136	425	246	41
Leather, furs, etc.	3,770	2,947	556	255	12
Rubber & plastics	2,184	1,558	287	272	67
Chemicals	1,095	538	227	239	91
Oil, coal & derivatives	123	46	35	31	11
Non-metallic minerals	5,280	3,948	712	542	78
Metallurgical industries	59	15	3	15	26
Metal mfr.	14,685	13,219	842	522	102
Machinery mfr.	4,465	3,482	561	372	50
Electrical	5,308	4,554	380	283	91
Transport equipment	13,365	12,142	781	365	77
Other mfr. industry	3,899	3,471	286	132	10
All industry	128,988	109,291	11,030	7,139	1,528

Source: EOMMEX, Greece.

national pattern. Magnesia had its largest concentration of employment (Table 3.25) in metallurgical industries with five companies employing an average of 169 each. Only the clothing (32) and paper (47) sectors had more than an average of 20 employees per firm. The overall average was 6 per firm. More firms were in the food sector than any other. In Phthiotis (Table 3.26) textiles was the largest employer followed by food and then the metallurgical industry. The latter consisted of two firms each with over 500 employees. The presence of these two firms did not seem to have had any impact on potential subcontractors as in the machinery industry which had an average size of 2 employees. The average employment per firm in Phthiotis is 5.

In Greece, 93 per cent of enterprises employ fewer than 10 people. In both Magnesia and Phthiotis the figure is 95 per cent. In both, only 1 per cent of companies employ more than 100. However, in both regions those companies employing more than 200 are of significance in that they employ more than one-third of workers (Table 3.27).

Magnesia essentially consists of two industrial structures. An area of Volos was declared an industrial zone in the 1960s and a combination of incentives and the presence of two large base industries attracted some heavy engineering industries. It now has the largest steel foundry in Greece, a large metal alloy producer, a large cement factory and the largest metal construction fabricators in Greece. Two of the nation's six steel mills are located near Volos. All of these major plants have their headquarters in Athens. The other industrial structure is a mass of small firms well over 2,000 in a community with a population of 182,000, and involved in every sector. Of 19 sectors, in only 6 is the average employment above 10.

Greek industry has a unique structure of a very large mass of very small firms employing a large percentage of total employment, with few in the middle-size ranges and then a number in the larger size also employing a large percentage. Greek industry has a weak engineering sector and exhibits signs of technological weakness overall. It is a structure paralleled to some degree by that of the Mezzogiorno, and like the Mezzogiorno it has a high entrepreneurial potential in that there are very many small family businesses. Growth and expansion are difficult, however, with such a weak technological base and probably also for other reasons, not unconnected with the strong centralisation of the country and a very conservative financial sector.

Ireland

As with Greece, one-third of the population of Ireland is concentrated in the Dublin region. Ireland had shown a decline in population at each census since the 'great hunger' of the 1840s. The 1971 census showed for the

Table 3.25 Breakdown of industrial activity in Magnesia by sector, 1980

	No. of companies	Mean annual employment	Average no. per company	Percentage share	
				No. of companies	Mean annual employment
Food	494	1,897	4	20.0	12.7
Beverages	31	280	9	1.2	1.9
Tobacco	6	101	17	0.2	0.7
Textiles	52	1,666	32	2.1	11.3
Clothing	337	2,092	6	13.6	14.2
Wood, cork	340	642	2	13.7	4.3
Furniture	189	469	2	7.6	3.2
Paper	4	189	47	0.2	1.3
Printing	34	214	6	1.4	1.4
Leather, furs	11	22	2	0.4	0.1
Rubber, plastics	27	232	9	1.1	1.6
Chemicals	15	170	11	0.6	1.1
Oil, coal, derivatives	4	12	3	0.2	0.1
Non-metal, minerals	124	1,568	13	5.0	10.6
Metallurgical industries	5	844	169	0.2	5.7
Metal manufacture	301	2,295	8	12.2	15.5
Machinery/manufacture	127	556	4	5.1	3.8
Electrical goods	108	738	7	4.4	5.0
Transport equipment	228	715	3	9.2	4.8
Other manufactured goods	39	106	3	1.6	0.7
Total	2,476	14,788	6	100.0	100.0

Source: Statistical Service of Greece, Industrial Census, 1978.

Table 3.26 Breakdown of industrial activity in Phthiotis by sector, 1978

	No. of companies	Mean annual employment	Average no. per company	Percentage share	
				No. of companies	Mean annual employment
Food	1,661	8,529	5	100.0	100.0
Tobacco	365	1,621	4	22.0	14.8
Beverages	14	202	13	0.9	2.4
Textiles	56	1,997	36	3.4	23.4
Clothing, footwear	237	461	2	14.3	5.4
Wood, cork	202	426	2	12.2	5.0
Furniture	60	108	2	3.6	1.3
Paper	8	311	39	0.5	3.6
Printing	17	42	2	1.0	0.5
Leather, furs	2	2	1	0.1	0.0
Rubber, plastics	26	51	2	1.6	0.6
Chemicals	8	103	13	0.5	1.2
Non-metal, minerals	63	789	13	3.8	9.3
Metallurgical industries	2	1,095	548	0.1	12.8
Metal manufacture	271	656	2	16.3	7.7
Machinery	45	108	2	52.7	1.3
Electrical goods	43	453	11	2.5	5.3
Transport equipment	215	428	2	12.9	5.0
Other manufactured goods	34	37	1	2.1	0.4

Table 3.27 Greece: employment and firm size in two regions, 1978

	Company size (by nos employed)				
	0–9	10–99	100–199	200+	Total
Enterprises					
Magnesia					
No. of firms	2,351	105	9	11	2,476
(%)	95	4	0.5	0.5	100
Phthiotis					
No. of firms	1,579	71	4	7	1,661
(%)	95	4	0.5	0.5	100
Employment					
Magnesia					
Nos employed	4,735	3,329	1,258	5,466	14,788
(%)	32	22	9	37	100
Phthiotis					
Nos employed	3,046	1,825	582	3,077	8,530
(%)	36	21	7	36	100

first time a net increase in population due to both a decline in emigration and return of emigrants. The latter were attracted back by the economic growth of the 1960s and the greater opportunities this brought. The consequences have been not only a fairly rapid expansion in population, 13 per cent between 1971 and 1979, but a dramatic shift in the age profile. Over 50 per cent of the population are under 25. Very recently there has been a sharp increase in emigration, especially of the young.

Industrial employment in Ireland increased by almost a quarter between 1961 and 1979. Most of this increase, however, was due to the increase in the number of foreign-owned establishments. Domestic industry, which suffered some changes in the 1960s nevertheless had grown in employment until 1974. Since then there has been a substantial decline in domestic industry, mostly in larger firms. Overall, the larger manufacturing firms tend to be foreign-owned. They have had very weak spin-off or linkage to indigenous industry (O'Malley 1985).

Kennedy and Healy (1985) found that in the period 1973–80 there was scarcely any net change in employment in small establishments existing in 1973, as against a net decline of 16 per cent in larger establishments (Table 3.28). They point out that the figures illustrate the volatility of small industry since gross losses and gains both exceeded those in large industry. Of the total increase of 37,000 jobs in expanding establishments

Table 3.28 Ireland: percentage changes in employment during 1973–80 in establishments existing in 1973

Establishment size	Net change	Gains	Gross changes		Total losses
			Closure	Contractions	
Small	-0.1	32.9	-22.3	-10.7	-33.0
Other	-16.1	12.2	-13.0	-15.4	-28.4
Total	-12.4	17.0	-15.2	-14.3	-29.4

from 1973 to 1980, 45 per cent were in establishments of less than 50 employees. Of the 51,800 jobs in establishments founded after 1973, 61 per cent were in establishments which started small.

However, the relative importance of small firms has declined (Table 3.29). The number of small firms increased until 1958, declined and increased again until 1975. Employment total increased steadily but small firms' share of total manufacturing employment has declined steadily and that of large firms has increased. Less than 4 per cent of all industrial

Table 3.29 Ireland: size distribution of Irish manufacturing industry 1929–75 (CSO data)

Establishment size	1929	1938	1946	1958	1968	1975
No. of establishments						
0–49	1,912	2,716	2,376	2,511	2,305	2,464
50–199	263	425	384	452	576	661
200–499			83	112	142	143
500+	11	15	21	31	51	52
Total	2,186	3,156	2,864	3,106	3,074	3,320
Employment nos (000s)						
0–49	22.2	32.8	32.5	37.5	38.2	39.8
50–199	32.0	53.4	34.7	42.3	56.5	63.8
200–499			23.9	32.4	42.1	43.1
500+	11.8	14.2	18.9	29.6	47.2	48.1
Total	66.1	100.2	110.0	141.8	183.9	194.8
Employment shares (%)						
0–49	33.6	32.7	29.5	26.4	20.8	20.4
50–199	48.5	53.2	31.5	29.8	30.7	32.8
200–499			21.7	22.8	22.9	22.1
500+	17.9	14.2	17.2	20.9	25.7	24.7

Source: Kennedy and Healy (1985).

firms employ more than 200 employees and less than 20 per cent more than 50.

The engineering sector is the largest in terms of employment in Ireland and includes the very largely foreign-owned data-processing equipment and electronics sectors (Table 3.30). The mechanical engineering and metal products sectors are weak relative to more developed countries. As Table 3.31 shows, this sector has shown a strong growth in the number of small firms, perhaps an indicator of improvement in the technological base of Irish industry.

The food sector is dominated by a few large dairy-farmer-owned co-operatives which have had considerable growth in processed output and employment. These represent the most progressive indigenous large-firm sector and some have had successful spin-off of sponsored or subsidiary firms in engineering and other subcontract supply.

The clothing, footwear and textile industries, largely indigenous, have seen a decline in the number of and employment by larger firms, but there has been an increase in the number of small firms. As in the more industrialised countries of Europe, the small firms have shown greater resilience in the recession. Whilst this pattern of decline of larger firms in the traditional sectors is that of Europe generally, the significance of the decline in Ireland is that indigenous industry lies largely in these sectors.

Of the regions of Ireland, the West and Mid-West are similar in population, with 287,000 and 308,000 respectively, but differ in their industrial structure. The Mid-West has its own regional development authority responsible for both industrial and tourist development. Since 1978 it has had a special responsibility to undertake new initiatives to support small-firm start-up and development. Industrial employment in the West has grown by 70 per cent since 1973, largely through the introduction of foreign firms, which now employ 49.7 per cent of manufacturing employment. The Mid-West had one of the lowest growths in industrial employment from 1973 to 1982, 14.8 per cent. Here 52.3 per cent are employed in foreign firms.

The engineering sector employs virtually 45 per cent in each of these regions, apparently strong but dominated by larger foreign plants. The small firm of under 50 employees is more important in the West, with 35 per cent of manufacturing employment, than in the Mid-West, with 25 per cent of employment (Tables 3.32 and 3.33). The East has had a substantial decline in manufacturing (Table 3.34) but has still nearly 40 per cent of manufacturing employment in the country. Ireland presents a mixed picture. It gives indications of an entrepreneurial potential, which has maintained itself through the recession. But this potential appears to be frustrated in its ability to expand.

Table 3.30 Ireland: Percentage manufacturing employment by sector and selected regions, 1982

Region	Non-minerals	Chemicals	Metals engng	Food	Drink, tobacco	Textiles	Clothing, footwear, leather	Timber, furniture	Paper, printing	Misc.
Mid-west	9.0	5.0	44.6	20.6	1.4	5.7	2.5	4.8	3.3	3.0
West	4.5	5.4	45.0	15.1	1.9	4.7	9.1	7.5	3.3	4.0
East	7.3	7.1	25.6	17.2	6.5	4.6	10.1	4.6	12.2	4.8
Ireland	7.3	6.3	29.1	19.9	4.9	6.4	9.2	5.1	6.7	5.1

Table 3.31 Ireland: changes in number of small firms* by sector, 1968–79

Sector	Percentage change in no. of firms 1968–79		Small firms as percentage of all firms	
	Small	Large	1968	1979
Wood, furniture	88	23	87.3	91.3
Cement, glass	145	97	77.6	81.2
Paper, printing	52	19	76.7	80.7
Mechanical engng.	204	76	68.2	78.7
Other manufacturing	96	110	77.8	76.7
Food, drink, tobacco	-21	33	81.4	72.0
Chemicals	9	66	77.6	69.5
Clothing, footwear	25	-2	62.4	68.0
Textiles	20	-14	53.0	61.0
Total	50	36	75.0	76.0

* Firms having less than 50 employees.

Table 3.32 Ireland: industrial employment by size of firm and region

Region	Size of firm by numbers employed						
	1–2	3–50	51–100	101–200	201–500	500+	Total
Mid-West	43	5,207	3,014	3,517	5,551	3,559	20,891
West	64	4,994	1,634	2,293	2,903	2,235	14,123
East	119	24,693	12,926	14,216	20,368	19,111	91,433
South-East	82	7,650	3,750	5,620	6,942	4,464	28,508
South-West	60	8,831	4,412	6,451	7,191	9,207	36,152
North-West	49	1,459	822	1,085	648	788	4,851
Donegal	30	2,141	1,650	1,886	1,200	—	6,907
Midlands	63	4,936	2,440	3,479	2,137	2,111	15,166
North-East	49	4,754	3,849	4,111	3,690	2,010	18,463
Total	559	64,665	34,497	42,658	50,630	43,485	236,494

Source: IDA Employment Survey, 1982.

Table 3.33 Ireland: percentage industrial employment by size of firm and region

Region	Size of firms by numbers employed					
	1–2	3–50	51–100	101–200	201–500	500+
Mid-west	0.2	24.9	14.4	16.8	26.6	17.0
West	0.5	35.4	11.6	16.2	20.6	15.8
East	0.1	27.0	14.1	15.4	22.8	20.9
South-East	0.3	26.8	13.2	19.7	24.4	15.7
Sout-West	0.2	24.4	12.2	17.8	19.9	25.5
North-West	1.0	30.1	16.9	22.4	13.4	16.2
Donegal	0.4	31.0	23.9	27.3	17.4	—
Midlands	0.4	32.5	16.1	22.9	14.1	13.9
North-East	0.3	25.7	20.8	22.3	20.0	10.9
Total	0.2	27.3	14.6	18.0	21.4	18.4

Source: IDA Employment Survey, 1982.

Table 3.34 Ireland: employment in industry, 1973 and 1982

Region	1973	1982	Change (%)
Mid-West	18,191	20,891	14.8
West	8,275	14,123	70.7
East	107,204	91,433	-14.7
South-East	23,166	28,508	23.1
South-West	34,708	36,152	4.2
North-West	3,287	4,857	47.8
Donegal	5,359	6,907	28.9
Midlands	9,179	15,166	65.2
North-East	18,071	18,463	2.2
Total	227,404	236,494	4.0

Source: IDA Employment Survey, 1982.

Italy

Italy is normally thought of in terms of the North and South, almost a black and white of industrial development. In reality the North does have regions not unlike the South and there is an East-Centre region which has begun its own pattern of development. This is based on many small independent firms which are innovative and dynamic, but this development is not observable in the data as yet.

The South, the Mezzogiorno, is one of the poorest regions in the EEC. Before the entry of Greece, the eight regions of the Mezzogiorno, including Sicily and Sardinia, occupied eight of the bottom nine places in a 1977

Table 3.35 Italy: number of manufacturing units by size of firm and by region

Region	No. employed in firm					
	1–5	6–49	50–199	200–499	500+	Total
Piemonte	260,966	32,720	2,813	459	218	297,176
Valle d'Aosta	8,252	926	49	4	4	9,235
Lombardia	493,413	83,509	7,121	1,101	387	585,531
Trentino-Alto Adige	58,761	9,308	501	62	15	68,647
Veneto	271,782	40,498	2,972	371	123	315,746
Friuli-Venezia	74,653	10,582	790	107	48	86,180
Liguria	108,927	11,725	875	127	83	121,737
Emilia-Romagna	298,732	38,664	2,987	400	114	340,897
Toscana	235,428	34,953	2,172	241	103	272,897
Umbria	46,403	6,299	470	50	18	53,240
Marche	101,680	14,455	952	87	30	117,204
Lazio	209,339	25,802	2,623	422	185	238,371
Abruzzi	65,372	7,701	591	63	31	73,758
Molise	17,191	1,664	129	14	2	19,000
Campania	201,196	20,182	2,062	290	120	223,850
Puglia	171,663	16,953	1,550	178	70	190,414
Basilicata	29,550	2,929	240	19	8	32,746
Calabria	82,593	7,698	645	62	24	91,022
Sicily	203,781	17,844	1,708	183	75	223,591
Sardinia	74,197	7,676	696	71	33	82,673
Italy	3,013,879	392,088	31,946	4,311	1,691	3,513,742

Source: ISTAT, Census of Industry and Trade, 1981.

ranking of EEC regions by GDP. Calabria, which occupied bottom place, is three times poorer than the richest Italian region, Valle d'Aosta. Urban domination in the Mezzogiorno is significant only in Campania, which includes Naples.

The contrast between North and South shows up in some aspects of industrial structure. Northern industry has more large firms with greater capitalisation. The Mezzogiorno is based more on small firms in traditional industries with larger firms being controlled from the North or from overseas. The small firms tend to be, as in Greece, family units of less than five employees per firm, and the numbers of such units is very large, as is the employment in them (Table 3.35–3.36). The north of Italy, for example Piedmont, also has a very large proportion of employment in such firms, but the percentage of employment in these is very much

Table 3.36 Italy: number employed in industry by size of firm and by region (thousands)

Region	No. employed in firm					
	1–5	6–49	50–199	200–499	500+	Total
Piemonte	466	430	251	137	329	1,613
Valle d'Aosta	15	11	5	1	6	38
Lombardia	907	1,118	631	328	449	3,433
Trentino-Alto Adige	111	116	43	18	15	303
Veneto	483	531	261	108	129	1,512
Friuli-Venezia	136	135	68	31	60	430
Liguria	194	149	77	38	110	568
Emilia-Romagna	520	497	269	115	121	1,522
Toscana	423	450	183	70	121	1,247
Umbria	81	81	42	15	25	244
Marche	176	187	81	26	23	493
Lazio	383	342	235	129	285	1,374
Abruzzi	112	101	50	19	33	315
Molise	28	22	11	5	3	69
Campania	326	274	178	89	164	1,031
Puglia	283	218	131	54	96	782
Basilicata	46	40	20	5	7	118
Calabria	130	107	52	18	23	330
Sicily	329	240	146	54	94	863
Sardinia	125	102	60	20	32	338
Italy	5,274	5,151	2,794	1,280	2,124	16,623

Source: ISTAT, Census of Industry and Trade, 1981.

Table 3.37 Italy: number employed in industry analysed by sector and region (thousands)

Region	Chemicals	Art fibres	Minerals	Metals & engineering	Food	Conf. drinks tobacco	Textiles	Leather & fur	Clothing footwear household linen	Wood & furniture	Print packng	Rubber & plastics	Other manu-facturing industries
Piemonte	18	5	45	403	21	16	73	4	40	27	32	42	14
Valle d'Aosta	—	—	6	1	—	—	1	—	—	1	—	—	—
Lombardia	103	9	111	697	46	28	174	15	125	92	93	72	25
Trentino-Alto Adige	2	—	11	25	4	2	3	—	3	13	4	3	1
Veneto	22	2	49	191	24	11	54	15	104	73	26	21	12
Friuli-Venezia Giulia	2	1	12	60	5	4	7	2	6	30	6	2	1
Liguria	9	—	24	73	6	3	2	1	5	6	5	3	2
Emilia-Romagna	19	—	69	231	35	18	39	7	53	37	21	17	7
Toscana	19	—	61	106	15	7	82	22	93	41	18	11	12
Umbria	5	2	17	20	5	5	9	1	15	7	4	1	1
Marche	3	—	10	39	6	4	8	5	71	27	6	6	9
Lazio	25	1	30	97	17	9	8	1	18	20	32	10	7
Abruzzi	3	—	14	25	6	2	4	3	19	8	4	3	1
Molise	—	—	2	6	2	1	—	—	1	1	—	—	—
Campania	6	1	24	113	25	11	9	9	35	18	9	6	3
Puglia	7	—	42	52	18	9	11	1	29	16	6	6	1
Basilicata	1	3	3	6	3	1	1	—	2	2	—	1	—
Sicily	11	—	22	44	12	6	4	1	13	16	6	5	2
Sardinia	6	4	17	13	7	2	3	—	2	7	2	1	—
Calabria	2	—	8	8	7	1	2	—	3	6	1	1	—
Italy	264	29	576	2,208	264	141	493	86	636	448	274	212	101

Source: ISTAT, Census of Industry and Trade, 1981.

higher in Sicily and Calabria (Table 3.38). Campania, which contains Naples, is the most urbanised region of the Mezzogiorno and has a higher concentration of employment in larger firms than other Mezzogiorno regions.

The engineering sector is the largest in Italy (Table 3.37), employing 38 per cent, followed in employment by clothing and footwear (11 per cent) minerals (10 per cent) and wood and furniture (7.8 per cent). In the

Table 3.38 Italy: percentage employment in industry by size of firm in selected regions

Provence	Firm size				
	1–5	6–49	50–199	200–499	500+
Piemonte	28.9	26.6	15.5	8.5	20.4
Lombardia	26.4	32.4	18.4	9.5	13.1
Siciliy	38.1	27.8	16.9	6.2	10.9
Calabria	39.4	32.4	15.7	5.4	6.6
Campania	31.6	26.6	17.3	8.6	15.9

Source: ISTAT Census of Industry and Trade, 1981.

Table 3.39 Italy: number of small firms (less than 50 employees) in each industry sector, 1981

Sector	No. of firms
Chemicals	7,373
Artificial fibres	132
Minerals	41,247
Engineering	174,742
Basic food manufcture	39,015
Sugar, confectionery, drink & tobacco	7,877
Textiles	58,265
Skins and leathers	11,831
Footwear, clothing & household linens	98,061
Wood and furniture	112,237
Print and packaging	24,251
Rubber and plastics	18,109
Other mfr. industry	19,387
Total	612,527

Source: Census of Industry and Trade, 1981.

Campania (Table 3.37) the engineering sector accounts for 19.8 per cent of establishments and 26 per cent of employment; in the Mezzogiorno as a whole it accounts for 21 per cent of establishments and 23 per cent of employment. Northern Italy has substantially more employment in the engineering sector. Lombardy has 41 per cent and Piedmont 54 per cent. The northern industrialised regions have twice or more the number of engineering firms of the South.

In small firms of under 50 employees, the engineering sector is again the largest nationally, at 28 per cent, followed by wood and furniture (18 per cent), footwear and clothing (16 per cent) and textiles (9 per cent) (Table 3.39).

In terms of employment, transport equipment, food and clothing each account for around 13 per cent of employment. In the Mezzogiorno (Table 3.40), mechanical engineering accounts for 23 per cent of employment followed by food (13.6 per cent) and clothing and footwear (23 per cent). In Salerno (Table 3.41), the subject of a survey reported in Chapter 6, the food industry dominates but the engineering sector displays the same level of importance as in the rest of the Mezzogiorno.

Table 3.40 Campania: manufacturing plants and employees by sector, 1981

Sector	Campania		Mezzogiorno	
	Plants (%)	Employees (%)	Plants (%)	Employees (%)
Food	11.7	13.3	14.4	13.6
Textiles	3.3	3.4	4.7	4.1
Leather	3.8	3.3	1.5	1.6
Clothing, footwear	21.8	13.0	19.0	12.4
Wood, furniture	21.6	6.8	22.7	8.8
Metal, coke	0.6	4.8	0.4	5.6
Mech. products	19.8	26.0	21.4	23.5
Transportation	0.7	13.3	0.5	7.6
Non-metallic minerals	4.4	6.0	5.8	8.7
Chemicals	1.1	2.9	1.0	5.4
Oil, nuclear fuels	0.1	0.6	0.1	1.4
Rubber, plastics	3.4	2.2	3.0	2.8
Paper, printing	4.1	3.2	3.2	3.4
Other	3.6	1.3	2.2	1.0
Total	100.0	100.0	100.0	100.0

Source: ISTAT, census of Industry and Trade, 1981.

Table 3.41 Salerno: ranking of manufacturing sectors

	No. of firms	(%)	No. employed (%)
Food	204	28.3	33.7
Mechanical engineering	132	18.3	22.5
Wood	101	14.0	4.8
Non-metallic minerals	96	13.3	14.1
Textiles, clothing	72	10.0	14.6
Paper	39	5.5	3.5
Plastics	32	4.4	3.0
Chemicals	27	3.7	1.8
Others	18	2.5	2.0
Total	721	100.0	100.0

Source: Salerno Chamber of Commerce.

Whilst Italian industry has a very large proportion of smaller firms, the North has a distinctly stronger technological base as illustrated by the size of the engineering sector. The South is much more dependent on larger non-indigenous firms and an indigenous small-firm, traditional low-technology sector. The entrepreneurial potential in Italy as a whole is very strong but in the South it is, as in Greece, very frustrated.

The Netherlands

Although The Netherlands is divided into twelve provinces, it is more usually looked upon as consisting of three large zones. The Inner Zone is the more urbanised, linking the three main centres of Rotterdam, The Hague and Amsterdam. It contains 40 per cent of the population and is known as the Randstadt. The Intermediate Zone surrounds the Randstadt, and contains 25 per cent of the population and centres such as Eindhoven, Apeldoorn and Nijmegen. The remaining area, the Peripheral Zone, is more sparsely populated in Dutch terms. Population trends have followed the European pattern of a drift from the inner Randstadt to the Intermediate Zone.

The Randstadt consists broadly of South Holland, Utrecht and North Holland; the Intermediate Zone consists of Zeeland, North Brabant, Gelderland (except the extreme east) a part of Overijssel and the Ijsselmeerpolders. The Peripheral Zone consists of Groningen, Friesland, Drente and Limburg with parts of Overijssel and Gelderland.

Employment in manufacturing industry has contracted in all regions in recent years and there has been high unemployment. The Peripheral Zone has been the hardest hit. The most important sectors are food (13 per cent) and chemicals (11 per cent). Engineering is the largest sector at, 24.6 per cent, if one aggregates the metalworking, machinery and electrical industries. The engineering sector is in fact relatively weak if one compares it to another small country like Denmark or to those of France, West Germany or north Italy.

Tables 3.42 and 3.43 confirm the dominance of the Randstadt provinces as the most industrialised. They also show the greater concentration in larger firms in sectors such as the chemical industry.

Small firms in The Netherlands are officially those with less than ten employees and medium sized are of between ten and 99 employees. Firms with 100 or more employees make up 3.5 per cent of the total number of firms, and employ 62 per cent of labour. SMEs therefore are of considerable importance in all regions of The Netherlands (Table 3.44). They are, however, not as strong a sector as in Denmark, but better than the French average. They are inevitably strong in the traditional sectors of industry such as leather, textiles and furniture but they are also significant in the publishing and optical industries. Of firms under ten employees, 28 per cent are in the engineering sector. They are thought to have been more resilient than larger firms in the recession, but have declined in number.

The entrepreneurial potential of The Netherlands appears to be very good, 38 per cent of employment being in firms of less than 100 employees, a figure comparable to Denmark's 39 per cent. The engineering sector is, however, much weaker than Denmark's.

United Kingdom

The United Kingdom is another centralised state like France, and has some 31 per cent of population concentrated in the South-East region. Since 1961 the population has tended to drift to the Midlands and South, particularly the South-East. Since 1971, there has been some change in that the South-East has declined by 0.8 per cent but this seems to have been a shift to the 'intermediate zones' of East Anglia and the South-West. As elsewhere, inner cities declined and the areas on the edges of large conurbations grew.

Manufacturing employment fell by 35 per cent in the period 1965 to 1983, a period which saw a significant fall in overall employment. In the regions, the changes in employment have been more favourable in East Anglia, the South-West and East Midlands. The West Midlands, which had the greatest concentration of manufacturing industry, has been the area with the largest decline in overall employment, 19.6 per cent.

Table 3.42 Netherlands: employment in manufacturing, industry by sector and by selected regions, 1983

Sector	Groningen	Friesland	North Holland	South Holland	Zeeland	North Brabant	Netherlands Total
Food, drink & tobacco	5,881	10,001	14,426	22,328	2,071	28,647	122,557
Textiles & clothing	1,013	1,271	4,990	2,649	802	11,592	41,836
Leather	27	86	274	286	52	6,593	85,459
Wood & furniture	907	1,681	3,444	4,321	387	6,323	31,860
Bricks, pottery, glass	530	1,297	1,244	6,280	774	3,862	50,306
Paper	2,756	384	2,699	2,298	141	2,896	24,266
Publishing	2,204	1,918	18,279	14,022	713	8,061	69,376
Oil & coal	330	82	1,263	10,701	639	1,294	16,454
Chemicals	2,738	1,085	11,867	27,483	5,153	13,807	104,756
Basic metals	747	86	18,725	2,434	3	2,583	29,755
Metal working	2,541	3,650	9,758	18,085	3,967	18,659	96,934
Machinery	2,571	2,744	9,352	10,823	1,179	15,680	77,394
Electrical industry	736	1,105	8,892	10,860	92	11,308	53,242
Transporting goods	1,723	3,093	10,823	22,105	3,532	16,321	88,576
Optical industry	796	692	3,881	6,576	283	3,238	30,296
Total							923,067

Source: Databank of the Netherlands Chamber of Commerce.

Table 3.43 Netherlands: number of firms by sector and by selected regions, 1983

Sector	Groningen	Friesland	North Holland	South Holland	Zeeland	North Brabant	Netherlands Total
Food, drink & tobacco	119	176	455	575	109	572	3,266
Textiles & clothing	82	90	1,021	579	119	752	4,070
Leather	7	12	75	65	11	508	868
Wood & furniture	125	143	427	579	66	793	3,697
Bricks, pottery, glass	80	85	206	364	43	337	1,975
Paper	24	7	96	60	2	51	408
Publishing	211	186	1,755	1,429	106	773	6,562
Oil & coal	5	4	101	167	5	21	366
Chemicals	72	44	407	460	23	381	2,215
Base metals	3	2	32	38	1	30	185
Metal working	269	290	1,254	1,679	219	1,405	8,227
Machinery	104	95	475	628	18	228	2,855
Electrical industry	43	28	369	310	18	228	1,525
Transporting goods	125	292	552	712	80	333	2,962
Optical industry	111	137	889	807	63	468	3,650

Source: Databank of Netherlands Chambers of Commerce.

Table 3.44 Netherlands: numbers employed by size of firm and region, 1983

Province	Size of firm				
	1–4	5–9	10–49	50–99	100+
Groningen	1,237	1,161	5,080	2,972	15,069
Friesland	1,540	1,245	6,432	4,176	15,402
Drente	848	665	3,339	3,357	8,519
Overijssel	2,966	2,556	12,297	8,613	38,764
Gelderland	4,745	4,236	20,267	15,389	71,530
Utrecht	2,458	2,217	8,403	4,932	24,032
N. Holland	7,312	5,854	20,551	12,498	73,702
S. Holland	7,346	6,349	28,030	16,850	104,828
Zeeland	947	729	2,848	2,044	13,220
N. Brabant	6,294	5,729	26,733	16,753	95,360
Limburg	2,979	2,406	12,365	7,273	49,962
Ijsselmeerpolders	242	147	1,139	231	1,089
Netherlands total	38,914	33,294	147,484	95,088	511,477

Source: Databank of The Netherlands Chambers of Commerce.

Table 3.45 Netherlands: number of small manufacturing firms (less than 10 employees) in each industry sector, 1983

Sector	Number of small firms
Food, drink & tobacco	1,913
Textile & clothing	3,256
Leather	673
Wood & furniture	2,850
Bricks, pottery & glass	1,370
Paper	179
Publishing	5,115
Oil & coal	225
Chemicals	1,298
Base metals	103
Metalworking	6,189
Machinery	1,585
Electrical industry	1,056
Transporting goods	2,316
Optical industry	3,026

Table 3.46 United Kingdom: percentage employment in manufacturing industries, 1975 and 1978

Manufacturing sector	Year	Firm size					
		10–49	50–99	100–199	200–499	500–999	1,000+
Non-metallic	1975	12.4	9.3	11.8	25.6	17.5	23.4
mineral products	1978	14.3	12.8	16.5	21.2	15.5	19.6
Chemical industry	1975	8.3	5.1	8.5	16.2	15.8	46.1
	1978	10.0	10.4	10.2	21.0	15.5	32.9
Manufacture of metal	1975	18.3	11.2	13.9	24.3	12.7	19.6
articles	1978	22.1	13.8	15.5	20.1	13.6	14.9
Mechanical engineering	1975	14.4	8.3	11.6	21.4	16.6	27.7
	1978	17.0	13.1	11.6	21.1	14.7	22.5
Electrical engineering	1975	5.2	3.2	7.7	16.9	16.1	50.9
	1978	6.0	7.0	10.1	20.0	15.0	41.8
Motor vehicles	1975	4.1	2.6	4.7	9.6	10.4	68.6
	1978	4.7	2.4	3.4	9.3	7.5	72.8

Other transport	1975	2.2	1.8	4.3	6.0	6.3	79.4
	1978	4.0	3.5	3.5	6.5	5.0	77.6
Instrument engineering	1975	10.8	6.8	11.6	17.3	18.4	35.1
	1978	24.5	9.2	10.8	16.7	17.1	21.7
Food, drink & tobacco	1975	6.6	7.5	9.3	23.5	16.4	36.7
	1978	11.5	10.0	10.1	25.0	16.5	26.8
Textiles	1975	10.3	9.5	19.7	32.0	15.2	13.8
	1978	13.0	13.6	18.4	33.2	12.2	9.6
Paper & paper products	1975	14.8	9.4	12.7	23.9	14.7	24.5
	1978	18.3	12.9	13.4	23.0	12.7	19.8
Other manufacturing	1975	15.5	13.7	11.8	20.6	14.3	24.1
industries	1978	24.6	18.5	15.0	19.4	9.2	13.0
Construction	1975	29.5	19.8	6.4	14.7	6.0	23.6
	1978	37.1	16.1	9.7	12.7	5.8	18.7

Source: ABT (1982).

As indicated earlier (Table 3.12), the United Kingdom has the second highest degree of concentration in establishments in Europe and the highest concentration in firms of any industrialised country. Table 3.46 gives the breakdown of manufacturing industry by size and sector. The pattern is much the same as in other major European countries, with small firms dominating in most traditional industries but also in instrument engineering. Table 3.47 shows a deconcentration in industry. The fall in employment has been much greater in larger firms than in small. All sectors other than motor vehicles have shown an increase in the number of firms employing 10–199 people as a percentage of all firms.

Table 3.47 United Kingdom: company size in manufacturing industries, 1975–8

Sector	Percentage of SME's*		Change (percentage points
	1975	1978	
Other manufacture	41.0	58.1	+17.1
Instrument engineering	29.2	44.5	+15.3
Non-metallic minerals	33.5	43.6	+10.1
Chemicals	21.9	30.6	+8.7
Food, drinks, tobacco	23.4	31.6	+8.2
Metal products	43.4	51.4	+8.0
Paper	36.9	44.6	+7.7
Mechanical engineering	34.3	41.7	+7.4
Construction	55.7	62.9	+7.2
Electrical engineering	16.1	23.1	+7.0
Textiles	39.5	45.0	+5.5
Other transport	8.3	11.0	+2.7
Motor vehicles	11.4	10.5	-0.9

* Company size 10–199.

Table 3.48 shows the breakdown of total manufacturing employment by selected sectors for the two years 1979 and 1983. The decline in manufacturing employment was sharp in this period with textiles, footwear and clothing, motor vehicles, mechanical engineering and metal products all showing sharp falls. The pattern of decline is therefore not only in traditional sectors as in Baden-Württemberg but also in engineering sectors.

In more recent times, there appears to have been an increase in the number of firms being founded and some decline in the failures (Table 3.49). The South-East and the West Midlands have the greatest excess of births over deaths. In terms solely of births, the South-East dominates, with the South-West, West Midlands, Yorkshire, and North-West each

Table 3.48 Great Britain: employment (thousands) in selected industries, 1979 and 1983

	1979		1983		Change (%)
	Nos	Percentage of total	Nos	Percentage of total	
Non-metallic mineral products	273	3.8	198	3.6	27.5
Metal products	516	7.2	378	6.8	26.7
Mechanical engng	1,011	14.2	789	14.2	21.9
Office equipment	820	11.5	75	1.3	12.7
Electrical & electronic			641	11.6	
Motor vehicles	433	6.0	306	5.5	29.3
Other transport	432	6.0	323	5.8	25.2
Instrument engng	126	1.8	108	1.9	14.3
Food, drink & tobacco	715	10.0	623	11.2	12.9
Textiles	376	5.3	240	4.3	36.0
Leather & leather goods	433	6.0	25	0.4	30.5
Footwear & clothing			276	5.0	
Timber & wooden furniture	249	3.5	203	3.6	18.5
Paper, printing & publishing	547	7.7	489	8.8	10.6
Rubber & plastics	240	3.4	175	3.2	27.0
Other	106	1.5	80	1.4	24.5

Table 3.49 United Kingdom: births and deaths of firms by region, 1980–1

Region	Births		Deaths		Excess	
	1980	1981	1980	1981	1980	1981
South-East	41,500	44,200	40,100	37,200	1,400	7,000
East Anglia	3,400	4,000	3,300	3,300	100	700
South-West	10,600	11,900	10,500	10,700	100	1,000
West Midlands	9,900	11,500	9,500	9,200	400	2,300
East Midlands	7,500	8,100	7,300	7,300	200	900
Yorkshire & Humberside	8,700	10,000	9,100	9,200	(400)	800
North-West	11,100	12,800	12,200	11,900	(1,100)	900
North	4,500	5,300	4,800	4,600	(300)	700
Wales	5,200	6,200	5,400	5,100	(200)	1,000
Scotland	7,600	8,000	7,500	6,800	100	1,200
Northern Ireland	2,900	2,500	2,200	1,800	700	700
Miscellaneous	400	300	3,400	2,900	(3,000)	(2,600)
Total	113,300	124,800	115,300	110,000	(2,000)	14,800

having a new entry rate approximately one quarter of that of the South-East. The West Midlands had a higher surplus in 1981 than any region other than the South-East.

The north of England typifies the difficulty created by the inappropriateness of administrative boundaries to analysis of localities with or without capability for self-generated growth. It includes very large rural areas such as the Border country, the English Lake District, and the Pennines, a physical and historical boundary dividing the region. The east of the region contains declining coal and steel areas and an urban region, Tyne and Wear, once heavily industrialised, which is representative of industrial regions in decline formerly based on heavier engineering such as shipbuilding.

In the period 1965–83, the region saw a fall in employment of 16.7 per cent. The major job losses have been in the older manufacturing industries, particularly shipbuilding, steel and heavy engineering. The national trend towards a higher percentage of SMEs in a smaller manufacturing sector is even more marked in the North. Nevertheless, the small firms sector has traditionally been weak and underdeveloped relative not only to the European Community but to elsewhere in the United Kingdom. The area has been dominated by large plants such as those in shipbuilding and latterly by branch plants attracted by government relocation policies and aid.

The sectoral distribution of smaller industry, Table 3.50, in Tyne and Wear, shows that 37.6 per cent of firms in this size category were in some aspect of engineering, a relatively high percentage, perhaps derived from the tradition of the region. The sectoral distribution of the firms otherwise follows the pattern of most European countries—smaller firms are located within the more traditional industries of furniture, food, paper and printing.

Table 3.50 Industrial structure of Tyne and Wear county

Sector	Percentage employing 1–250 workers	Percentage employing 10–250 workers
Food, drink and tobacco	9.4	10.2
Coal and petroleum products	0.4	0.4
Chemicals and allied industries	3.1	3.9
Metal manufacture	2.0	1.5
Mechanical engineering	14.3	18.1
Instrument engineering	3.4	1.7
Electrical engineering	4.8	5.4
Shipbuilding and marine engineering	2.9	3.7
Vehicles	1.4	1.5
Metal goods not elsewhere specified	10.8	11.2
Textiles	2.1	1.7
Leather, leather goods and fur	0.6	0.6
Clothing and footwear	8.1	6.3
Bricks, pottery, glass, cement, etc.	4.3	4.3
Timber, furniture, etc	14.3	13.6
Paper, printing and publishing	12.5	10.2
Other manufacturing	5.5	5.6
Total all manufacturing industries	100.0	100.0

Role of Size Distribution

In summary, a table produced by Storey (Table 3.51) shows the relative employment in small firms in the EEC, Japan and the United States, mainly in the early 1970s. At this level of national economies, having a large employment in small firms is obviously not a guarantee of economic progress. Nevertheless, the figures are indicators of a potential which if activated with other elements will produce economic growth. The eastern coast of Italy is now apparently witnessing such an activation. Japan which has a very high employment in small firms also demonstrates the result of such an activation.

Table 3.51 Contribution of smaller enterprises to employment in manufacturing

Country	Year of data	Percentage of manufacturing employment in small firms	
		1–99	1–199
United Kingdom	1976	17.1	22.6
Denmark*†	1973	36.6	52.1
Ireland†	1968	33.0	49.8
Italy*	1971	n.a.	47.3
Netherlands	1973	36.0	47.8
Belgium	1970	33.2	43.4
West Germany	1970	28.8	37.0
France	1976	25.2	34.2
Luxembourg	1973	19.1	28.2
Japan	1970	51.6	n.a.
USA	1972	24.8	n.a.

* Includes energy and water industries.

† Figures for these countries exclude employment in very small enterprises and understate the contribution of small enterprises.

The indicators of entrepreneurial potential in the numbers of small manufacturing firms and relative proportion of people employed in small firms appear to be good in Italy, Greece, Netherlands and Denmark. In the United Kingdom and West Germany, they are not good and in between lie France, Belgium and Ireland.

Denmark has a strong and prosperous economy with a high percentage of employment in firms of less than 50 employees. The Netherlands has shown weakness in recent years although before that an apparently strong economy. Greece and southern Italy are not prosperous or showing real signs of self-generated growth. On the other hand, the southern *Länder* of West Germany have exhibited growth and maintained prosperity with a small-firm sector, stronger than in other parts of West Germany, but much weaker than Denmark or other countries. The United Kingdom, with the weakest small-firm sector has suffered decline in all branches of industry.

A strong small-firm manufacturing sector is of critical importance because it has the major incubator role for new small firms. Most new firms are founded by people who previously owned a small manufacturing firm or worked in one. However, it is not the only factor nourishing

Table 3.52 Employers, self-employed and family workers, 1970–9

	1970		1979	
	Numbers	Percentage of total	Numbers	Percentage of total
(*a*) *Agriculture*				
FRG	1,967	87.0	1,289	83.5
France	2,239	79.4	1,498	80.2
Italy	2,642	68.1	1,898	63.0
The Netherlands	252	76.6	209	74.9
Belgium	160	92.0	106	89.8
UK	316	40.3	267	42.3
Ireland	246	86.9	196	89.1
Denmark	204	76.7	157	75.5
(*b*) *Industry*				
FRG	774	6.0	668	6.0
France	629	7.8	584	7.6
Italy	1,167	15.4	1,090	14.3
The Netherlands	122	6.9	98	6.6
Belgium	118	7.5	107	8.0
UK	438	4.0	507	5.3
Ireland	20	6.4	27	8.1
Denmark	97	11.1	82	10.9
(*c*) *Services*				
FRG	1,681	15.3	1,613	13.2
France	1,595	16.9	1,526	13.2
Italy	2,598	33.5	2,778	28.9
The Netherlands	389	15.7	341	11.9
Belgium	415	21.8	413	18.0
UK	1,149	9.1	1,112	7.7
Ireland	62	13.8	57	11.5
Denmark	178	15.2	167	10.9

Source: ABT (1982).

the entrepreneurial potential. Another is the extent of self-employment in an economy (Table 3.52).

Agriculture, a prime family source of entrepreneurs, has been in severe decline in all countries although still a very important sector in terms of self-employment. Ireland has the highest self-employment, the United Kingdom the lowest, indicating the high degree of concentration of ownership in this sector. Agriculture follows the general British pattern of concentration. France and West Germany have both still a large population in self- or family employment in agriculture. Industry, which has also declined in numbers of self-employed, shows Italy and Denmark with the largest percentage of self-employed. Ireland has shown a distinct improvement between 1970 and 1979, as has the United Kingdom, which is still at the foot of the table.

Italy leads with the highest number of self-employed in the services sector, followed by Belgium. Denmark has had a strong relative decline as has The Netherlands. The indicators here are of a trend to concentration in the services sector. Indeed, ABT (1982) comments that the services sector is polarised in Europe between small firms and very large firms.

The services sector has had the strongest employment growth in all countries, and it is the sector with lowest barriers to entry. One would expect a higher level of start-ups in this sector than anywhere else. There was, however, a decline in the number of 'establishments', except in Italy.

A segment of employment difficult to compare from country to country is the 'crafts and small trade' sector, as it is termed in Germany. This sector consists of both manufacturing and services. Almost half of the supplies and services were provided to private households, 40 per cent to industry and more than 10 per cent to public services. Compared to other states in West Germany, the crafts and small trade sector in Baden-Württemberg, with 670,000 employed, is highest in number of firms and second highest in number of employed after Bavaria. This sector probably contains the equivalent of many of the small family units of the Mezzogiorno.

Denmark has its 'trade and minor industry' sector. In 1975, this sector consisted of 87,100 firms with 464,000 employed, including owners and their wives (Hastrup 1977). These minor firms include small manufacturing units with not more than 19 employed, building contractors, laundries, shoe repair, car repair and other services. This sector, after a decline in the 1950s, had substantially increased its numbers employed from 362,000 in 1948 to 464,300 in 1975.

In Europe generally, self-employment and small firms both in manufacturing industry and the services have been in a process of long-term decline. The recession seems to have halted this process. The number of small manufacturing firms is tending to show some increase in most countries and between 1976 and 1979 the number of self-employed in industry increased, as it did in the services sector from 1977 to 1979.

The causes of this halt to decline may be variously interpreted. 'In a sluggish economic climate, small businesses are more likely to maintain certain levels of demand for labour than larger ones' (ABT 1982). Small firms may be more resilient because they are more flexible, meeting change more quickly than large firms. This flexibility is not simply a characteristic of each firm. Very many may not have flexibility, but the small firm sector as a dynamic sector has a volatility in its number of deaths and births. Its flexibility comes from this volatility. Unemployment is also a strong stimulant to setting up one's own business.

It may also be that small firms are meeting the growing market demand for diversity more effectively than the large firms and the large mass producers.

The recession may have shown up the potential role of the small-firm sector more clearly than might have been possible in a time of full employment and general prosperity. Large firms which, through the application of efficient mass-production technology, did bring a new level of prosperity, seem to be dependent on an environment which is increasingly prosperous and therefore on a longer product and technology cycle. At the same time, the growth of the large firm and the large corporate bureaucracies may itself be the cause of the recession. Their failure lies in the lack of innovation in new products, the concentration on short-term profits and investment in rationalisation rather than expansion. These were the factors which OECD's experts (1980) saw as the major cause of the recession.

The trend may not be towards a true deconcentration. The small-firm manufacturing sector, including the self-employed, has proved a degree of resilience which is very creditable against the background of decline. The reasons for this background of decline remain—the increased domination of the large firms, the restriction to certain sectors and difficulties in obtaining finance, and other resource inputs.

Europe displays a very mixed entrepreneurial potential. A country like Denmark is fulfilling its potential but others, like Greece, southern Italy and Ireland, do not seem able to convert their potential entrepreneurs into new economic activities. Industrially declining regions, some only recently starting decline, have weak entrepreneurial potential. At the other end of the spectrum lie the southern *Länder* of West Germany which, relative to Denmark have a weak entrepreneurial potential but are retaining their prosperity. The empirical evidence and the evidence of countries like Denmark, and regions like that around Milan, do point to the size of the small firm sector as important. The evidence of regions like the Mezzogiorno and Baden-Württemberg show that there are other factors involved in addition to the size of the small-firm sector or the numbers employed in small firms.

One is the number of large firms and the balance of size distribution. There appears to be more vitality where there are also a sufficient number of firms of over 500 and even 1,000 employees. Where the industrial structure is predominantly in the smaller size categories and particularly in the less than ten employees category, the large size of the small-firm sector generally does not result in growth. Equally, where there is a dominant concentration in very large firms or establishments of over 1,000, there has been a decline in prosperity, an inability to generate new growth. In other words, areas with a balanced industrial size distribution, that is, having a small firm sector employing 40 per cent or more of industrial labour and a strong but not dominant (in employment terms) number of firms of over 500 employees, have a propensity to greater prosperity.

There are also other factors at work since Baden-Württemberg does not in fact follow this pattern of industrial structure. Its smaller firms are lively but it does not have a mass of them. And at the other end of the scale, and described later, lies the Prato region of Tuscany, very heavily dominated by very small firms but exhibiting a considerable vitality, growth and prosperity. Both have features associated with technical progressiveness and by being almost exceptions in other respects demonstrate how essential are features associated with technical progressiveness.

References

Tables, unless otherwise stated, are taken from Sweeney, G. P. (1985). *A Study on information networks designed to support technological innovation in less-favoured regions of the Community*, Dublin, IIRS.

ABT Forschung (1982). *An overall view of employment in small and medium sized enterprises in the EEC: report prepared for the Commission of the European Communities*. Bonn, September.

Boeckhout, I. J. and Molle, W. T. M. (1982). *Technological change, location patterns and regional development*. Rotterdam, Netherlands Economic Institute, 1982.

Bouvier, F. (1984). 'Setting up of technological networks—theory and practice'. Six Countries Workshop, Limerick.

Eurostat Review (1974–83). Luxembourg, Office for Official Publications of the European Community.

Hastrup, B. (1977). *The trades and Danish economic development since 1945*. Copenhagen, The Chamber of Danish Trade and Crafts.

INSEE (Institut National de la Statisque et des Etudes Economiques) (1982). *Disparité et diversité des regions françaises—à la veille du IXe Plan*. Paris, October.

Kennedy, K. A. and Healy, T. (1985). 'Small scale industry in Ireland' in Fitzpatrick, J. and Kelly, J., *Perspectives on Irish industry*. Dublin, Irish Management Institute.

Malecki, E. J. 'Science, technology and regional economic development: review and prospects', *Res. Policy*, 10, 312–34

Marsh, D. (1986). 'French regional policy: an unequal dash for advantage', *Financial Times*, 14 February.

O'Malley, E. (1985). 'Performance of Irish indigenous industry: some lessons for the 1980s', in Fitzpatrick, J. and Kelly, J., *Perspectives on Irish industry*. Dublin, Irish Management Institute.

OECD (1980). Technical change and economic policy. Paris.
Progress (1983). 'Année européenne des PME et de l'artisanat'. No. 78. Brussels.
Storey, D. J. (1982). *Entrepreneurship and the new firm*. London, Croom Helm.

CHAPTER 4

The Innovative Potential

Great or small, a long leap or a small increment, innovation is what entrepreneurs invest in. They feel that they have something through which they can create wealth even if it is only at the mundane level of 'earning their own living'. Creation of a new economic activity through the foundation of new firms occurs through the union of entrepreneurial and innovative potential. Innovative potential is complex. Its presence, like entrepreneurial potential, does not guarantee the creation of new economic activities and therefore growth. It is in essence the stock of knowledge of a locality. The conversion of this into innovation is dependent on characteristics associated with technical progressiveness—the willingness to give and to receive information, buy rather than make policies and decentralisation of decision-making.

The innovative potential of a region, like entrepreneurial vitality, is determined by whether it is a central core region or a remote region, whether it has autonomy in information or receives information, eventually, as a transplant from the centre. It depends on the flows of nutrient information, and on the cycle time for logistic information.

Sectoral distribution of industry is one of the factors considered to be significant to innovative potential and entrepreneurial vitality. 'Regional competitiveness, then, is largely a function of the industrial mix and technological capability that reinforce each other in a dynamic manner' (Malecki 1981). Sectoral distribution is a major part of the diversity which leads to higher creativity and innovativeness and entrepreneurial vitality.

Generally, the small-firm sector tends to be more dominant in traditional industrial sectors such as food, textiles, leather, clothing, wood products and furniture. These sectors have also witnessed a decline in the number of large firms, with impact on the regions which had specialised in these sectors. This can be seen, for example, in the textile and clothing sector of the Nord-Pas de Calais in France, the North-West of England and Ireland. The number of small firms in these sectors has, however, shown an increase. They are more flexible and can respond to the market demand for greater diversity and quality more readily than large firms.

Where they adopt new technologies and the latest best practice, they can compete against standardised products from developed or developing countries, as the formerly declining clothing industries of New England are now showing. For this to happen, a region needs a mix of sectors and technologies and occupations so that there is awareness of new technologies.

Less-favoured peripheral regions tend to have an even heavier concentration of small firms in the traditional sectors and agricultural resource-based sectors. But here the quality tends to be lower. There is a very slow uptake of the best practice and they are usually a long way down the innovation chain. So also are the industrially declining areas, areas once dominated by one or two sectors and lacking the sectoral and technological mix. In both peripheral and industrially declining regions some confusion is created at a macro-data level by relocation or decentralisation policies. These have in recent years brought into the regions plants in newer industries and have increased at least in appearance the sectoral mix in these regions.

The importance of the sectoral mix lies not only in the creation of awareness through the diversity of information in the information flows but also in the creativity spurred by this diversity. The ideas around which an entrepreneur founds a new firm is a result of the mix of diverse and disorderly bits and pieces of information flowing in casual and business conversation. 'Heard by chance' and 'browsing' are far from infrequent sources of innovation. Creativity which results in innovation happens when two concepts, bits of information previously unassociated, strike one another and spark off something which did not exist before in quite that way in that market or in that locality.

The critical component in sectoral diversity seems to be the strength in the indigenous engineering sector, and in there being a sufficent number of medium to large firms in this sector. Southern Germany has high employment in this sector, Denmark less but a significant 39 per cent. France has 43 per cent of employment in this sector, 30.5 per cent without the transport equipment sector, but this is regionally concentrated, a quarter being in the Île de France. The north of Italy is strong in engineering, but the Mezzogiorno, Greece and Ireland are weak. The United Kingdom has a high percentage also, but the sector has declined severely in recent years.

The strength in size terms of the engineering sector is an indicator but it is probably much more the size in qualitative terms of the engineering industry which has the strongest influence in the mix of sectors and technologies. Where the engineering sector is one with a high level of best practice it gives a strong technological orientation to the region and diffuses the best practice to other sectors. It gives other sectors a capability to develop new technology.

Where a region is an importer of technology and does not build its own improvements on this technology and then export this in the form of engineering products or in plant, machinery and equipment, then it remains an economy without self-generated growth. This is the theme of Jane Jacobs (1985)—that prosperity is led by import-substituting cities. If a region is an exporter of materials or agricultural produce to self-generating prosperous regions, it may gain a level of prosperity. If this prosperity is not put to use to generate technologies and economic activities to replace imported industrial and technological products, its prosperity is fragile. Anyone who has visited Lesvos, an island of 12 million olive trees, an extraordinary sight in itself, will also not forget the decayed and decaying houses of the former 'merchant princes'. Jane Jacobs uses Uruguay as her example of the failure of a region, once the most 'European' of South American countries, to generate its own skills, technologies and industries. It was deluded by a temporary prosperity brought by selling the products of its farms and ranches to a Europe which eventually found alternative sources. Demand for olive oil from centres such as Lesvos has declined because import-substituting regions, more technologically advanced and self-sufficient than the olive oil producing regions have turned to other sources for cooking and other oils.

Uruguay and Lesvos provide a contrast to Denmark, which developed even its traditional industries to a high level of technical excellence. The technical progressiveness of its agriculture and engineering sectors enabled it to develop an agriculture machinery sector. Its dairy equipment remains in the forefront through the incorporation of the most recent technology and best practice—microelectronics. Inevitably its food products are of high quality with a high added value.

Stuttgart also, the engineering heart of Baden-Württemberg, demonstrates the role which a strong and progressive engineering sector can play in a regional economy. 'Stuttgart's sinews are its small and medium-sized companies, often family owned, which excel in precision engineering, machine tools and electronics, where the brainpower is at least as important as industrial brawn' (Cornwell 1986). The skills and products of this sector influence the technological orientation and ability to be an exporter rather than an importer and to be self-generating.

The engineering sector has a lead role—it is the technology of making things and hence the strength of the engineering sector is an essential part of that technical culture which provides the environment for innovation and for the rapid diffusion of innovation. For example, Denmark is a country with a reputation for pottery, furniture, cutlery and other products produced by good technology. The awareness and respect for design, quality and technological excellence is high. Its technical culture is strong and pervasive. It is strong like Stuttgart's because the mix of sectors and technologies led by a progressive engineering sector results in a wide range of higher-level technological skills. Availability of skills, a well-trained and qualified labour force, continually recurs as an essential requirement for the entrepreneurial foundation of a new firm. Without availability of a skilled labour force, the perception of an innovative opportunity cannot be turned into an activity which creates wealth.

Where the engineering sector is tied to a dominant sector, as happened in the Manchester area of England, then as the dominant sector firms become more concentrated and less progressive, the engineering sector declines. The basic skills remain but have no opportunity for expression in entrepreneurship and innovation.

Regions which are without a mix of sectors, technologies and occupations are regions with dominant firms and sectors. Where these sectors or firms are in decline, the region has a weak technical culture and innovative potential. It becomes difficult for entrepreneurs to perceive an innovative opportunity. There is a lower level of best practice. The awareness is narrow because the nutrient information flows lack diversity and are far downstream. Others have taken out the nutrients earlier.

Agriculture can be one such dominant sector. In the less-favoured regions, there is still a relatively high agricultural labour-force which, in the Western half of Ireland, the Mezzorgiono and Greece, is of low productivity and technical skills. Table 4.1 shows the relative proportions of employment in the major sectors of the ten-member EEC and the

Table 4.1 Sectoral distribution of civilian employment (per cent) and GDP per capital (US dollars)

Country	Agriculture (%)	Industry (%)	Services (%)	GDP ($)
Greece	30.3	30.2	39.5	3,769
Ireland	19.2	32.4	48.4	4,885
Italy	14.2	37.8	48.0	6,123
France	8.8	35.9	55.3	10,552
Luxembourg	6.3	38.4	55.3	10,556
West Germany	6.0	44.8	49.2	11,076
The Netherlands	4.6	32.0	63.3	9,861
Belgium	3.0	34.8	62.2	9,651
UK	2.6	38.0	59.4	8,886
Denmark	2.0	26.4	71.6	11,350

Notes: Sectoral data for Belgium refers to 1979, for Denmark to 1982, otherwise to 1980. GDP per capita figures are for 1984.

Sources: Trend of Employment and Unemployment: Basic Statistics of the Community; Danish National Statistics; OECD.

relative GDP. Denmark and The Netherlands which have still a high value in exports of agricultural produce, have high productivity and technical skill in the sector, and have developed agricultural machinery and chemicals industries of international competitiveness. In Ireland, although there has been very high investment in agricultural equipment in the last decade, it has been virtually all imported. Employment in the agricultural machinery sector is less than in 1914. In Greece and Italy, the agricultural employment figures hide considerable underemployment. Underemployment in agriculture in Ireland has declined but there is still some in the poorer agricultural regions of the Midlands and West. Outside the East region, agricultural employment is high in Ireland as in Greece outside of Athens (Table 4.2).

Italy shows a similar picture of a large agricultural sector occupying a significant proportion of total employment (Table 4.3) with the percentage much higher in the South than in the North.

Table 4.2 Ireland: employment by sector and region, 1981 (thousands)

Region	Agriculture		Industry		Construction		Services	
	Numbers	(%)	Numbers	(%)	Numbers	(%)	Numbers	(%)
Mid-West	22.7	22.7	22.5	22.5	10.3	10.3	44.4	44.4
West	29.0	32.2	15.6	17.3	7.1	7.9	38.4	42.6
East	18.2	4.0	105.1	23.3	40.1	8.9	288.0	63.8
Ireland	186.5	16.4	259.8	22.9	100.3	8.8	588.2	51.8

Table 4.3 Italy: employment by sector and region, 1981 (thousands)

Region	Agriculture		Industry incl. construction		Services	
	Numbers	(%)	Numbers	(%)	Numbers	(%)
Campania	316	18.0	492	28.0	946	53.9
Mezzogiorno	1,326	20.9	1,706	26.9	3,292	52.0
Rest of Italy	1,219	8.9	5,892	41.0	7,243	50.4
Italy	2,545	12.3	7,598	36.7	10,353	50.9

Baden-Württemberg had in 1982 4.9 per cent of its employment in agriculture, 50 per cent in industry and 45 per cent in services. The agricultural sector here is characterised by an exceptionally high share of special crops—wine, fruit, tobacco, and asparagus. The contrast with the agricultural sectors of the peripheral regions is sharp. Baden-

Württemberg's agricultural sector demonstrates the appreciation of quality, specialisation in higher added value crops and technical skills in the management of these crops. The technical culture and technological orientation of the industrial sector is apparent also in the agricultural sector. In the peripheral regions the indigenous manufacturing sectors find difficulty in achieving quality. They exist in an environment and culture with a low technological orientation. Indigenous industry is a relatively small sector in employment terms overawed by the agricultural sector. In Western Ireland, for example, the indigenous industrial sector employs only 8.5 per cent of total employment in the region. The Mezzogiorno is little different. The influence of a dominant weak agricultural sector on overall performance can be gauged from the external view of products from Denmark as against those from Greece, Italy and Ireland. As is clear from Table 4.4, two countries have a low reputation for quality, market response and interaction, and progressiveness. Italy's reputation is mixed, perhaps illustrating the contrasts of North and South. All three countries, however, compare poorly to Denmark which has a consistent ranking.

Table 4.4 EMF survey 1984: indicators of quality and innovativeness: ranking in 22 OECD member states

	Denmark	Greece	Italy	Ireland
Product quality	4	21	12	18
Product design and styling	2	21	1	19
Product safety	5	20	17	18
Packaging of consumer goods	3	20	11	18
On-time delivery of products	4	15	17	18
After sales service	5	21	15	17
Company attitude to marketing	6	15	19	22
Attention to studying the market	4	19	9	21
Innovativeness in production techniques	6	21	8	19
Innovativeness in product lines	5	20	7	21
Extent plan effectively towards the future	6	21	17	18
Readiness to exploiot inventions	3	21	8	20

The Higher Education System

A very major influence on the technological culture and orientation of a region is the educational system. Whilst tradition and history have played a strong role in the way in which higher-level university education has developed in Europe, there has been considerable expansion in technological and technical education in the post-war period. No attempt is made here to describe the educational systems of various countries but to give only an overall impression of the orientation of the educational system of various regions of the European Community.

France, Belgium, Denmark and Ireland have high concentrations of students in their respective capitals, whereas in The Netherlands, Germany, United Kingdom, and Italy there is a wider diffusion of universities and student populations throughout the country, as is illustrated in Figure 4.1. The distribution is such that no correlation between student numbers and prosperity of a region can be drawn except perhaps in Baden-Württemberg, which has the highest concentration of students in the Federal Republic of Germany. On the other hand, the South of Italy has in some regions much higher proportions of students in the total population than Piemonte or Lombardia. The more even distribution present in England is superficially at least independent of the heavy concentration of research in South-East England, whereas in France, Paris dominates in both respects.

A more important factor would appear to be the technological orientation of the education system, albeit a complex factor. Germany has, like England, a long tradition in mechanical crafts and trades and developed in the nineteenth century a strong technical and technological education system. It was followed in the earlier years of this century by Denmark. Whilst Germany was building on a strong existing technical culture, Denmark would seem to have developed its technical culture as a consequence of the remodelling of its educational system. England, however, retained the focus of its educational system on the arts, humanities and science rather than developing a new technological focus. This was attempted in the post-war period, but seems not to have broken the boundaries of the traditional education/class system.

In contrast, the southern regions of Italy and France have high student populations. But as in Ireland, Wales and Scotland the higher-level education system has maintained its traditional cultural orientation to the classical professions, humanities and sciences (Kormoss and Cerych 1979). In both France and Italy the South is overrepresented in the national administration. In Ireland, only one engineer is produced to Denmark's three in relative terms.

The educational system is a major source of the skills and expertise which make up the stock of knowledge of a region, and in its orientation it

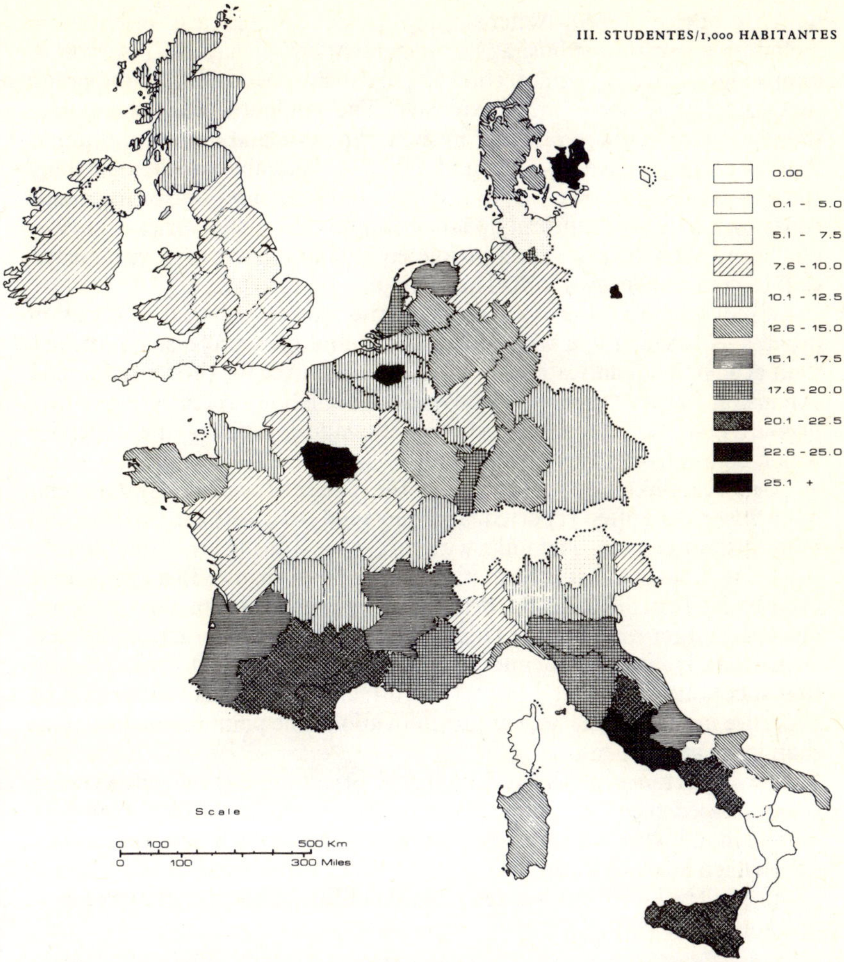

Figure 4.1 Number of students per thousand inhabitants.
Source: Kormoss and Cerych (1979).

is a major determinant of innovative and entrepreneurial culture. Where there is a strong technological orientation, observable particularly in the number of engineers produced, then there seems to be a higher likelihood of a region having a capability for self-generated growth.

The higher-education structure of a region also contains a very large reservoir of knowledge and expertise. For the most part, the expertise in the education system is transferred to industry and into innovative products through the graduates and this transfer process may be long and tenuous (Price 1966). Where there is a technological orientation, including scientific and business management knowledge, the reservoir of knowledge relevant to the technical progressiveness and the innovation potential of a region is more extensive. The graduates who emerge will therefore also be more relevant in their expertise and more importantly they will tend to have skills around which it is possible for them at some stage to create their own job, to become entrepreneurs. One of the major consequences of the cultural divide, reinforced by a snob or class divide, has been that so many young people emerge into the world without the skill to create their own jobs. They can only be employees.

Employees are also necessary in the entrepreneurial innovation process. A labour force with diverse skills and high professional, rather than academic, qualifications is a required resource for the founding and expansion of new economic activities. This labour force is a product primarily of the education system, with industry giving the expertise which comes from experience.

The direct links with industry from the higher educational system tend to be fewer than often reported, and they tend to be with larger firms and more distant centres. The links with larger local firms are important. As will be seen later, most information passes from firm to firm, the larger progressive firm diffusing the best technical practice to smaller firms, but often the larger firm acquires its awareness of the best practice and new knowledge from its academic consultant. The SAPPHO project found that successfully innovating firms had direct personal links with research expertise in the specific area of the innovation. The point is valid for more than innovations *per se*.

The importance of the technological orientation is evident even in science-based faculties which either result in new knowledge or in new high-tech industries. It is the technological orientation of universities like MIT which leads to Route 128s. On the other hand, a complete technical culture will be increasingly a determinant of future success. Piatier (1981) has noted that

> the educational system can play another role in promoting innovation: the development of imagination and creativeness is essential to provide fertile ground for innovation. This is probably underrated today in our countries whereas in Japan it is given priority from infant school onwards.

Culture is the basis of product innovation.

The Services Sector

A further influence in the sectoral mix is the services sector but its influence arises from more than simply a further mix of occupations. Services have had the strongest growth in employment since the 1950s and this sector has become the largest of the macro-sectors in numbers employed and the dominant sector in many countries. Analyses of this sector such as those by Machlup and Porat referred to in Chapter 2 have shown that one must divide the services sector into two very distinct sectors. One, the tertiary sector, is the traditional services sector, mainly composed of personal services such as laundries, street cleaning, hotels and so on. The other is a new quaternary sector, the information sector, the sector of the late twentieth and twenty-first centuries and the source of much of the wealth of the information society. This sector is again divisible according to Porat (1977) into two subsectors—the primary and the secondary. The primary sector consists of all the activities in knowledge and information generation, storage and dissemination such as research, education, computing, software, publishing, libraries, consultancy, and so on. The secondary sector consists of all the private and public bureaucracies. Obviously, all the activities in a bureaucracy concerned with generation of information such as a national statistics office belong in the primary sector. The bureaucracies as here classified as being the secondary subsector of a quaternary sector are all the administrative activities, the administration as such in a public service sense.

Unfortunately, national statistics and, particularly, regional statistics, do not as yet provide easy access to data on these sectors and subsectors. However, within the role of the quaternary sector lies the basis for determining more effective regional policies and therefore one must look at each in turn.

Tertiary (Services) Sector

The 'services sector' as a whole accounts for 44.4 per cent of employment in the Mid-West of Ireland, and 52 per cent in the Mezzogiorno. In Baden-Württemberg, services of all types account for 43.5 per cent of employment. Within these figures is employment in retailing, personal services such as laundries, repair and maintenance, hotels and catering, and transport. Public sector employment at the local and regional level tends to be at the routine service and administration level, and the more centralised a country the higher the percentage of regional public sector employment is at this lower level. Peripheral regions also tend, as in Greece or Portugal, to have a relatively high tourist service employment, which is in effect a transfer payment from other regions for personal services. It tends to be price-sensitive for the mass tourism attracted to the sun, rather than quality-sensitive.

This tertiary sector wields little if any influence on the technical culture of a region, and especially the mass tourism segment which may even depress it further. On the contrary, it seems in its quality of service and management of its micro- or macro-environment to be a dependency on the producing sectors. If these are good, then this tertiary sector reflects that quality. It provides a useful and immediate indicator in the quality of hotel services, maintenance of the environment, litter on the streets, particularly outside the central urban area. The cumulative influence which pervades a society, driving it upwards to a consciously good management of the quality of all aspects of the environment and of products and services, or downwards to neglect, apathy and mismanagement, is reflected in this tertiary services sector.

Relocation of government offices carrying out routine processing and administration does not affect the technical culture. They are the services-sector equivalent of branch plants and the truly information intensive functions are left behind in the centre. Indeed, many of these routine functions are very sensitive to the job-displacing impact of information technology reinforcing the negative impact on the local technical culture. The job-reinforcing impact of information technology takes place in the autonomous centres.

However, wherever there is a substantial decentralisation of government then there is a higher level of autonomy in decision-making and information-intensive functions. Where the rest of the mix is right this decentralisation enables the entrepreneurial and innovative potential as in Denmark to merge into self-generated activity. Where the mix is not right, and the educational system is a major component, then, as in the Mezzogiorno, there is a lack of innovative potential or, as in North Rhine-Westphalia, a lack of entrepreneurial potential.

The Quaternary Sector

The growth in the quaternary information-providing sector represents in some degree a shift out of manufacturing of certain productive activities, and also a reinforcement of traditional activities. Information-generating, storage, processing, disseminating and communicating activities provide the inputs on which the technical progress, innovativeness and competitiveness of manufacturing companies depend to an ever-decreasing extent in an information-intensive economy. It is therefore an economically productive sector, generating and providing much of the information component of the end product, the component on which non-price competitiveness depends.

As with the manufacturing industry sector, a mix is probably essential, for example in research creativity: a mix of technologies and sciences, of consultancies, libraries, professional associations. The greater is this mix the more nutrient the information flows and the higher the probability of innovation—if this mix is matched by an industrial mix of sizes as well as sectors.

The information sector is concentrated in core regions, especially in more centralised countries. It consists, as described earlier, of public and private research, information centres and major libraries, government information-processing activities such as statistics, standardisation, software development, computer databases, marketing, advertising, publishing, financial institutions and public and private bureaucracies, and other activities. The influence of these can be considerable in giving a region information autonomy and 'the half-hour information-intensive contact', diverse and richly up-to-date information flows. They also make up a large segment of the innovative potential of a region. Thwaites *et al.* (1984) quote Schmookler (1972) as defining 'the technological capacity of an economy as the accumulated body of technical knowledge weighted by the number of persons who have access to this knowledge'. Where there is a concentration of information-intensive functions and a concentration of more skilled and highly qualified personnel within the half-hour contact potential then the capacity is high and a lot of people have access to it. And conversely, where it is low there is less access to it. Thwaites *et al.* (1984) refer to work which has shown that establishments in areas like the northern region of the United Kingdom make fewer contacts either by telephone or through meetings in a given period than their counterparts in the core region of the South-East and in particular Central London (James *et al.* 1979). There are fewer information-intensive contacts which can be made.

The concentration of population in Athens, London, Paris and Dublin is an indicator of the concentration of the information sector. These cities contain the main administrative departments and therefore the main decision-making functions of centralised national governments. The half-hour information-intensive contact is important not only for information gathering but also for influencing a decision with information and 'informed opinion' and for obtaining a decision. It is part of the logistics in the cycle time between need and supply and between the identification of the opportunity or creation of the innovative idea and its entry on the market.

Hence, such centres also contain the headquarters of large corporations. Table 4.5 shows the concentration of industrial headquarters in a number of countries. In West Germany, a federal country, there is a distribution amongst the more industrialised *Länder*, but North Rhine-Westphalia still holds a central place with 42 of the top 100 companies located there. The United Kingdom, a centralised country with a high degree of concentration in its industrial and business structure, has 80 of its top 100 companies located in the South-East, and France has 87 in the Île de France. The Netherlands has 67 in the Randstadt. Belgium is more distributed, but shows the discrepancy of Flanders and Wallonia which is reflected in their respective growth and decline.

Table 4.5 Regional distribution of industrial headquarters in Europe, 1976

Country and region	Number of companies identified	Sales ($m)	Sales/national total (%)
Germany	100	230,602	
North Rhine-Westphalia	42	97,524	42
Hamburg	11	28,177	12
Hesse	10	23,330	10
Baden-Württemberg	9	21,186	9
Bavaria	11	18,734	8
Lower Saxon	6	17,437	8
Rheinland Pfalz	2	10,750	5
Berlin	3	7,156	3
Rest	6	6,308	3
United Kingdom	100	162,231	
South-East	80	145,918	90
West Midlands	7	7,893	5
Scotland	5	3,092	2
North-West	5	2,906	2
Rest	3	2,422	1
Italy	100	82,219	
Lazio	14	42,278	51
Lombardia	44	20,333	25
Piemonte	14	10,679	13
Liguria	10	6,062	7
Rest	18	2,867	4
France	100	153,779	
Île de France	87	140,989	92
Rest	13	12,790	8
Netherlands	100	112,334	
West	62	71,826	64
South	19	21,384	19
East	12	10,583	9
North	7	8,551	8
Belgium	49	27,260	
Brabant	16	12,949	47
Flanders	21	10,339	38
Wallonia	12	3,972	15
Denmark	50	9,493	
Zealand	31	7,092	75
Rest	19	2,401	25

A. S. Økonomisk Literatur, *Europe's 500 largest companies.*

Along with headquarters of government and business go many other activities such as research and computer installations. An assessment has been made of the relative distribution of these in the regions of the United Kingdom (Table 4.6). The table indicates one very interesting phenomenon. A major result of the activities of the Location of Offices Board has been to move offices only from Central London to its immediate surroundings in South-East England. The pull of the information-intensive contact is irresistible, whether it is the need to be close to the information-intensive and decision-making activities of others or to have close to oneself, one's own such activities.

This region dominates in the United Kingdom in the number of research establishments and computer installations and, as Table 4.7 shows, the research establishments of private sector industrial firms do not differ from this pattern. Yet the South-East of England contains only a quarter of manufacturing employment. Furthermore, Thwaites *et al* (1984) have shown a systematic regional variation not only in on-site R & D effort, with less-favoured regions having fewer such units but also fewer people in the units which do exist.

The distribution of innovation tends to follow this pattern of concentration of research although by no means to the same extent, a point worth observing. Thwaites *et al.* (1984) quote from work of the Science Policy Research Unit, University of Sussex, to show the regional trends in innovation between 1945 and 1980 (Table 4.8). The South-East has a share of significant innovations well above its share of manufacturing employment, although declining a little, whilst 'intermediate' areas have shown a distinct improvement. Development regions have declined considerably in their innovation output. The Sussex study also reveals that the South-East is the area to benefit most from the transfer of significant foreign technologies to Britain.

Incremental innovations, or innovations at a less than major significance level, are possibly even more important to the overall prosperity of an economy in maintaining competitiveness and market share and in opening up new markets. Thwaites *et al.* (1981) therefore looked at three industries well represented in all regions—machine tools, instruments and electronic components—to examine whether they were making major contributions or to increasing their use of micro-electronics. The South-East recorded the highest incidence of product innovations. The propensity to innovate in plants with under 100 employees is nearly 2.5 times higher in the South-East and West Midlands than in regions containing most of the United Kingdom's 'assisted areas' (Oakey *et al.* 1979). Diffusion of innovation tends to be concentrated. Oakey and his colleagues found that whilst the South-East is the most important source of innovations it is also the main beneficiary in this process. Adoption of the best practice is associated with innovativeness.

Table 4.6 United Kingdom information sector: regional indicators

Region (largest city)	Distance of largest city from London	Number of research estabs	Research estabs per 100,000 population	Computer installations		LOB regional destination of relocation
				Net	per 100,000 pop.	
SE England (London)	0	579	3.4	7,260	43.1	77.4
SW England (Bristol)	120	60	1.4	838	19.6	7.3
East Anglia (Norwich)	110	38	2.8	436	23.5	2.3
East Midlands (Nottingham)	120	55	1.5	689	18.3	3.2
West Midlands (Birmingham)	110	106	2.1	1,052	20.4	0.4
Wales (Cardiff)	160	29	0.9	345	12.5	0.2
NW England (Manchester)	180	107	1.6	1,387	21.3	3.9
Yorkshire and Humberside (Leeds)	190	71	1.5	808	16.6	3.6
NE England (Newcastle)	280	48	1.5	503	16.1	1.4
Scotland (Glasgow)	400	86	1.7	1,068	20.5	0.3
Northern Ireland (Belfast)	450	15	0.9	122	7.9	0.0

Source: Ward and Newman (1981).

Table 4.7 Great Britain: location of research establishments in private sector industrial firms

Region	1968 (%)	1980 (%)
South East	45.6	47.0
East Anglia	2.0	2.6
South West	5.6	7.2
West Midlands	11.5	8.9
East Midlands	5.0	5.5
Yorkshire and Humberside	6.5	6.2
North West	11.1	11.5
North	4.9	5.0
Wales	1.5	2.2
Scotland	5.8	3.8

Table 4.8 United Kingdom: distribution of 'significant innovations' by location, 1945–80

Period	South-East	Non-assisted areas excluding the South-East	Intermediate areas	Development areas
1945–59	36.7	27.5	19.1	17.5
1960–9	31.2	28.4	24.8	14.5
1970–80	34.0	24.9	30.3	10.6
1945–80	33.7	27.0	25.5	13.7
Total number	770	616	583	313
% of manufacturing employment: 1978	24.9	30.6	24.6	19.9
% of manufacturing units: 1978	31.0	29.6	23.4	15.9

Source: Townsend (1981).

The distribution of information-intensive occupations follows much the same pattern except that the proportion of skilled manual workers is below the national average in the South-East, and higher than the national average in almost all other regions (Table 4.9). Most significant is that industry in the South-East is more information-intensive than in any other region. The proportion of professional and managerial workers is considerably higher than elsewhere, the numbers of low-skilled workers

Table 4.9 Great Britain: percentage of manufacturing employment

Region	Low skilled	Professional & managerial	Skilled manual
South-East	24.70	19.58	33.32
East Anglia	33.21	13.98	36.71
South-West	28.29	14.86	38.08
West Midlands	32.82	12.83	37.91
East Midlands	31.45	12.71	39.58
Yorkshire & Humberside	34.33	11.89	38.51
North-West	34.75	12.27	36.51
North	33.41	10.06	41.16
Wales	36.52	10.29	38.20
Scotland	32.50	10.86	40.18
Great Britain	30.94	13.88	36.87

relatively lower than elsewhere but skilled manual workers are lower in number.

One effect of this concentration is that it has been noted (Goddard *et al*) that 'in general plants in development areas mention relatively few local useful technical contacts. They appear to prefer or are forced to use technical sources at a greater distance than are firms located elsewhere'—a consequence both of lack of autonomy and information impoverishment.

The pattern of concentration in France is much the same. Table 4.10 gives the number of researchers per thousand economically active persons and the numbers of research staff for each region. The Île de France has a dominant place but the attraction of researchers to Provence-Côte d'Azur, as to California, has given this region the highest number of researchers relative to the working population. Rhône-Alpes is also a research-intensive region. The Île de France has a strong concentration of the laboratories of the CNRS, the national research organisation, 54 per cent of whose staff are located in the Paris region.

The Midi-Pyrénées, a concentrated region within itself, lies fourth in France in its 'innovation potential' as measured by research activity and wealth of high-tech firms. But there are strong contrasts. With 8.6 per cent of the national agricultural population, only 2.5 per cent of food-processing added value is contributed from within the region. Six of the ten largest firms are in Toulouse, which also contributes 41 per cent of the region's industrial value added. Toulouse has become a national research centre, with 40 per cent of research in aeronautics and robotics. It is now also an important centre in microbial biotechnology and pharmacology. The industry links from research, however, are to large

Table 4.10 France: number of researchers per thousand active population, 1982

Region	Number of researchers per 1,000 active population	Researchers	'Effectives'
Alsace	3.92	394	1,086
Aquitaine	3.27	1,264	4,918
Auvergne	2.97	725	5,445
Bourgogne	1.8	407	1,460
Bretagne	2.47	448	1,459
Centre	1.87	506	2,427
Champagne-Ardenne	1.37	209	665
Corsica	0.07	—	—
Franche-Comté	2.21	417	2,136
Île de France	4.17	23,048	72,929
Langeudoc-Roussillon	3.90	218	1,143
Limousin	1.60	98	409
Lorraine	3.37	417	1,627
Midi-Pyrénées	3.78	966	4,395
Nord-Pas de Calais	1.63	622	2,749
Basse-Normandie	1.45	180	665
Haute-Normandie	1.74	688	2,594
Pays de la Loire	1.61	565	2,682
Picardie	1.44	550	2,490
Poitou-Charentes	1.53	192	796
Provence-Alpes-Côte d'Azur	4.51	2,106	7,036
Rhône-Alpes	4.07	3,345	13,117
France	3.21	37,366	132,228

Source: *Atlas Français de l'Innovation* (1982); Piattier (1985).

firms outside the area. The contact between the research and education systems and SMEs outside Toulouse is from the professional (vocational) and technical schools. The local subsidiaries of major national groups appear, however, to have strong local decision-making which enables interaction with local suppliers. This region has the contrast of an agricultural peripheral region containing a centre with a strong high-tech large and small industry which bypasses the rest of the region.

Baden-Württemberg, as well as having a high percentage of the West German engineering industry within its borders, also has a rich infrastructure of universities, polytechnics and research institutes. There are twelve joint industrial research institutes, AiF. Thirteen of the thirty or so

Fraunhofer-Gesellschaft (applied research) institutes are located in Baden-Württemberg, as are three national research institutes and 230 'institutes of universities'. There are also 17 institutes of the Max-Planck-Gesellschaft (fundamental research) and 14 polytechnics. Baden Württemberg is rich in research and accounts for a quarter of all R & D spending in West Germany.

It is not a concentrated region in the sense of the Île de France or the South-East of England and there is a spread of these organisations through the state. It has, in addition, many 'consultancy' and information organisations such as the RKW (Rationalisierungskuratorium der Deutschen Wirtschaft) and Chambers of Commerce.

ISI Karlsruhe carried out an evaluation of the regional effects of various measures in West Germany introduced since 1981 (Krist 1984). This showed that innovating firms, those receiving R & D grants, and new innovating firms, those founded since 1969, were concentrated in central agglomerated areas and that the 'innovation potential' of regions of northern Germany, the border area and peripheral regions in the West, mostly assisted areas, was below the national average. The regional effects of information-intensive concentration are as visible in West Germany as elsewhere.

Branch Plants

Concentration of the information sector in core regions is one facet of a centralisation both in industry and administration which has its inevitable effect on other regions, drawing from them capabilities for creation of wealth and making them more dependent on transfers from the centre. Another facet is the concentration of this sector in core or autonomous regions in other countries. This growing phenomenon is visible in the spread of American branch plants in Europe and indeed in the spread of Japanese branch plants in the United States. In peripheral and declining regions, there has been considerable growth in the proportion of plants controlled from outside the regions in the last three decades and in the proportion of manufacturing employment in them. This has been one feature of the growth of the large corporation.

This growth in branch plants has been partly by independent decision of headquarters of these firms, but in the case of less-favoured regions (LFRs) has been strongly influenced by the national regional policies. Regional industrial policy has concentrated on amelioration of employment problems by attracting national or foreign large corporations to establish branch plants. This has been characteristic of policies for both declining and less-developed regions. Large firms have been able to take advantage of incentives and lower labour costs by locating production in LFRs.

This control of industry from outside regions together with the concentration of the information-intensive functions near the corporate headquarters of the firm has meant that many regions become branch-plant economies. 'Regions whose economies are principally involved in branch plant production have become increasingly recognised as being inhibited in both technological innovation and in the formation of new firms' says Malecki (1981), referring to studies such as that of Firn and Swales (1978). Branch plants which have no autonomy or local control of production technology, marketing and product development have little interaction with local industry in the region for the supply of a wide range of inputs of equipment, components, materials, sub-assembly and information.

There is little diffusion of the best practice from such firms into the regional economy, if only because their own information-intensive functions are very limited and highly production-orientated. Such buying or subcontracting as is done locally tends to be of low-technology parts rather than of locally designed components, sub-assemblies or equipment. And as Thwaites *et al.* (1984) observe:

> Independent enterprises are in principle unable to tap group resources for information but numerous executives in small enterprises obtain non-sensitive information from such sources through personal contact or from former colleagues. This type of contact is more frequently available in the South-East than in the North where the previous work experience of colleagues tends to be limited; in the latter region establishments operating in the same area of production are scarce and many group plants do not possess any research staff from whom information may be gleaned.

In France, the Île de France has the lowest percentage of manufacturing industry controlled from outside, 4 per cent, another indicator of the dominance of the Paris region. Alsace is next with 33.3 per cent, even though it is well penetrated by non-indigenous firms. Rhone-Alpes is the next least dependent, with a relatively strong indigenous base. In the 50–60 per cent external control range are Midi-Pyrénées, Aquitaine, Bretagne, Pays de Loire, Bourgogne, Franche-Comté and Languedoc-Roussillon. The most dependent are Provence-Côte d'Azur, Corsica, and the regions around the Île de France. Most others have a 40–50 per cent dependency. The Institute National de la Statistique et des Études Économiques (INSEE) has developed (1982) indices of control by major French financial groups and by foreign groups (Table 4.11) in the regions of France. The first column illustrates the centralisation in Paris, reinforcing Table 4.5. The second column gives a 'feel' for the degree to which French regions are comparatively dependent on foreign-owned plants.

Table 4.11 France: relative penetration of foreign firms

	Index of control by major groups	Index of control by foreign groups
Île de France	112	140
Champagne-Ardenne	72	80
Picardie	88	92
Haute-Normandie	117	253
Centre	76	88
Basse-Normandie	88	35
Bourgogne	97	36
Nord-Pas de Calais	91	51
Lorraine	109	50
Alsace	88	54
Francne-Comté	112	34
Pays de la Loire	97	70
Bretagne	82	37
Poitou-Charentes	85	42
Aquitaine	114	125
Midi-Pyrénées	76	52
Limousin	76	52
Rhône-Alpes	86	47
Auvergne	92	37
Languedoc-Roussillon	112	180
Provence-Alpes-Côte d'Azur-Corsica	118	234

Note: Index of control by major groups = $\frac{\text{Value added by major groups in the region}}{\text{Value added of region}}$

Index of control by foreign groups = $\frac{\text{\% of value added by foreign groups in the region}}{\text{\% of national value added by foreign group}}$

Source: INSEE 1982.

In the United Kingdom, externally controlled employment increased in the northern region from 54 per cent in 1963 to 79 per cent in 1973, that is, three out of every four manufacturing jobs are now controlled from outside the region. In the Merseyside region, external control has increased from 57 to 70 per cent. Sixty per cent of manufacturing activity was externally controlled in Scotland and Wales in the early 1970s.

Belgium has a relatively high concentration of foreign investment, with more than 1,000 American companies established there. Fifty per cent of this investment is in Flanders, with the rest evenly divided between Brussels and Wallonia. Given the high level of unemployment, the 18 per cent decrease in large-firm employment, this foreign investment does not seem to have had a multiplier effect on indigenous industry.

In Ireland as a whole, 35.2 per cent of industrial employment is foreign-owned, in the Mid-West 52.3 per cent, and in the West 49.7 per cent (Table 4.12). No figures are available for ownership by Dublin-based firms or firms in other regions, but observation would indicate that headquarters of larger firms tend to be in Dublin. Although Ireland, looked on as a single less-favoured region, has had a very successful rate of foreign investment and its marketing organisation, the Industrial Development Authority, has been the envy of regions elsewhere, Ireland has not as high an external dependence as many other regions in Europe.

The Mezzogiorno has also had substantial investment by foreign firms (Table 4.13) and in particular by state-owned companies with over 50 per

Table 4.12 Ireland: percentage employed by nationality of firms' owners by region, 1982

Region	Ireland	USA	UK	Germany	Other
Mid-West	47.7	29.2	1.8	11.5	9.8
West	50.3	37.4	1.5	2.7	8.1
Dublin	68.0	9.6	17.2	0.2	5.0
East (excl. Dublin)	74.7	10.5	3.5	2.2	9.1
South-East	73.7	9.7	1.6	9.2	5.8
South-West	61.0	14.7	8.0	6.9	9.4
North-West	51.1	23.5	3.6	12.5	9.3
Donegal	82.9	2.4	10.4	1.5	2.8
Midlands	47.7	29.2	1.8	11.5	9.8
North-East	65.0	18.3	10.7	0.4	5.6

Table 4.13 Foreign investors in the Mezzogiorno by country of origin, 1979

Country of origin	No. of firms in the Mezzogiorno
USA	76
Switzerland	27
UK	21
West Germany	19
France	19
The Netherlands	5
Belgium	5
Other (non-European)	6
Other European	5
Total	183

cent of manufacturing employment in externally controlled firms, adding to the overall impression of the dependence of less-favoured regions on external information-intensive functions, including that of decision-making.

Autonomy

One aspect of the cycle time of logistic information is the actual information supply from some source, the other is the external decision as to resources, such as a loan or grant, specification of a requirement by a customer, or infrastructural inputs. Information supply is potentially efficient in a region rich in information-intensive activities.

The information of the external decision is also largely resident in such regions with the managerial functions of business and government. Geographical distance indicates remoteness from decision-making. In Europe a small federal country like Switzerland has prosperity. Denmark, another small country, also has prosperity. Here, although much is located in Copenhagen, the decentralisation of much of the administration and the smaller size of business organisation has enabled the rest of the country to have a higher share in self-generated growth than might otherwise have been the case. West Germany, too, is a federal country and has probably benefited greatly from the decentralisation of much administration and information-intensive activity. But obvious imbalances have also developed. The strength of the information-intensive activities of Baden-Württemberg contrasts with the large plant domination of North Rhine-Westphalia. In the United Kingdom, highly centralised in all spheres, the lack of autonomy of the regions must be a very major factor in the impoverishment of most.

A factor which emerges in the next chapter is the role of the larger technically progressive firm which is also a firm decentralised in its decision-making. In France, before decentralisation most of the R & D grants and loans made by ANVAR went to large companies. After decentralisation of decision-making to the regions, most went to small firms. It is not only, as J. B. Hunt, Governor of North Carolina, has said, that 'People are essential in technological innovation, and people can more easily relate to state and local governments than to distant federal agencies'. It is also that the cycle time has been reduced to a level which gives opportunity and efficiency to the smaller firm.

Autonomy in decision-making within a region is an essential part of that local environment of responsiveness which supports entrepreneurial activity. Boeckhout *et al* (1984) report that 'Strikingly, in almost every region entrepreneurs call for more accessible and comprehensible consultation structures and a less bureaucratic and more business like treatment of applications for subsidies, premiums and licenses'. Accessibility and less bureaucracy demand more local decision-making.

R & D

Probably the most commonly and traditionally used indicator of 'innovation potential' is the level of R & D carried out in a country as a percentage of gross domestic product. The comparative percentages of nine EEC countries are shown in Table 4.14.

Table 4.14 Expenditure on R & D, 1979

	Expenditure on R & D as a percentage of GDP	Percentage of R & D expenditure funded	
		by government	by industry
Greece	0.80	100.0	—
Netherlands	1.88	48.0	47.3
Denmark	0.96	52.6	45.8
United Kingdom	2.20	NA	NA
Belgium	1.36	31.0	65.8
France	1.81	51.1	43.1
Germany	2.40	42.5	55.4
Italy	0.85	44.0	54.5
Ireland	0.74	56.0	35.1

Source: OECD.

The figures of expenditure on R & D as a percentage of GDP illustrate to a degree the indifference of R & D expenditure *per se* to growth or prosperity. West Germany, in its period of post-war economic expansion, had a level of R & D expenditure which was below that of either the United Kingdom or the United States—similarly Japan. Both West Germany and Japan had a negative technology balance of payments, the other two countries had positive balances. Both countries have now increased their R & D expenditure.

As Charpie found (CTAB 1967), there are other factors at work. Alexander King, the doyen of science policy administrators, many years ago pointed out that the function of an industrial R & D department was to identify and assess the relevance of externally generated information and knowledge to the objectives and products and processes of the firm. Hence, only 2 per cent of the information incorporated in a new product was in fact generated by the firm's own research. Project Hindsight (Insenson 1969), which analysed the role of research in the development of the first post-war generation of space launchers and weapons, found that 92 per cent of the knowledge had been in existence before the war, some well before the war. The post-war researchers indentified and used it. Thwaites *et al.* (1984) have made the same point: 'the staff in these R & D units tend to be "information oriented" frequently systematically monitoring technical advances in their field and collecting information from a wide variety of resources'.

Where there is a technical progressiveness and a technological orientation, then the major factor in growth is early identification and adoption of new knowledge and others' innovations. Sciberras (1986) states that

> in many industries, R & D constitutes only a small share of total technical effort. Improvements in product design, performance and specification undertaken outside of a formal R & D facility may constitute a very important aspect of technical development. Subcontract design, support from research associations and universities or from central laboratories in the case of diverse company groups can also contribute very significantly to a firm's technical effort in an industry. In some industries this wider technical effort may be many times larger than formal R & D. Formal research and development did not appear to play a major role in the relationship between technical change and competitive success.

Dynamic firms supplement and even substitute for their own research effort by an ongoing active programme of external information acquisition.

Another way of seeing the role of research is to consider the result of a study of academic research in the United States (Sirbu *et al.* 1976). Only a small percentage of university research, 4 per cent, was funded by industry in the 1970s. Yet American industry is considered to have much closer links with academics than European industry. This was because industry used the academics as consultants for their expertise. The importance of their research was that it had provided them with a know-how and expertise often at the front-end of knowledge. The research as such was not of interest.

Again we are turned back to the characteristics of technically progressive firms—and regions—in information-giving and -receiving.

Table 4.14 also shows that statistics, as always, can obscure the reality. The 0.96 per cent of Danish GDP spent on research is very much higher than the 0.74 per cent of Ireland. Other factors are the level and role of defence R & D expenditure. This is high in both France and the United States, and therefore West Germany's R & D expenditure on civil research is considerably higher than that of these two countries. The role of defence R & D is more complex. The spin-off of defence in the United States into new industrial technologies and products is the result not only of clever specification of requirements and placing of contracts by the Department of Defense but also of both the technical progressiveness and entrepreneurial potential which took up the new technologies to make non-defence products. This kind of spin-off has not happened in the United Kingdom. It may be happening in France.

In the private sector, research expenditure is heaviest in the more science-based industries of chemicals and electrical/electronics. Large firms dominate in all research and in the high research-expenditure sectors. In Belgium, for example, large firms accounted for 70 per cent of expenditure. Overall distribution of research expenditure in Belgium is given by sector (Table 4.15) and by firm size (Table 4.16). The firm size of 500 means in all probability that much of the expenditure and most of the personnel are in medium-sized enterprises, and that firms of less than 100 employees carry out little research as officially defined. Generally, small firms carry out little research in any visible sense. They also carry out little R & D in Ireland. The Irish small firms of under 50 employees are probably more representative of small firms' R & D activity as measured

Table 4.15 Belgium: change in distribution of R & D expenditure by industry sector, 1971–9

Sector	1971	1979
Agriculture	1.2	1.2
Extraction	0	0.5
Distribution	0.6	0.6
Ferrous and non-ferrous metals	9.6	7.3
Ceramics, glass, cement	5.0	3.6
Pharmacy	6.7	6.7
Chemicals	26.5	26.3
Metal products	4.6	4.6
Mechanical engineering	5.9	6.9
Electrical & electronic	22.8	23.0
Transport equipment	1.2	4.4
Food	2.23	2.24
Textiles, leather	4.8	2.9
Wood, paper	1.1	1.0
Rubber, plastics	1.1	1.4
Printing	0.1	0.1
Other manufactures	0.1	0.3
Construction	1.5	1.3
Commerce	1.1	1.3
Transport and communication	0	0
Other services	1.6	2.1
Consultancies	1.7	2.1

Source: Programmation de la Politique Scientifique (1983).

Table 4.16 Belgium: distribution of R & D expenditure between large and small enterprises, 1979

Sector	SMEs*		Large enterprises	
	Percentage of expenditure	Percentage of R & D personnel	Percentage of expenditure	Percentage of R & D personnel
Agriculture	100.00	100.00	—	—
Extraction	54.86	20.54	45.14	79.46
Energy	34.30	37.19	65.70	68.81
Ferrous and non- ferrous metals	10.13	9.72	89.87	90.28
Ceramics, glass, cement	25.82	28.90	74.18	71.10
Pharmacy	31.80	31.80	68.20	68.20
Chemicals	21.18	15.92	78.82	84.08
Metal products	29.53	27.48	70.47	72.52
Mechanical engineering	44.99	44.98	55.01	55.02
Electrical and electronics	15.45	15.00	84.55	85.00
Transport equipment	14.71	12.22	85.29	87.78
Food	55.32	39.11	44.68	60.89
Textiles, leather	53.19	53.29	46.81	46.71
Wood, paper	46.21	47.78	53.79	52.22
Rubber, plastics	79.30	85.25	20.70	14.75
Printing	100.00	100.00	—	—
Other manuf.	60.72	73.74	39.28	26.26
Construction	76.54	73.81	23.46	26.19
Commerce	69.18	77.09	30.82	22.91
Transport and construction	57.24	53.76	42.76	46.24
Other services	4.27	9.68	95.73	90.32
Consultancy	78.88	82.73	21.12	17.27

* Defined as less than 500 employees.

Source: Programmation de la Politique Scientifique (1983).

by official statistics or science administrators than the Belgian figures. Sectoral and size distribution of research activity by industrial companies in Ireland is shown in Tables 4.17 and 4.18. Sectoral distribution shows a heavier concentration of expenditure in the food sector than the more general national distributions. This is not surprising in view of the higher

Table 4.17 Ireland: sectoral analysis of private R & D expenditure

	Percentage of all R & D expenditure
Industry	
Chemicals/drugs	18.4
Food, drink and tobacco	21.3
Paper and printing	0.4
Stone, clay, glass and cement	4.1
Textiles and clothing	3.8
Wood and furniture	0.0
Machinery and instruments	7.1
Electrical/electronic	15.9
Fabricated metal products	6.9
Rubber and plastics	4.5
Other	2.5
All manufacturing	84.9
Non-industrial	
Agriculture	0.5
Mining and peat	3.2
Construction	0.5
Services	11.9
Total	100.0

Table 4.18 Ireland: analysis of firms performing R & D by size of firm

Firm size	Percentage of firms performing R & D
3–9	0.8
10–49	2.7
50–99	6.7
100+	21.3

dependence of Ireland on agriculture and food processing and the heavier concentration of large indigenous companies in this sector.

R & D expenditure in industry is important in so far as it relates to the level of technical progressiveness of a company and assists in giving it an open mind, reaching out for new information and being receptive to it. It is also important in big industry in developing big technology. But elsewhere, except perhaps in the regulation-dominated drug industry, innovation springs from nearly anywhere. Entrepreneurs and small firms so often outperform big firms in innovation that one can use the R & D statistics only with caution when one is examining the role of R & D in growth and in creation of new economic activities.

Nevertheless and bearing in mind what has been said earlier, the carrying out of public and academic R & D does enhance the expertise within a country. From this simple point of view peripheral countries have a lower expenditure on R & D and industrially declining regions in more prosperous countries have weaker R & D activities than more prosperous regions. Their level of expertise is lower.

The effectiveness of the expertise as part of a stock of knowledge from which flows a nutrient supply of information to entrepreneurs within the region is another matter. Again one must focus on the local networks of information, and as Diana Crane (1974) found, in developing countries the academic networks are generally external to the country. In less-favoured regions they seem to be external to the region—with the core central region or with such regions in other countries.

As in all human situations, the statistics show only a part of the picture; one has to then add all the human, personal and social dimensions.

The occurrence of innovative activities in a region is dependent on a complex mix. As Boeckhout *et al.* (1984) have said:

> It also depends on the presence of certain locational factors. Certain kinds of information appear to be highly conducive to the initiation and realisation of innovations, as is the availability of high quality staff. Good access to clients and suppliers, availability of appropriate and cheap work accommodation, an attractive residential environment, and the active stimulation of regional development by the regional authorities are of influence as well.

As are other factors. One cannot adopt a simplistic solution. An *esprit* is also needed.

In discussing innovation as the main preoccupation of regional redevelopment programmes in France, Gaudemar (1984) makes the point that 'the "poles of conversion" are often originally areas which are highly underdeveloped in these (new technology) fields and often areas where to date innovation had penetrated least of all. Not only innovation in its factual form, but what is possibly more serious, the spirit of innovation.' The 'poles of conversion' roughly correspond to job areas which are greatly affected by the 'single-activity crisis'. Restoration of innovation potential should be accompanied by restoration of the spirit embodied in entrepreneurial potential if new economic activities are to be founded.

Conclusions

What emerges is that the factors which make up the innovative potential of a region seem to be a complex mix of the following:

- the sectoral and technological mix of the industry in a region;
- the strength of the engineering sector;
- the autonomy of decision-making in the industries and infrastructure of a region;
- or the dominance of branch-plant employment;
- the dominance of employment in one or two sectors, especially where these are of low use of best technical practice or are declining industries.
- the strength or weakness of the quaternary information sector;
- the technological orientation of the educational system or lack of it.

Innovation potential is the stock of knowlege of a region. In one way or another the above factors influence this, building it up or detracting from it. This stock, however, is an inert factor. Its conversion into innovation lies in influences associated with technical progressiveness. Having a large concentration of information-intensive occupations in a region and in particular a large concentration of research does not bring about a proportionate increase in innovation, as South-East England demonstrates.

Technical progressiveness has not been discussed in this chapter *per se*. Yet in discussing the innovation potential of a region it is a factor which keeps emerging. Even calling it a factor is misleading, since it is not quantifiable. As was outlined in Chapter 2, it embraces a set of characteristics which have been associated with the behaviour and performance of firms which have been found to be commercially successful and to have a high technical performance. Being non-quantifiable, technical progressiveness has eluded those who seek to measure its contribution to economic growth. It is the residual which, when all other quantifiable factors have been subtracted from the total of economic wealth created, seems to be responsible for the creation of most economic wealth and indeed employment.

It is a social and human phenomenon as much as a technological or production one, stemming from a dynamic participation in spatial and professional social information networks. Technical progressiveness is complex in other ways, too. It is a major contributor to the innovation potential of a region and a major influence on the entrepreneurial. Where a region has the R & D, the skills, the autonomy of information and decision, the mix of sectors and technologies, the technologically-orientated education system, a strong engineering sector, then it has innovation potential. Where there is a dominance of technical progressiveness in the larger firms both manufacturing buyers, distributive buyers and suppliers of resources (finance, education, consultancy) then there are open networks carrying a free movement and flow of information. Where there is also entrepreneurial potential, then this and the innovative potential are converted into entrepreneurial vitality and investment in innovation.

The information communication networks which characterise technical progressiveness unify the entrepreneurial and innovative potentials.

References

Atlas Français de l'Innovation (1982). ANVAR.

Dept of Industry (1983). A White paper: regional industrial development. London, HMSO.

Boeckhout, I. J. *et al*. (1984). 'Innovation profiles and regional policy in The Netherlands'. Six Countries Programme, Workshop, Limerick.

Cornwell, R. (1986). 'Stuttgart: Germany's job creation machine', *Financial Times*, 20 March.

Crane, D. (1974). *An inter-organisational approach to the development of indigenous technological capabilities: some reflections on the literature*. OECD, Development Centre (Industry and Technology Occasional Paper, no. 3).

CTAB (Commerce Technical Advisory Board) (1967). *Technical innovation: its environment and management*. Washington, DC, Dept of Commerce (Charpie Report).

Firn, J. R. and Swales, J. K. (1978). 'The formation of new manufacturing establishments in the central Clydeside and West Midlands conurbations, 1963–1972', *Regional Studies*, 12. 199–213.

Gaudemar, J. P. de (1984). 'Regional measures backing up innovation in France: some food for thought'. Six Countries Programme, Workshop, Limerick.

Goddard, J. B., Thwaites, A. T. *et al*. (1983). 'Technological innovation in a regional context: empirical evidence and policy options'. OECD, Workshop on research, technology and regional policy, October.

Hemer, J. (1984). '*Information networks designed to support innovation in less favoured regions of the European Community: case study in Baden-Württemberg*'. Karlsruhe, Fraunhofer-Institut für Systemtechnik und Innovationsforschung, October.

Hunt, J. B. (1982). Editorial, *Science*, 215(4533), 5 February, 617.

INSEE (Institut National de la Statistique et des Études Économiques) (1982). *Disparité et diversité des regions françaises*. Paris, October.

Isenson, R. S. (1969). 'Project Hindsight: an empirical study of the sources of ideas utilised in operational weapon systems' in Marquis, D. J. *Factors in the transfer of technology*. Cambridge, MA, MIT.

Jacobs, J. (1984). Cities and the wealth of nations: principles of economic life. Toronto, Random House.

James, V. Z. *et al.* (1979). *Telecommunications and office locations. Final report to the Dept. of the Environment*. University of Newcastle, Centre for Urban and Regional Development Studies.

Kormoss, I. B. F. and Cerych, L. (1979). 'The regional distribution of higher education in Europe: two maps', *European Jnl of Education*, 14(3), 233–8.

Krist, H. (1984). 'The promotion of new technology based firm foundations as part of regional innovation policies'. Six Countries Programme Workshop, Limerick.

Malecki, E. J. (1981). 'Science, technology and regional economic development: review and prospects', *Res. Policy*, 10, 312–34.

Oakey, R. P. *et al.* (1979). *The regional distribution of significant British industrial innovations*. University of Newcastle, Centre for Urban and Regional Development Studies.

OECD (1980). *Technical change and economic policy*. Paris.

Piatier, A. (1981). *Barriers to innovation in European Community Countries: summary of the general report*. Brussels, CEC.

Piatier, A. (1985). *Les regions en France: leur role et leurs moyens financiers: évolution recente et vues prospectives*. Paris, CNRS/GRAL, Vol. I.

Porat, M. U. (1977). *The information economy*. US Dept of Commerce, 9 Vols.

Price, D. J. de Solla (1966). 'Is technology historically independent of science? a study in statistical historiography', *Technology and Culture*, 6(4), 553.

Programmation de la Politique Scientifique (1983). *Les dépenses de recherche et de développement*. Brussels.

SAPPHO (1972). *Success and failure in industrial innovation: report on project SAPPHO*. London, Centre for the Study of Industrial Innovation.

Schmookler, J. (1972). 'Patents, invention and economic change: data and selected essays' edited by Griliches, Z. and Hurwicz, L. Cambridge, MA, Harvard University Press.

Sciberras, E. (1986). 'Indicators of technical intensity and international competitiveness: a case for supplementary quantitative data with qualitative skills in research', *R & D Management*, 16(1), 3–14.

Sirbu, M. A. *et al.* (1972). *The formation of a technology oriented complex*. Cambridge, MA, MIT Press.

Thwaites, A. T. *et al.* (1981). *Industrial innovation and regional development: Final report to the Dept. of the Environment.* University of Newcastle, Centre for Urban and Regional Development Studies.

Thwaites, A. T., Goddard, J. B. and Gibbs, D. C. (1984). 'The provision of technical information and the stimulation of industrial innovation in lagging regions'. Six Countries Programme Workshop, Limerick.

Townsend, J. (1981). *Science and technology indicators in the U.K.: innovations in Britain since 1945*. University of Sussex, Science Policy Research Unit (Occasional Paper Series, no. 16).

Ward, T. B. and Newman, J. (1981). *Computer conferencing and post-industrial regional policy*. Ulster Polytechnic, June. Working Research Paper Series, U8.

CHAPTER 5

Information Flows and Needs

Information networks seem to be the factor which, above all others, make a rich environment in which small firms adopt a highly dynamic approach to technology and markets, and in which entrepreneurs are active in founding new firms and economic activities. That is, networks in which the giver is open and responsive to the needs of the seeker for information. Information networks are social. Entrepreneurs are people and small firms and large firms are staffed by people. All behave in a very human way in their acquisition and communication of information. There is much in common between people in small and large firms and there are many differences produced by environment and education and personality characteristics. In a progressive and supportive environment, there is a responsive and open giving and receiving of information. In other environments, the flow through the networks is restricted even though there is an apparently rich stock of knowledge or else the networks can provide only tardily and weakly because the stock of knowledge is impoverished. But what should one do to change the non-progressive to the progressive? What immediate steps can be taken to convert a dependent region to a self-generating one?

An understanding of the actual process of information transfer is necessary before beginning to answer these questions. Understanding is a prerequisite to constructive regional policy formulation. The objective of this chapter, therefore, is to delineate the way in which information flows, which sources of information are used by whom, whether information is pushed or pulled and by whom, and what kind of information is needed by whom. Chapter 6 then sets out data specifically related to small firms and entrepreneurs in less-favoured regions of the European Community.

A Spectrum of Behaviour

Informal person-to-person contacts are the main source of information. The half-hour information-contact potential is the ease with which one can have face-to-face contact with someone who has or appears to have the information which one wants. The one-to-one relationship is replicated many times so that each person has a network of contacts, his own invisible college. Each person with whom he is connected has his or her own further personal network, so that for each there is a range of contacts who can provide a further contact. The networks obviously overlap, people as well as being at the centre of their own network are members of their contacts' networks.

All people in science, technology, industry, business and administration have a high dependence on informal networks of information but the degree of dependence and the use of formal resources of information varies significantly from pure physicists at one end of the spectrum of information-seeking behaviour to the small firm entrepreneur in a low-technology traditional industry in a peripheral region at the other end of the spectrum. Nevertheless, there are general patterns of behaviour because all are human, there are patterns of behaviour specific to a profession and there are patterns specific to organisational types.

The transition from one part of the spectrum to another is a gradual one. Large firms and small firms do not behave absolutely differently from each other. Their behaviour is determined by the people in them as well as the needs of the organisation. Chemists and engineers do not change radically when employed in a university or a small innovative firm. However, as one approaches the small-firm sector, and in particular the information profile of the entrepreneur, there is an apparently major shift in the behaviour pattern. This is due to the organisational context. 'There is a great deal of difference between personal and group or organisational use of information' (Lamberton 1986). The principle of division of labour of the larger bureaucracy no longer applies. Where, in the larger firm, the engineer in the research department has a narrower job specification, his information behaviour is near to that of an academic engineer. Production, marketing, finance and management/decision-making are separate information activities, whereas the engineer/entrepreneur is responsible for all the information-intensive activities of his firm. He acts more as a person than an organisation and his information behaviour and needs become more complex and assume different priorities.

Although the shift across the spectrum is gradual, segments of the spectrum can be used to highlight the appropriateness and use made of different sources of information and therefore the relevance of different sources, channels and services to different types of user. In other words, the key to understanding of information transfer lies in identification of the population segments. From this understanding can then be identified or developed the types of information and modes of transfer appropriate to the particular population segment. For example, one should then be able to define policies which promote self-generated regional growth and support entrepreneurs and SMEs in less prosperous regions and in regions which have low entrepreneurial vitality in a more effective manner.

Formal Published Information

There are considerable differences in the use of formal published sources of information by scientists and engineers, depending on the discipline itself or the activity, be it research or production. Seventy per cent of all reading by scientists and engineers is in journals but the number read varies widely (Table 5.1). In terms of reading material generally, scientists make more use of journals, reviews and abstracting journals, whereas engineers and technologists read very little professional literature. They mainly use trade journals, textbooks, data compilations and technical reports. Allen (1977), in his studies of communication in industrial R & D laboratories, reported that engineers spent three times as much time on informal literature (unpublished reports, etc.) as on formal literature (books and journals). Technologists and industrialists prefer not references but direct and immediately usable information. Thus, small firms tend to use journals for specific rather than general information, a purpose for which they are not designed (Thwaites *et al*. 1984). As they become more involved in production or in design of products which embody component parts or in development of products and processes in more traditional industries, there is increasingly heavier use made of practical handbooks, technical literature of suppliers (and therefore exhibitions) and of competitive products. Advertisements in trade and technical journals become an important source of awareness and information sourcing as do new product announcements. The growth in

Table 5.1 Journal reading

	Scans	Reads	Buys
Average scientist	3,000 articles per annum or 5–15 journals per week	300 articles per annum	3 journals
Pure scientist	10 journals per week	7.4 per week	
Applied scientist			1.3 journals
Town planner	5–6 journals per week		
Engineer	0.5 journals per week 20% read more	1.5 articles per week	

Source: Sweeney (1978).

the number of controlled circulation new product magazines is an indicator of a real need rather than of the wealth of advertising budgets.

There are other differences. Researchers in well established fields are more likely to make use of the journal literature than those in newly-emerging cross-disciplinary fields. These latter use more informal semi-published literature. They have more need of current awareness and ideas.

Currency of the literature read is a common trait across all disciplines and types of activity. Between 65 and 80 per cent of all reading has been published in the last twelve months, and of this, 50 per cent is of journals just published. This reliance on current reading is more marked the more applied the activity, from research to production.

Browsing is also more common at the technologist end of the spectrum. They not only browse but browse and read in areas very marginal to their apparent main interest. Scientists not only browse less, their reading is more restricted to a narrow band of interest. This latter point is further emphasised by the finding that researchers in universities and polytechnics receive less journals than those who describe themselves as teachers.

Browsing is not only an important mode of information acquisition, it is also a source of ideas, and is the major activity in the occurrence of 'chance' in finding information and as the source of an innovative idea. Eighteen per cent of new ideas are said to come from browsing, 'finding in the book next to the book' (Shapero 1973).

Referral

Abstract journals are used by scientists rarely and somewhat patchily. For the most part, when used, they are used as current awareness journals, and this use, together with the growth of *Current contents* and computerised SDI (Selective Dissemination of Information) services further confirms that a primary objective of scientists is awareness of what is currently happening. Use of abstracting journals for archival search by scientists is limited. Overall, scientists use these and other bibliographic aids only when they cannot avoid it and engineers and technologists use them even less, most never. Reviews of the literature do, however, rate more highly with scientists; they are the most highly used bibliographic source of information. Someone else has identified the important references and evaluated them. On-line literature searches have grown in importance, overcoming the difficulty of manual searching particularly where an intermediary is used. The on-line search thus fulfils one of the functions of the review—someone else has done the searching and identification of possibly useful articles.

Table 5.2 gives the result of some surveys of users as to first choice of the most effective retrieval methods. The first column was a survey of the use of technical literature by industrial scientists (Scott 1959). The second was a survey of information-gathering habits of workers in pure and applied science (Herner 1954), and the third of medical scientists (Herner 1959). The fourth column is from a survey on literature-searching by research students (Martyn 1964). The fifth column cites 'how scientists actually learn of work important to them' (Glass and Norwood, 1959). There is a bias to the literature in some of these results given the objectives of the survey and yet even here the importance of current reading, personal contact and chance are significant as sources of referral to formal published literature. The fifth column, giving the results of a more broadly-based survey, is more indicative of the relative importance of different sources to research scientists.

Another study (Rosenberg 1967) ranked certain information sources in order of preference of industrial personnel (Table 5.3). Allen (1977)

Table 5.2 Most effective retrieval methods, percentage of respondents

	1	2	3	4	5
Citation in current reading matter	5	19	13	19	7
Abstract/index	4	15	12	13	6
Bibliography	—	14	6	4	2
Library catalogue	18	8	9	4	—
Reviews	—	8	9	—	4
Personal	30	19	11	28	33
Chance	41	17	12	17	33
Other	2	—	28	14	15

Source: Ford (1977).

Table 5.3 Preferred information sources

Search personal library	1
Search material in building where you work	2
Visit a knowledgeable person nearby	3
Telephone a knowledgeable person	4
Use a library not within your organisation	5
Consult a reference librarian	6
Write a letter	7
Visit a knowlegeable person 20 miles away or more	8

found that references to formal literature were obtained from personal files, colleagues and 'others' 73 per cent of the time as against the formal methods of personal search of a library, use of an information officer or abstracts.

Overall, the main sources of reference to the literature can be classified according to their users as follows:

- Research workers in pure science rely more on direct use of the literature, mainly through current journals and current contents, reviews of the literature and more recently but to a lesser extent on-line searching; personal contact is, however, second only in importance to current journals as a source of literature references.
- Researchers in newly emerging fields rely much more on the current literature, with personal contact relatively much lower.
- Applied scientists rely more on personal contact for references to the literature with, then, a pattern similar to that of pure scientists, but at a lower level of dependence.
- Academic engineers have a pattern similar to that of applied scientists but a tendency to shift in use of the literature to a more technological mode of behaviour.
- In industry, those in research make more use of the literature as a source of reference than those in production. There is similarity between academic scientists and scientists in high-level industrial research.
- Engineers and technologists in design and production rely heavily on personal contact and browsing of more informal technical literature.

The pattern of behaviour shifts both with qualifications and with tasks. PhDs are more common amongst those who use the formal literature and are in research, than amongst those who are more dependent on informal sources and are in more applied and production activities. The closer the task moves to industrial or corporate decision-making the more personal contact and informal literature are used.

Generally amongst scientists, there is only a moderate interest in the literature, and a dominant reliance on the informal sources and channels. Even university research scientists tend to avoid use of the formal aids to finding information in the literature, consulting librarians only when there is no alternative. Indeed there is some evidence that the more creative a scientist the less likely he is to refer to a library, a characteristic indicative of the difference between nutrient and logistic information. The formal published literature and modes of referral to it tend to be used for direct specific data and information; informal sources and informal use of literature such as browsing tend to be used for ideas and awareness. This latter statement must, however, be further qualified in that the more research-based the activity the more conceptual information sources are used.

However, there is evidence to suggest that the use of and reference to published information is influenced by the mode of its provision. Where it is made more accessible and presented in a mode suited to the end-user, then there is greater use. *Current contents* and SDI services have been cited as examples, as has on-line literature searching. This correlates with the ease-of-access syndrome referred to below.

The Preferred Source

Many studies and virtually all reviews of the literature emphasise that the primary criteria for selection of an information source are accessibility and ease of use. This remains so even when the anticipated value of the information to be obtained is low. Furthermore, the intrinsic value of an information source has virtually no bearing on the frequency with which it is used. The existence of a psychological barrier of some sort lowers frequency of use even to zero.

The preferred source common to all information seekers, except for a few at the pure physics end of the spectrum, is the personal source. This personal source is used as a direct source of information, the information seeker uses the information obtained as the final information, or a referral point. Even here, the referral is made after discussion of the problem and options. The referral given is given as, in effect, a solution to the problem. Use of personal sources is subject to constraints which are common to the use of any information source, but its predominant use arises from its additional advantages.

To be used, there must be not only no psychological barrier—it must be easy to approach the person concerned—but they must also have some kind of professional status or social authority. For example, those without PhDs in a research context will tend to approach those with PhDs. PhDs approach other PhDs. Or, the person approached has some other status, such as being one grade higher and/or of longer service in the organisation. Invisible colleges are built first around one distinguished researcher or professor by his former students. Objectivity of the source is another characteristic determining use—he is disinterested in terms of personal gain. Leonard-Barton (1983) has remarked that:

> Individuals who serve as information intermediaries are not always formally recognised authorities on the topics. They may be peers who have faced problems very similar to those of the information seeker, and who therefore are invested with the wisdom born of experience.

> Peers serve as influential information sources because they are possessed of two types of credibility: this person is enough like me to have similar views—and—this person is technically competent.

Nevertheless, whilst there are strong indicators that a contact is used when he has some authority, natural or professional, which renders the information credible, ease of access is the ultimately determining factor in use of a personal or any source of information.

Geographical proximity, even within the same building, affects frequency of contact. The probability of two persons communicating at least once a week drops from 0.98 at a separation distance of 2 metres to 0.06 at 50 metres. Being on separate floors reduces the probability further. Distance between organisations has the same effect.

There is, however, one exceptional personal source which is used more frequently than other personal and easily available sources—the high communicator or gatekeeper. These are people who in a research context read more, give more papers, attend more conferences, have a wide range of personal contacts, more interorganisational contacts, and are high technical performers. In all contexts, they are people who tend to be referred to more often by colleagues in their own organisation and by their counterparts in other organisations. They are also people who are the leaders in a sector of industry, recognised as progressive and followed by others when they adopt a best practice.

Such people are the pivotal or nodal points in the social spatial, that is local network, or the professional network of a wider region, and they provide the linkages to the wider networks outside the locality and outside the regional profession or industrial networks.

They exhibit authority and are easy to approach. Such people seem to exist in all networks, their superficial characteristics changing with the tasks performed and the institutional context. The industrial design engineer, for example, visits exhibitions rather than professional conferences.

High communicators reach their position as a nodal point also because they are likeable. Not merely is there no psychological barrier but they are easy and pleasant to talk to.

Use of informal personal channels is not merely a result of human laziness in overcoming barriers. Face-to-face communication has a richness which written communication and even telephone communication with a known or an unknown person does not have. Both parties participate in exploration and definition of the problem and the questions to be answered. Value judgements are given by oral and facial expression. There is immediate feedback, there is acknowledgement of receipt of the message, its nature and urgency. The questions and the responses are corrected and amplified as the communication proceeds.

This richness in personal communication results in higher creativity and productivity. Higher use of informal communication has been associated with professional productivity in a number of studies. High performers make more use of informal and interpersonal sources than low performers and use a wider variety of sources including formal sources. In one study of 300 award-winning technical products, informal sources and channels of information accounted for 75 per cent of the sources and channels used in the progress from idea to final product (Shapero 1985).

Studies of technically progressive companies show them to have characteristics similar to those of high communicators, in this case related to their rate of adoption of best technical practices. They use a wider variety of information sources and channels and have more interpersonal linkages internally and externally. Successfully innovative companies have been shown by studies such as the Sappho project to have direct personal links to specific external expertise and to users of the product.

The richness of the personal source lies not merely in the richness of the face-to-face mode of communication but in the direct referral to the most relevant and approachable source.

The referral may also be to documents and is the most frequent means of identification of appropriate documents. Documents contain the exact statement, the precise description, data and figures. They have therefore an essential role to play in the process of communication of information to solve a problem. Indeed, one study (Hawthorne 1971) on technology transfer to less-industrialised countries concluded that too great a reliance was placed on personal communication and too little on provision of documentation. Hence the transfer process was ineffective. Exact data and information are a requirement of all types of user but the access to these tends to take place within the overall framework of personal contact networks.

Frequency of use of the personal contact varies with degrees of uncertainty and of stress—the complexity of the problems faced and the time within which a solution must be found. The greater the complexity and stress, the more frequent the personal contact. As the problem is solved the frequency of contact declines as does the ratio of face-to-face to phone contacts. On the other hand, where there is normally frequent use of personal communication, the periods of uncertainty and stress are less frequent and are of shorter duration. There is also a strong relationship between productivity and creativity or the creative solution to a problem and the number of work-related conversations an individual has with colleagues. Productivity rises sharply when the average frequency of information-intensive contacts arises from weekly to semi-weekly to daily and when the contact group numbers some 15–20 individuals. Such contact groups usually have amongst their number a high communicator who links the group not only to other local groups but also to the wider professional groups. This communicator brings awareness, information and knowledge of other contact points and sources of information within the range of the group.

Informal Networks

Person-to-person contact takes place within informal networks of personal contacts. Each member shares some of his contacts with other members but also has further contacts which are not shared until a moment of need arises. Each network is thus linked or overlaps with other networks. Informal networks are of two types with a number of subdivisions, spatial and professional.

Spatial networks are based on a physical and social propinquity such as exists within an industrial research laboratory or amongst entrepreneurs in an inner city but they also include the networks of friends which exist in a neighbourhood or locality. These latter spatial networks of friends can have an important connecting role, making the connection between different organisational or professional networks.

Professional networks are networks such as the classic invisible college of academic science which link specialists of a particular discipline or profession and have no geographical boundaries *per se*. In academic research, members of such a network hear of advances and have access to research results often a considerable time before publication. Similarly, computer specialists, for example in industry and business who have stayed at the forefront of development, hear of new developments before full commercial launch or of research of interest to their company at an early stage. This scenario can be repeated through the technically progressive firms of virtually any sector. The professional network enables such a company to be early in the identification of new information of potential for innovative developments and to be early in adoption of a new best practice.

Some professional networks are also spatial. Centres of expertise develop which contain the prime professional network. London is a leading financial centre, Paris a centre of fashion, Milano-Como of fashion textiles, Silicon Valley of microchip design and production and so on. With such centres, one must stay in touch. Those in the same profession but located elsewhere must still be part of the spatial professional network of such centres and hence must by frequent contact maintain this membership. And they must also contribute. Members of invisible colleges who are not contributing as well as receiving soon find themselves dropped from the network.

In localities with high entrepreneurial vitality there are intensive and extensive series of person-to-person networks between entrepreneurs and suppliers and customers and between entrepreneurs and the suppliers of financial, technical and other resources.

One use of these networks is for nutrient information, the maintenance of awareness and the state-of-the art of fashion or design, new technology, competitive success and failure and emerging opportunities. The other use is for logistic information, obtaining the information directly from the contact or using the contact as referral to the source of direct information. Most use of formal information systems is by referral from the informal network.

Informal Networks and Telecommunications

Networks are person-to-person. The need for people to meet face-to-face is high and sometimes urgent, hence the desire to be located within the half-hour contact potential. Once having met, the telephone provides an alternative for face-to-face contact with reinforcement of the contact by occasional face-to-face meetings. Video conferencing has, for example, been found useful as a renewal of face-to-face contact or as a means of making more informal the telephone contact between people who had not previously met. However, at times of stress or uncertainty, of facing a difficult problem, there is increase in person-to-person contact, first largely by phone, but then with an increase in face-to-face contact. As the stress or uncertainty is resolved, there is a fall back to phone and to the normal frequency of contact.

There is a trade-off between phone and face-to-face communication (Shapero 1985). When people are located on the same floor, most communication is face-to-face. When on two different floors, face-to-face drops to one third and the phone makes up the rest. When distance or other barriers intervene further there is a greater trade-off.

The relationship between person-to-person contact and productivity, efficiency and creativity, which has been found to exist at the micro-level of an organisation, would seem to obtain also at the microeconomic level of a region. That there is a correlation between economic development and the intensity of the telephone network has long been observed. The nature of the relationship was unclear. However, recent work by ITV (International Telecommunications Union) and OECD (1983) has demonstrated that installation of a telecommunications system is 'one of the "causes" or contributory factors of development' and has considerable multiplier effects. The studies were largely carried out in developing countries, with the exception of one comparing France and Spain.

A major finding was that whilst business telephone installation leads economic development in industrial countries, it is the residential domestic telephone which leads development in developing countries. This last finding is significant. It highlights the interdependence of entrepreneurial development, the entrepreneur's dependence on personal informal networks and their urgent need to get in touch. A larger number of domestic phones allows greater freedom to make contact by someone under continuous time pressure with others under equal time pressure or only contactable at home in the evening. The empirical data on regional development, technically progressive firms and the role of communication and informal networks and contact, all corroborate the findings of ITU and OECD (1983) and point to the potential of network-based technologies for the enhancement of entrepreneurial and innovative vitality.

Observation of videotex information service for industry in France has shown that these are used for the most part not for the information provided, but to send messages to other members of the club or other subscribers. More recently, a representative of a multinational company has privately stated that the recently installed private international network of the company has increased interpersonal communication between some people by a factor of five. The telephone bill has declined drastically. The terminal has become a trade-off with the phone as the phone has been with face-to-face communication but the effect is a greatly intensified person-to-person contact which the data show to lead to greater productivity and creativity with fewer periods of stress or uncertainty.

Characteristics of Small Firms and Entrepreneurs

The information-seeking behaviour of the entrepreneur is very personal. He behaves as a person who is a chemist or engineer or technologist or craftsman, but in this behaviour he is biased further to the informal end of the spectrum by being an entrepreneur. Small firms as personified by their entrepreneurial owners and managers have distinct characteristics which determine, rather than simply influence, their information behaviour and needs.

The essential characteristics which distinguish a small entrepreneurial firm from other firms are two. Firstly, there are not more than three people who take all major decisions and most often there is only one. These people or this person manage the enterprise personally, having for the most part founded it themselves, and they bear all the risks of the enterprise because they own it. Secondly, the decision-makers are the major information processors making the majority, if not all, of the external contacts on all aspects of the business. They also bear the responsibility for all the information-intensive functions of research and development, marketing, finance and production.

Although categorised and often approached as a group or sector standing on its own, small firms do not in fact form a homogeneous group. Whilst now concentrated in a small number of sectors, they are spread across all sectors and thus have a wide diversity of information needs. Intrinsically, they have the same problems and needs for information as large companies. The emphasis however is different. The need for finance is greater and the ability to obtain and manage it less. The product cycle is shorter and more sequential because the product range is smaller. Internal skills are narrow and more technical than business management.

Within his firm, the entrepreneur tends to be the main information-processor because he has little or no freedom to delegate. It has been suggested that the characteristic which fundamentally differentiates 'small firms' as a group is that a small firm has no staff member whose function is information collection and evaluation. Although skilled in the main-line technology of his firm, he may have to tackle a wide range of technical problems over a period, many falling outside his direct skills. Any single major input takes time to absorb and implement. Hence his contact with a single source of expertise for in-depth input is highly infrequent and often unique. Continuing contact or relationship from a research centre or technological institution is therefore difficult, particularly from a national or centralised institute. Distance adds to the difficulty of contact, as does the psychological barrier of passing through an anonymous switchboard when the problem may be difficult to articulate.

He is under constant pressure and is a relatively isolated individual, as both Shapero (1984) and Capital Planning Information (1982) have remarked. He himself bears the responsibility for gathering information, assessing it and making decisions regarding all aspects of the company—business, finance, marketing, production and product development. He is wholly involved, caught up in day-to-day problems and yet simultaneously having to deal with policy problems. He works under harsh time constraints and for long hours. If information is not available virtually immediately, he does without. The problem is arbitrarily solved because he is forced into consideration of another problem. 'Many problems in the enterprise demand prompt solution causing lack of sufficient time to arrive at an optimal choice of information sources' (PIPIN 1983). But putting off a problem can lead to a crisis. Capital Planning Information (CPI) (1982) observed of the small businessman and his seeking of finance:

> He tends not to react to information until a crisis is upon him, and when the crisis occurs he does not know the appropriate person to turn to, unless he has a well-established relationship with his accountant or bank manager.

His contacts for information are friends—other entrepreneurs or people professionally associated with him such as bank officers or accountants—and other acquaintenances, people whom he has met or been referred to by friends as a good contact. They are the local spatial network or are connected to it. They may be the equivalent of local, like the technical representative of a supplier who comes to him at his own office—no effort is required to make contact. For the most part, because of all the constraints on him, he uses his friends and personal contacts for what they can give him. He rarely goes beyond them. The ease-of-access factor is particularly symptomatic of small firms' information-seeking behaviour. The entrepreneur under pressure with unique needs has not the range of professional skills within himself or his firm to overcome psychological, technological, and communication barriers in sourcing and interpreting information.

The CPI (1982) study, one of the most comprehensive studies on information and small firms carried out in the United Kingdom, concluded that:

- small firms do not form a coherent homogeneous group;
- information needs of small firms are closely related to day-to-day problems and facts which are needed to make decisions at short notice;
- small firms are a difficult target for national initiatives and centralised services; local initiatives relying on local contacts are more likely to prove useful and to be used;
- most information passes by word of mouth, especially involving suppliers and customers;
- small firms need informal contacts, a need reflected in the rapid growth of small business clubs;
- small firms cannot readily identify agencies appropriate for them and rarely establish continuing relationships with most agencies

Types of Small firms

As was remarked earlier in Chapter 2, small firms are a major source of innovation and change, partly because they are in continual pursuit of a new venture in order to survive. Piatier (1981) put forward the view that the life of a small firm is not a continuum but a succession of projects. There are, however, differences in the innovativeness and progressiveness of small firms. The Dutch PIPIN (1983) project investigated the information behaviour of a group of small firms in higher technology industries. Four types of entrepreneur were distinguished:

- Dynamic entrepreneurs, who represented 18 per cent of the PIPIN population of 1,600 mechanical engineering, electrotechnical, optical and instrument industries. These are described as having a high absorption capacity for external information and a well-developed propensity to analyse, a 'democratic and social attitude *vis-à-vis* the enterprise, an open eye for long-term strategy etc'.
- Technically orientated entrepreneurs representing 40 per cent of the population. These have excellent qualities in a limited area of entrepreneurship but have clear gaps in knowledge and experience of which they are aware.
- Entrepreneurs with 'traditional attitudes', 25 per cent, with a low 'adoption capacity'.
- Crisis entrepreneurs, 14 per cent, who are in difficulty and facing severe problems.

Bouvier (1984) divided the 2,300 firms of the Midi-Pyrénées into three categories:

- The first, containing around 300 firms, consists of highly innovative small and medium enterprises, managed by top-level men, often university educated. They are able to communicate directly with the research centres, being familiar with the language and reasoning of the latter. Most of these are in Toulouse and linked to the aerospace and other high-technology industries;
- The second group, made up of the majority, some 1,600 of the regional firms, mostly outside Toulouse, will never make a demand on the research centres. They are often managed by men with an anti-university complex. Whilst seemingly unaware of technological possibilities or accessibility they are nevertheless open to transfer when it is transmitted on a client-to-supplier basis or from local technical schools;
- The third type consists of firms which, due to the age of their management or their financial situation, are no longer open to external impulses.

In practice, these analysts may well be differentiating between those firms lying towards the more formal end of information behaviour and those at the more informal end. Their middle groups of firms may be no less involved in new venture search and development but, behaving more as persons, they act as technologists where the high-tech behave more as scientists.

Innovative or dynamic firms tend to have a high degree of specialisation and a more than local or regional market. They have need for expert and tailor-made inputs. They tend to have innovation as their business, one new product succeeding another. They have high-quality products. The technically orientated or progressive firms tend to seek the best technical practice and to obtain much of their information and impetus for new product development from their customers who are often technically advanced or progressive companies. They are concerned with quality in process and product. Traditional firms tend to supply local markets with more traditional products using traditional expertise but of a lower technological quality. They are not easily open to new information inputs. Crisis firms tend to be traditional firms overtaken by succession problems, or by technological and market change.

No matter how they are classified, supply of information to small firms is made yet more difficult by the fact that, whatever characteristics may be common to small firms and entrepreneurs, each is unique. Each small firm and its owner are unique in technology, market, product and geographical location. Its skill and labour force are unique to itself and the problems which occur are in a different time sequence and a different context to those of another. Their innovations and adoption of technical change require unique inputs and the day-to-day need for specific information requires a unique response. Hence the dependence on the personal contact and on the richness of the personal contact which allows a unique response.

Sources of Information

Use of information sources even by large industry seems to follow the same pattern of behaviour as do individuals. They have a place in the spectrum of information behaviour. An Irish survey of over 2,000 firms undertaken in 1973 highlighted this (Murray *et al.* 1973). Firstly, higher-technology firms such as chemicals or firms with a high proportion of graduates such as consultants have a more intensive use of information (Table 5.4). Smaller firms in these sectors have a more intensive use than small firms in other sectors.

This bias in behaviour is also evident in the pattern of enquiries handled by the Information Services of IIRS, the principal technical information service to industry in Ireland (Table 5.5). Sixty-eight per cent of the enquiries it receives are from firms of less than 50 employees. The more technologically based industries make more use of this service than the more traditional industries. They also make more use of on-line information services (Table 5.6) through IIRS intermediaries. This particular table must be seen against a background where a number of larger and/or more science-based industries operate their own on-line searches through intermediaries trained by IIRS.

Table 5.4 Overall information effort by field of activity

	Information effort		R & D		Size	
	Total	Rank	(%)	Rank	(%)	Rank
Chemicals, drugs	570.7	(1)	56.2	(1)	27.6	(4)
Technical services	545.8	(2)	40.0	(7)	0.0	(18)
Electrical, electronics	527.3	(3)	39.4	(9)	36.4	(2)
Non-technical services	492.9	(4)	54.5	(2)	12.0	(16)
Rubber and plastics	487.5	(5)	43.8	(5)	17.5	(10)
Agriculture, forestry & fisheries	436.2	(6)	38.8	(10)	12.1	(15)
Machinery manufacture	434.7	(7)	42.5	(6)	15.0	(12)
Glass, clay, cement	425.1	(8)	45.9	(3)	21.7	(8)
Textiles	407.0	(9)	39.9	(8)	31.3	(3)
Metal and metal products	401.9	(10)	42.5	(6)	19.0	(9)
Mining, peat	400.7	(11)	45.8	(4)	37.6	(1)
Shipbuilding and vehicles	397.5	(12)	25.0	(14)	17.5	(10)
Food and drink	396.8	(13)	24.9	(15)	24.9	(6)
Clothing, footwear	366.3	(14)	30.1	(12)	26.1	(5)
Miscellaneous	360.0	(15)	38.5	(11)	13.9	(13)
Construction	349.3	(16)	17.1	(17)	22.4	(7)
Paper, printing	336.4	(17)	22.1	(16)	13.7	(14)
Wood, furniture	296.6	(18)	27.1	(13)	8.4	(17)

Note: The criteria used in compiling the information ranking were: the percentage of firms in the sector taking more than five journals and attending more than five exhibitions, using each source frequently or occasionally, having an information person and spending more than £100. For the R & D ranking the criterion was the percentage of firms performing R & D and for size the percentage employing more than 100.
Source: Murray *et al*. (1973).

Tables 5.4 and 5.7 further reinforce this point that the more technological or science based the firm the more intensive the use of information. Carrying out R & D is in any type of firm at the minimum an indication of a more technological orientation and of a search for better technical performance, and undoubtedly in each of the three size groups, R & D firms have a more intensive use of all information sources than non-R & D firms.

Size is clearly another factor. Large firms also have a more intensive use or as Piatier (1984) expressed the point, a more diversified use. This is as a result both of size and of having more qualified personnel. Small firms have a narrow range of contacts and have to rely much more on themselves. Table 5.7 illustrates the relative isolation of small firms and in particular of the small firms which do not carry out R & D.

Table 5.5 Ireland: source of enquiries to IIRS information services, 1984

Source of enquiries sector	Employment* (%)	Percentage of total enquiries
Mining & quarrying	5.21	0.6
Chemicals & pharm.	6.03	10.0
Engineering	21.85	32.0
Electronics	7.14	12.1
Food, drink & tobacco	24.79	11.6
Textiles & clothing	13.12	2.9
Timber & furniture	4.0	2.3
Printing & packaging	6.75	3.5
Plastics & rubber	4.10	3.4

* Numbers employed in the sector as percentage of total manufacturing employment.
Source: IIRS.

Table 5.6 On-line searches by IIRS, 1983

	No.	Percentage of lit. searches	Percentage of enquiries from the sector
Chemicals & pharmaceuticals	50	18.45	10.80
Engineering	23	8.49	1.73
Electronics	14	5.17	2.06
Food, drink & tobacco	30	11.07	7.25
Textiles & clothing	2	0.72	1.43
Plastics & rubber	4	1.48	2.09
Printing & packaging	1	0.37	0.66
Self-employed and start your own business	11	4.06	1.37
Building and civil engineering	5	1.85	0.80
Govt & semi-state	21	7.75	1.89
Medical	51	18.82	
Consultants	33	12.18	4.33
Educational	26	9.95	4.56

Source: IIRS.

Table 5.7 Business enterprise sector—characteristics of firms carrying out R & D in 1970 and not: average within a particular size category

	Criterion	All Firms	All R & D Firms	(Less than 25)		(25–100)		(Over 100)	
				R & D	Non-R & D	R & D	Non-R & D	R & D	Non-R & D
In Ireland									
Journals	5 and over	23.0	40.5	22.6	5.5	30.5	15.0	69.1	41.5
Conferences	3 and over	41.5	59.9	42.8	21.4	56.2	36.0	82.4	58.6
Supplier/customer	Freq. and occ.	69.8	74.9	71.2	63.2	74.9	69.9	78.8	71.9
Sci/tech library	"	25.9	41.1	39.0	16.0	37.4	17.3	51.0	19.5
Res/trade org.	"	42.4	53.3	47.0	27.6	51.6	42.6	61.3	51.8
Tech inf/adv.	"	37.8	49.2	46.2	26.2	47.7	35.2	54.8	41.8
Associate co.	"	20.8	28.5	20.7	11.1	31.4	18.1	32.9	28.0
Overseas									
Supplier/customer	"	51.3	67.2	57.3	33.7	67.5	46.7	78.9	59.6
Sci/tech library	"	15.8	28.9	20.3	7.3	27.3	7.9	39.3	14.9
Res/trade org.	"	25.8	39.0	28.8	11.9	33.8	19.9	54.4	33.9
Tech inf/adv	"	24.7	35.6	30.9	14.3	32.6	22.0	43.7	26.1
Associate co.	"	22.8	31.9	18.2	6.6	34.2	22.6	43.3	41.2
Inf. Person	% employing	9.0	19.0	18.2	2.6	16.8	4.5	22.5	7.0
Difficulty in getting inf.	Extremely and fairly	28.9	34.6	37.2	26.3	33.9	24.0	32.7	27.0
Difficulty in keeping up-to-date	Extremely and fairly	34.0	38.3	42.0	33.5	38.6	29.2	34.8	29.3
Expenditure	over £100	23.1	43.8	23.0	5.0	42.0	12.5	67.6	39.7
Total no. of firms		2,270.0	728.0	248.0	726.0	238.0	501.0	235.0	214.0

Source: Murray *et al.* (1973).

Table 5.8 Information sources used by industry in Japan (%)

Source	SMEs' information		Large firms' information	
	On demand	On technology	On demand	On technology
Database	6.7	2.0	12.4	7.2
Newspapers, TV	40.0	16.9	41.2	16.7
Business & technical periodicals	72.8	66.6	81.3	75.4
Government and official publications and reports	3.5	3.0	3.6	5.7
Financial institutions	6.8	0.9	9.1	1.4
Parent companies	26.1	27.0	22.5	24.1
Enterprise in the same business	24.4	24.9	15.6	18.9
Clients & customers	29.7	13.0	37.4	10.3
Seminars	4.3	11.9	5.7	16.8
Guidance by private experts	1.5	5.0	2.7	8.1
Regional inf. centres, res. insts.	7.3	12.5	3.4	7.2
Academic institutions	1.5	6.6	1.9	17.7
Sample fairs	14.8	26.4	16.2	25.6
Meetings among different businesses	3.3	3.7	3.3	2.7

Source: MITI (1984).

Another significant point made by Table 5.7 is the very high use of suppliers and customers made by firms of all sizes. Carrying out R & D does not substantially change this high dependence. The heaviest flow of information is that from firm to firm.

Capital Planning Information (1982) noted that the links between small manufacturing firms and large companies 'are often significant if not crucial, to trading and information'. They noted three kinds of link:

- as an incubator and then patron of the entrepreneur with orders, advice and even equipment;
- as customer, using the small firm as subcontractor or supplier of parts;
- as supplier of materials and equipment and very often of advice and technical information especially as regards production, materials and processes.

This firm-to-firm relationship, as is well known, exists also in Japan. The SME sector there, composed of firms containing less than 300 employees, has a very important role, employing in 1981, 74.3 per cent of all manufacturing employment. A survey of the information sources used by SMEs and large firms showed a heavy reliance by both groups on clients and customers which includes in Japan the separately identified category 'parent company' (Table 5.8).

As elsewhere, large firms tend to make more extensive use of all sources of information other than 'parent companies' which largely means companies for whom subcontracting is carried out and regional information centres and research institutes which are more oriented to SMEs. The high use of newspapers, business and technical periodicals is a known feature of Japanese information dissemination. Japan has a very high readership of such publications and they are of high quality, containing reports by experts on international and national technology and market trends. They provide perhaps a confirmation of the point that when information is made easily accessible, it is used more frequently. Overall, informal sources such as newspapers, suppliers, customers and other businessmen are used significantly more than formal sources.

The PIPIN project in its first phase found a very wide range of sources used by the smaller higher-technology firms surveyed (Table 5.9). Many were used only rarely. Predominant were informal contacts and internal expertise, two sources not investigated by the earlier Irish study. Suppliers had a relatively high ranking and if one takes suppliers and customers together industrial firms are the third most used information source.

In a later phase of the PIPIN project, data was collected on sources of information used by 1,600 firms. Table 5.10 gives the sources of information cited by more than 10 per cent of the population and analysed according to 'entrepreneurial categories'. The informal contacts

Table 5.9 Information suppliers

Information supplier	Times mentioned	Percentage
Information contacts	40	20
Internal solution	34	17
External experts	26	13
Banks	25	12
Furnishers (suppliers)	21	10
Auditors	20	10
Consultancy bureaux	20	10
Chambers of Commerce	16	8
Books, etc.	15	7
Periodicals, etc.	14	7
Regional labour offices	14	7
Trade fairs	14	7
FME/Metal Union	14	7
Customers	11	5
Ministry of Economic Affiars	10	5
TNO	10	5
State Industrial Service	10	5
Lawyers	9	4
Architects, contractors	8	4
Universities	8	4
Municipalities	7	3
Embassies	6	3
Furnishers of means of production	6	3
Netherlands Credit Insurance Company	5	3
Other public services	5	2
Patent offices and agencies	5	2
Economic Information Services (EVD)	5	2
Agents	4	2
Branch organisations	4	2
Trade unions	4	2
Others (mentioned only a few times)	21	10

Source: PIPIN (1983).

had a higher score in this survey. The conclusion of the PIPIN project put its emphasis on the informal contact.

> People, not documents, are the most important information suppliers to SMI. These people form an integral part of the social infrastructure of enterprise and entrepreneur: business connections, personal contacts of the entrepreneur, enterprise staff, suppliers, the local bank, the auditor etc. Information to be found in journals and books, or

Table 5.10 Important sources of information by entrepreneurial category (per cent)

Information source	Entrepreneur in category			
	I	II	III	IV
Informal contacts	47	43	38	39
Trade fairs	29	35	50	15
Reading six or more trade journals	60	35	33	0
Information services of public agencies	53	30	16	23
Employers (branch) organisations	41	38	54	46
External experts	12	18	8	8
Bank services	12	7	4	15
Technical and other universities	6	15	17	—
Chambers of Commerce	41	28	17	23
Total population ($N = 1{,}600$)	288	688	400	224

I = Dynamic entrepreneurs; II = Technically entrepreneurs; III = Entrepreneurs with traditional attitude; IV = Crisis entrepreneurs.

Source: PIPIN (1983).

Table 5.11 Sources of information of small firms (per cent)

Personal communication	71.0
of which customers, suppliers, fairs, external discussion groups, seminars, other enterprises	56.0
external advice, universities, advisors, information transfer agencies	15.0
Documentary information	17.0
Patent and environmental	6.8
Databanks	4.5

Source: Piatier (1984).

through formal information suppliers such as ministries, public information services, universities, embassies, etc. is much less in demand.

Piatier (1984) also found that, of the 'factors' determining innovation, internal R & D had the highest score followed by the client firm (Table 5.12).

PIPIN emphasised not only the role of informal contacts but also the importance of internal sources of information, a source ignored in many studies. All firms have a high dependence on internal sources of information, as Rothwell (1975) showed in illustrating the sources of

Table 5.12 Factors determining innovation

R & D in the enterprise	77	Rationalisation of the firm	33
Collaboration with a client	57	New investment possibilities	31
Marketing	50	Licences and patents acquired	29
Access to pertinent information	49	Subcontracting	26
Licensing and patents held	49	Other	10
Training	42	Total	453

Source: Piatier (1984).

Table 5.13 Sources of ideas for innovative developments (per cent)

	Sappho	Bolton	Langrish
In-house	53	53.70	—
Private industry	18.5	17.60	64
University	10	2.53	10
Government agencies	13.5	6.88	21
Individuals	5	1.25	—
Research associations	—	4.20	—
Abroad	—	13.74	—
Second World War effort	—	—	7

Source: Rothwell (1975).

ideas for innovative products. He drew on the Sappho project, a study of 86 innovations, Langrish's (1971) study of 82 award-winning innovations, and data on 1,667 innovations compiled for the Bolton Committee (Freeman *et al*. 1971).

All firms are dependent on internal sources of information, but large firms have a wider range of internal skills to use directly. These skills in numbers of people and disciplines give the larger firm a much more extensive range of external contacts. It is not surprising, therefore, that the larger firm has not only a more intensive use but also uses a wider range of sources. In contrast the entrepreneur is limited internally to his own skills for the most part and externally to his own range of contacts.

Most entrepreneurs found their firms around their own ideas and skills, and these skills are usually technical and production skills. This technical and production orientation of entrepreneurs has been referred to in many studies as for example in one study of Flemish entrepreneurs ("X" 1983), that by Scase and Goffee (1980) or the classic craftsman entrepreneur of Smith (1967). Of the 92 per cent of interviewees in the CPI (1982) study who were owners or founders, 54 per cent had a production or technical background, 12 per cent had administrative or personnel experience, 8 per cent sales and marketing and 23 per cent claimed no relevant skills. The production area was reported a source of less problems than the sales, marketing and finance areas. The lack of business skills is the major problem, and most young and small firms fail because of it. CPI found that only 13 per cent of their entrepreneurs had business training. However, where the firm is founded by three or four partners with a mix of skills, it is much more likely to survive and grow (Roberts 1983). It has not only a better range of internal skills, it has a wider range of external contacts.

CPI found that in the 26 per cent of firms in which there was more than one manager there was a considerable difference in background, a possession of complementary skills which in some firms was pointed out as having been essential to the development of the firm. Where the background was similar (17 per cent), usually in production this appeared as a weakness and restriction on the range of contacts made.

Use of informal networks, as has been indicated earlier, is not merely a habit of information behaviour, it is a need of all people in science, technology, industry and business. Rothwell and Zegveld (1985), have emphasised this point in relation to small firms: 'Especially to smaller firms an adequate network of external relationships is of crucial importance ... relationships with other companies, banks, (regional) government agencies and elements of the technological and scientific infrastructure'.

The Role of the Customer

Studies of small firms, particularly in more-developed countries or regions, give a significant role to the customer as a source of ideas for their innovative products and as a source of information. But in this the customer is also revealed as a stimulus to adopt the best technical practice.

> The needs of small firms' customers determine to a large extent their technological position (level of technological demand) ... Where smaller firms are dependent on a few larger local firms as suppliers or especially as customers and where these customers are technologically non-demanding they can become 'locked in' to a local regime greatly deficient in terms both of the supply of, and demand for, technology-embodying goods and components (Rothwell and Zegveld 1985).

This technology demand or pull would appear to be the determining factor in the quality of information flows and in the diffusion of the best practice in a progressive self-generating region.

Subcontracting *per se* to larger firms including the previous employer is often cited as a frequent basis for starting up a new enterprise. However, it very often fails to move to development of new and own products by the subcontracting firm. A study of new entrepreneurs in Denmark showed a heavy reliance on subcontracting, particularly in start-up (Wickman 1983). The intention generally of the entrepreneurs was eventually to develop a new idea once sufficient resources had been generated. Only in a few cases had this happened. But, although these products were traditional, 50 per cent were exporting and some of these and most of the non-exporters were subcontracting.

The large firm stimulates innovation and adoption of the best practice when it develops 'buy' rather than 'make' policies for more sophisticated components and equipment. The role of the customer is very evident in Sweden, a country which can be classified as technically progressive. In an evaluation of the Swedish microelectronics campaign (Åsell 1984), of 44 companies interviewed, 32 said that their customers were the foremost or the only source of ideas for their product development. One argued that it was the leading one in its trade and could not get ideas from customers or other external sources. A third of the firms mentioned exhibitions and a quarter courses, journals and literature as important sources.

A French study (Sofres 1983) examined the sources of positive roles in the innovations of small firms. These are listed in Table 5.14. Whilst confirming the high dependence on internal sources, Table 5.14 also emphasises the role of the client or customer as a source of information and stimulator of innovation and entrepreneurship.

Table 5.14 Providers of positive roles in innovations in small firms (per cent)

The personnel of the enterprise	43
Clients	40
Banks	25
Suppliers	21
Researchers	13
Educationalists	3

Source: Sofres (1983).

A study of the role of the customer in product development in the United Kingdom and West Germany (Parkinson 1982) highlighted the significance of the quality or technical progressiveness of the domestic customer in development of products which were successful on the international market. West German suppliers were significantly dependent on inputs from their domestic customers throughout the product-development cycle. The user frequently initiated the product-development activity and influenced the way in which the supplier developed the innovation until the point of commercialisation. The Sappho project (SPRU 1972; Rothwell *et al.* 1974) made virtually the same point as to the very close linking to customers in successful innovation. The Parkinson study found that British domestic customers were less interested and less demanding in specification of quality and technology. This may partly have been due to the lesser independence of the British customers which often had to refer to a parent for decision, whereas the German customers took the decision in the company at the local level.

In the Midi-Pyrénées, the large-scale regional decision-makers, chiefly the subsidiaries of large national groups, are reported (Bouvier 1984) to be a major source of technology supply. 'Through the specifications which they transmit to their sub-contractors, but also during project follow-up, engineers and project managers effectively help to raise the technological level of small and medium sized industries', particularly in 'terms of quality requirements in mechanical engineering industries'. The customers are technically progressive and their decisions are made locally.

This role of the technically demanding customer who diffuses the best practice is one that has been exercised by Marks and Spencer in England with its suppliers in the clothing and knitting industries. The role of the larger Japanese firm in this regard is also well known, and it is interesting to note that the MITI (1984) study on small business remarked that contractors were becoming more exacting in their demand for quality and improved technology.

Pieper (1986) found a contrast between the sources of information for product innovation and those for process innovation. For product innovation informal contacts were used by 44 per cent of small firms, customers by 43 per cent and suppliers by 40 per cent. For process innovation, informal contacts were used by 12 per cent, customers by 16 per cent and suppliers by 34 per cent.

In Baden-Württemberg, ISI reported that the customer was the major innovative 'impulse', with internal sources a low 27.8 per cent (Table 5.15). This is a prosperous and technically progressive region with a preponderance of manufacturing employment in engineering. Not only do customers play a larger role but so also do other external sources. Similarly, the customer is the predominant source of information for the very small firms of Prato in Italy on new products and textile equipment suppliers, on new processes (ENEA 1984). Prato is, however, very different in its industrial structure, being highly entrepreneurial.

Table 5.15 Baden-Württemberg: innovation impulses (per cent) (multiple response)

	All sectors	Machine engng	Electrical engng
Internal	27.8	22.9	17.4
External	69.0	70.8	82.1
Customers	67.7	60.4	78.6
Suppliers	2.4	0.0	0.0
Competitors	28.6	8.3	3.6
Consultants	5.6		
Fairs, exhibitions, conferences	19.8	29.2	21.4
Printed media	18.2	8.3	32.1

Source: Hemer (1984).

The point was made earlier that in some countries with a very large number of small firms the entrepreneurial potential was frustrated in achieving innovation and prosperity. Prato provides an example of how the frustration can be released. Covering some 700 square kilometres, the Prato region is a mainly rural one centred on the town of Prato, 20 km from Florence. Its entrepreneurial activity is centred on the woollen textiles industry. Thirty years ago it was a 'reasonably integrated industrial system', based on medium-sized units producing mainly flannel, but in the face of international competition there has been a massive restructuring. In 1971, there were 8,740 firms with 42,000 workers. In 1984, there were 15,000 firms with 66,000 workers. The industry is composed of skilled craftsmen working in very small units supplying the remaining medium-sized firms and the *impannatori*, textile brokers unique to Prato. The number of firms providing services is also high.

Over the last ten years, there has been a high level of innovation and adoption of the best practice in production processes 'exploring everything that the textile technology market can offer, plus automation and electronics' (ENEA 1984). There has been a wide diversification in the products themselves outside the traditional Prato range, in new markets and in the raw materials used. The spread of innovation is stimulated by the close collaboration between the industry and the textile machinery suppliers, but most of all it is the *impannatori* who spread innovation. These number about three hundred, supply raw materials, supervise the entire production cycle through several small firms, and sell the finished products. They design new products, offer these to new markets and then organise production to meet orders obtained. Because they operate on world markets, with contacts at many levels, they bring an awareness of innovation and best practice taking place outside Prato.

They are the local gatekeepers and the local customers who provide the technology pull. There are intensive personal contacts and networks between the larger firms and the *impannatori* and the small firms.

> With all this, Prato's textile industry has been able to upgrade its production standards, winning new markets by offering higher quality fabrics. This has been achieved not only by raising technological levels but also by the projection of a new image, by creative design capabilities, greater product reliability, improved quality of materials, absolute guarantee of continuity of supplies, and punctuality of deliveries (ENEA 1984).

In other words, it is a technically progressive region with a wide diffusion of the best practice and autonomy of information. Logistic information supply is good and the nutrient information flow is rich but with a diversity less than ideal.

Whilst in frequency of use informal contacts and networks tend to dominate as the main sources and channels of information, the customer plays a significant role in stimulating the innovativeness of small firms and in diffusing the best practice in regions which have prosperity and progressiveness. The supplier supports this role in adoption of the best practice.

Formal Sources

In the preceding sections, data have been presented on the use of more formal information sources such as the literature, research organisations and universities. By and large these have tended to be at a relatively low level compared to informal sources or other firms (and many informal contacts are inevitably other entrepreneurs) with customers predominating over suppliers. Japan provided an exception, but it was an exception in which the ease-of-access syndrome had a strong influence, as in the quality of the newspapers, for example. Large firms tend to use a wider spread of sources and it is apparent that much of the supply of formal information from research largely passes through the larger firms to the smaller, certainly in areas outside the usually narrow expertise of the entrepreneur. For example, ISI paid special attention to the awareness and use of innovation and technology consultancy institutions, of which there are a large number in Baden-Württemberg. A large number of small firms know of the sources of consultancy supporting innovative development but only a small number have used them (Table 5.16).

Only 5 per cent of CPI's firms had made use of consultants, but it was apparent that certain outsiders were used as consultants, not often, but they had high influence. Such informal consultants were diverse—a member of the family, a customer, someone in a university. However, no

Table 5.16 Awareness and use of consultancy organisations (per cent)

	All surveyed manufacturing sectors	Machine engineering only	Electrical equipment only
Publicly sponsored technology and innovation consultants or technology transfer agencies:			
not known to firm	38.9	39.6	21.4
known, but not utilised	45.2	45.8	57.1
known and utilised	7.1	6.3	7.1
Institutions for contract research (e.g. FhG, Batelle):			
not known to firm	38.9	50.0	25.0
known, but not utilised	51.6	39.6	60.7
known and utilised	1.6	4.2	0.0
Institutes of AIF*			
not known to firm	52.4	47.9	46.4
known, but not utilised	34.9	37.5	35.7
known and utilised	2.4	4.2	0.0
External contract research through the AIF*			
not known to firm	25.4	10.4	39.3
known, but not utilised	48.4	52.1	35.7
known and utilised	19.8	33.3	10.7

* AIF = Union of Industrial Associations.
Source: Hemer (1984).

general awareness problem was found in regard to the public or public-supported services on offer. But the proliferation of services in some parts of the United Kingdom may be the cause of a good general awareness and of confusion as to what could be obtained from which agency. This was specifically so with regard to the availability of grants and loans. Many of the contacts made therefore lead to frustration.

Small firms tend to use the less formal literature and sources, behaving like technologists. CPI found that 46 per cent of firms had used trade shows and exhibitions for promotion and as a source of information. Many firms used them to find out what the competition was doing, to purchase new equipment, to obtain new ideas, and make new contacts. Not unexpectedly, trade journals were read by 54 per cent, and 33 per cent received other types of periodicals, with 27 per cent receiving newsletters and bulletins from trade associations and so on. Directories were mentioned—Yellow Pages by 34 per cent, other directories by 26 per cent. Yellow Pages was particularly important. Commercial literature (catalogues, product literature etc.) was mentioned by 35 per cent as being important. These results confirm the low use of literature and, at that, the literature used is that more likely to give direct information. CPI found 9 per cent of firms had used a public library and a further 10 per cent other libraries usually in universities or polytechnics. In France also the literature was less used by smaller innovating firms (Table 5.17).

Universities, research and technological organisations and other technical services are not used frequently, but PIPIN reported a high use of regional information centres of public agencies reinforcing the point that to be used a source of information should be near.

Table 5.17 Sources of information of innovating firms

Source	SMEs	Large firms
Literature	45	71
Fairs and exhibitions	36	45
Foreign countries	30	59
Technical centres	20	34
Professional organisation	14	30
ARIST	8	9
Internal	14	12
Centres of research	5	3
Market research	11	9
Specialised conferences	2	3
Others	8	7
Total sources per 100 innovators	193	282

Localisation of Information

Nearness is in fact pervasive and dominant. Economic development, innovation, entrepreneurial vitality are all local phenomena. Information networks are local. Subcontractors to larger companies and especially entrepreneurs who start up on the basis of subcontracting tend to be located in proximity to their customers. This is one aspect of the significance of distance in use of an information source. Donckels and Degadt (1985) state that

> from communication theory they know that the probability of an exchange of information between two individual entities is a decreasing function of the distance separating them ... A direct

consequence is that contacts with local authorities in general are much easier than with authorities at a higher hierarchical level.

Thwaites (1984) remarked of Industrial Research Associations in Britain that although they are important sources of information they are sited at one location, 'creating inevitable problems for regular contact'. the influence of distance is further illustrated by the regional origin of enquiries to the IIRS information service and to the AnCo 'Hot-Line' for small firms (Table 5.18).

Table 5.18 Ireland: clients by region, 1981 (per cent)

	IIRS	AnCo	Manufacturing firms percentage of total
Donegal	0.90		2.6
North-West	2.54	2	2.2
West	4.85	5	7.3
Mid-West	7.45	4	13.5
South-West	9.65	9	12.1
South-East	5.42	8	9.7
East	60.55	66	39.2
North-East	4.97	2	7.0
Midlands	3.78	4	6.2

Source: IIRS and AnCo.

When compared with the regional distribution of industry in Ireland use of these information services is seen to be determined quite heavily by distance. Equally significant to the 'ease-of-use' syndrome was the observation in Italy that the owner of a small craft-based firm is more likely to accept *and act* on information available locally than from far afield.

Thwaites *et al.* (1984) also confirm that 'research suggests that distance is an important barrier to communication, particularly for distances of over 20 miles', and Eriksson (1984) gives the other side of the coin—'our findings suggest that geographical proximity to knowledge is of crucial importance to fast modernisation'.

The PIPIN project concluded that 'information transfer is more effective the nearer the transfer agencies operate in the geographical and psychological environment of the enterprise'. It pointed to decentralised agencies as being regularly consulted by SME. The least effective were centrally located establishments, such as ministries and universities. PIPIN commented that information distribution is also more effective when the information can be orally transferred and commented on.

In the United States the Federal Government 'began to decentralise its service delivery in order to meet the needs of the small business sector at the grass roots level . . . At the grass roots level networks are a quick and cost effective means of accessing information and assistance' (Garber 1984).

These various conclusions confirm the role of the half-hour information potential, with its face-to-face contact, and the localised nature of networks. For the most part they are social and spatial, with certain members who provide links to non-spatial professional networks or distant but key spatial professional networks.

Information Needs of Small Firms

Finance, its sources, availability and management, is invariably quoted as the dominant information need of small firms, but in practice it often alternates as first priority with market information. Technology, *per se*, takes a lower ranking, but is inherent to other perceived needs. Market information and new products information are closely interrelated, both being part of that search for new business in order to survive which characterises many small companies. The top priority accorded finance is inevitable given the usually straitened financial resources available to a small firm and the usual lack of management skill of the founder or entrepreneur. In one banker's perception 'the majority of small businesses find it much more difficult to keep track of and hence to take advantage of, the enormous variety of terms and conditions of finance. Most small businessmen will readily agree that they find financial management an increasingly difficult subject to master' (Blackburn 1981). Yet the greater risk requires greater management input.

In Denmark, many entrepreneurs had financial difficulties and few sought the privileged loans available. They suffered from a lack of financial counselling and information on the administrative aspects of establishing a business (Wickmann 1983). Another report identified financing, market information and advice on available public subsidies as barriers to innovation (Nielsen 1979).

In Norway, 80 per cent of enquiries are said to be about financial problems and, in Baden-Württemberg, 50 per cent of enquiries to SfW (Steinbeis Stiftung für Wirtschaftsförderung) are about finance and sources of finance. Amongst 605 firms of under 200 employees surveyed in Scotland, the two areas where the need for external advice was most strongly felt were finance and administration, both 52 per cent (Scottish Development Agency, 1978). In the CPI study, 27 per cent of firms indicated difficulties in identifying and finding sources of finance and many indicated difficulties relating to finance in a more general sense. Another British study (Communications Studies and Planning Ltd 1978) of the information needs of small firms was carried out to determine the potential role of telecommunications and computing. In this, finance and various aspects of its sourcing, control and management were identified as a dominant problem (Table 5.19). This study concluded that to be attractive to small business, the enhanced Prestel Videotex service would require to focus on its function as a small business computing service rather than on its capability to retrieve information from public databases.

Table 5.19 Information technology and the information needs of small firms

Activity problem/ need	Funds transferred	Information retrieval from external database	Information retrieval from internal sources	Calculations and forecasting	Matching
Obtaining finance	×	×	×	×	×
Cash flow	×		×	×	
Inventory/stock control	×	×	×	×	
Production control			×		
Credit control	×	×	×	×	
Estimating & forecasting		×	×	×	
Tax returns	×	×	×		
Legislation			×		
Liaison		×	×	×	
Marketing		×	×	×	
Recruiting		×	×	×	

Other studies have put marketing as the first priority. In Ireland, a survey of the problems small firms considered most important, undertaken by AnCo, the Industrial Training Authority, showed that market, finance and new product information headed the list of requirements (Figure 5.1). Interestingly, information about where to obtain what from state agencies ranked fourth. Thwaites (1981) says that 'other studies have discovered that a lack of market information may form a major barrier to new product or market development'. This may reflect a simplistic attitude by some small firms in less-prosperous regions, who do not have the opportunity to be linked to demanding customers who supply the ideas of their needs. The Sappho study also pointed to the need to be in very close communication with users. Capital Planning Information (1982) set the need somewhat more pointedly: 'Without doubt, more difficulties and problems occur in the whole area of marketing, including

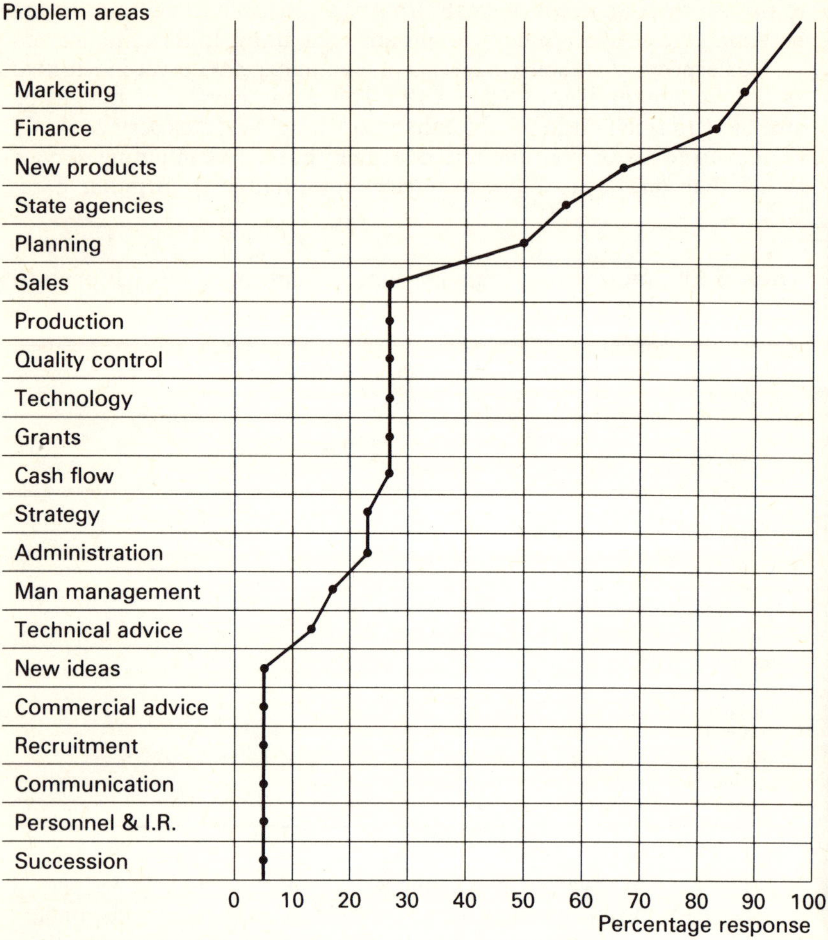

Figure 5.1 Ireland: problems and difficulties of small firms.
Source: AnCo (1984).

selling, promotion, market research, exporting, export documentation, etc. than in any other single area.'

In France, Sofres (1983) found that the most important needs of the heads of small firms were:

- Information on the French market and its evolution (83%);
- Finance available (83%);
- French regulations (78%);
- French competition (77%);

- Foreign competition (56%);
- Available support in research and technology (55%).

Significant of the more research-orientated firms was that 70 per cent of the electronics/electrical firms in this survey were concerned about available support in research and technology. Piatier (1984) also found that the most important obstacle to innovation was lack of finance followed by the poor economic situation and lack of skilled labour. Self-finance was the most frequent source followed by public subvention.

The PIPIN project took a different approach by analysing 203 cases of decision-making and related information-seeking reported by 157 respondents in its sample of 103 firms in phase 0 of the project. Table 5.20 gives a classification of the kinds of decision-making problems encountered. 'Decisions concerning the introduction of new entrepreneurial activities (new products, new markets, new production processes) most frequently give rise to queries for external information.' Marketing took second place with 21 per cent but financial decisions were a low 9 per cent. Nevertheless financial information was in frequent demand along with technical and legal information. There were therefore either multiple needs and/or the information needed for a technical decision, for example, was financial (Tables 5.20 and 5.21). For the 203

Table 5.20 Decision requiring external information (per cent)

Products/production processes	27
Market/marketing	21
Personnel	13
Real estate	10
Means of production	10
Finance	9
Organisation/management	7
Entire enterprise	3

Source: PIPIN (1983).

Table 5.21 Information needed for decisions (per cent)

Techical	37
Financial/economic	36
Legal	35
Commercial	25
Procedural	14

Source: PIPIN (1983).

Table 5.22 Number of needs per decision

	1	2	3	4	5
Products/production process	37	15	2		
Market/marketing	20	18	4		
Personnel	20	5	1		
Real estate	9	9	1	1	1
Means of production	12	8	1		
Finance	13	6			
Organisation	9	4	1		
Entire enterprise	2	3	1		
Total decisions	122	68	11	1	1

Source: PIPIN (1983).

decisions, there were 300 information needs (Table 5.22). A majority of decisions, 59 per cent, had one information need but 33 per cent had two needs. Technical information has a low priority rating, probably because the firm was founded around the experience of its owner/manager.

CPI found that

> the small manufacturing firm often contains considerable experience in the person of the owner or one of the founders (in production) which explains why there tends to be a lack of demand for information relating to products, processes and production generally ... young firms show a distinct tendency towards knowing it all.

Only between 4 and 5 per cent of firms in the CPI study showed interest in quality control, processes, plant, and so on. For the most part, the smaller firms relied heavily for technical information on their customers or suppliers.

> Nonetheless there is some demand for technical information which is not satisfied so easily and seems to arise as the smaller firm begins to grow and diversifies its products or installs new equipment ... Problems begin when the owner becomes involved with other matters.

The most frequently cited problem in the CPI study, was finding premises (32 per cent) and a further 14 per cent referred to problems of relocation. Whilst the problems may in fact have been more restricted than these figures indicate there was a broad consensus that information about premises is too fragmented and inadequate. Most firms in this study seemed well aware of legislation affecting them, some even complaining of too much information.

After finance and marketing, the Scottish Development Agency (1978) reported that 39 per cent of firms had a need for external advice in 'Manufacture and production, which included building and planning regulations (20% of the total) and location of premises (13%)'. Personnel and training needs were identified by 40 per cent .

Specific Information

The priority needs for information are reasonably clear. What is the kind of information demanded to meet these needs? For the most part it is in fact the specific data and information for day-to-day decision-making, referred to earlier, and, as will be seen, information for longer-term decision-making is also perceived in terms of specificity and urgency.

The type of information sought from the IIRS (Institute for Industrial Research and Standards) Information Services is given in Table 5.23. This illustrates the importance both of referral to expert sources and of direct immediately usable information. Most of the requests for specific information or data, as ARIST (Agences Regionales d'Information Scientifique et Technique) in France has also discovered, are for information on where to get materials, components and equipment or for specialised subcontracting—information on other firms. CPI (1982) found 18 per cent of firms identifying problems 'associated with finding details, such as names and addresses of suppliers and sub-contractors' and therefore the most important aspect of technical information. CPI also found that the main need for marketing information 'seems to be for specific information on firms, products, agents, addresses etc.'. CPI enquired of some public librarians and of the information centres of the

Table 5.23 IIRS: type of information sought and complexity (per cent)

	1984	1983	1982	1981
Standards	13.06	17.53	17.91	17.09
Products	22.39	23.34	24.33	22.58
Data	37.00	31.83	29.58	24.55
IIRS Services	17.36	17.86	13.40	16.78
Other	10.19	9.44	14.78	19.00
Complexity of enquiries				
Directional/referral			34	
Quick reference			40	
Extended subject search			23	
On-line literature search			3	

British Small Firms Service and found that the greatest demand was for directory-type information, particularly related to companies. In the Scottish Development Association's study 22 per cent of firms identified 'purchasing' as a need area. The main problem appeared to be identification of sources of materials and components needed in manufacture of their products.

The SPRINT (1984) project which studied the Prato entrepreneurs defined the information needs in much the same way—specific data and much of it names and addresses. The project team proposed that there were needs for data bases on:

- suppliers and subcontractors;
- suppliers of services;
- raw materials availability;
- machinery, spare parts, and prices;
- availability of experienced people (job seekers).

Whilst the Prato trade associations sent out a lot of information in their bulletins and other communications, this was not available in the firm when needed. They had no files or could not locate the specific information, much of it concerning regulations, laws, tax, labour, and other administrative decrees or requirements. A need was also identified for information on raw materials coming to the market, and outlets on foreign markets.

In France, studies reported by the Germon Committee (1985) state that most information provision is

- too detailed;
- too general;
- to imprecise;
- badly expressed or in a specialist language;
- too long to read;
- too theoretical.

When SMEs have identified some potential sources they are confronted with two questions—who does what and whom should I call in these organisations? Personal contact is essential. The Germon report concluded that for information to be be used by SMEs it should be

- short, precise, synthesised;
- expressed in a language open to the receiver;
- at an acceptable cost if it is sold;
- current or new and supplied without delay.

The analysis of the 'need for information on longer-term technological trends' in Baden-Württemberg illustrated the perception by small firms of their information needs in a different way. Whilst 44 per cent felt that they needed such information regularly, almost a third saw the need as occuring only seldom. Obtaining such information was seen to be no problem at all for many firms. More interesting was the reinforcement of the general finding that small-firm information needs are for specific information and data for immediate decision-making and problem solving. A third of firms felt that information obtained was either not specific or not enough for specific requirements (Table 5.24).

Table 5.24 Baden-Württemberg: needs for information on long-term technological trends by sectors (per cent)

Answer category	Sectors		
	All surveyed manufacturing sectors	Machine engineering only	Electrical equipment only
Regularly	44.4	33.3	46.4
Innovative ventures only	23.8	25.0	28.6
Seldom	30.2	39.6	25.0
Information procurement:			
No problem at all	10.3	4.2	17.9
Too much information is supplied	10.3	4.2	17.9
Not enough information for specific requirements	21.4	20.8	14.3
Available information not specific enough	10.3	12.5	3.6
Systematic search and evaluation of information is costly and time consuming	24.6	16.7	21.4
Information arrived too late	0.8	0.0	3.6
Information supply services are too expensive	11.9	14.6	10.7

Source: Hemer (1984).

Analysis (Table 5.25) as to whether information on long-term trends was required regularly, for innovative ventures or seldom, reinforced not only the specificity of the information needed but also the immediacy of perceived needs—even for long-term trends. Those involved in innovative ventures largely felt that information came too late. A good number of those seeing a regular need felt that the process of obtaining it was too time consuming.

Table 5.25 Baden-Württemberg: needs for information on long-term technological trends by frequency of need (per cent)

Problems mentioned	Answer categories	Regularly	Frequencies for innovative ventures only	Seldom
No problem at all	42.9	30.0	15.8	
Too much information is supplied	16.1	13.3	50.0	
Too little information for specific requirements	19.6	30.0	18.4	
Available information is not specific enough	12.5	6.7	10.7	
Systematical search and evaluation of information is costly and time-consuming	39.3	16.7	10.5	
Information arrived too late	1.8	86.7	50.0	
Information supply services too expensive	16.1	13.3	5.3	

Source: Hemer (1984).

Conclusions

Small firms behave more like people than organisations in their information-seeking behaviour, and they tend to the informal end of the spectrum of information-seeking behaviour. Indeed small firms in the more traditional industries tend towards the extreme informal end. They are highly dependent on their informal contacts but they are also highly dependent on their customers. The customer is usually a larger firm, but not necessarily so, as the *impannatori* of Prato demonstrate.

The customer plays a significant role in providing a pull to raise the level of technical performance of its supplier, to diffuse the best practice and to stimulate its innovative products.

Nevertheless, the small firm is dependent in its own area of specialisation on the skills and expertise of the entrepreneur. These were the foundation on which he set up his firm and which are continuously enhanced not only through his customer and supplier but also through his informal network and informal browsing.

The entrepreneur is highly local, dependent on the opportunities and networks of his locality and on the technical progressiveness of his customers and peers in his locality. His contacts are personal, face-to-face and by phone. He lives within a half-hour contact potential and his innovativeness and efficiency depend on the logistic and nutrient information available within that area of contact.

His main information needs are otherwise day-to-day, quick and specific data and information, mainly on finance or managing it and on markets. He prefers information sources which are locally accessible and personal. Only intermittently are his needs in depth and therefore continuing contact is difficult from a research centre or consultancy organisation, especially one at a distance. His needs, and his uniqueness, are difficult to serve through formal means.

References

The literature on sources and channels of information is extensive. The main sources used in compilation of the earlier sections of this chapter were the following:

Ford, G., ed. (1977). *User studies: an introductory guide and select bibliography*. University of Sheffield, Centre for Research on User Studies. Occasional paper, no. 1.

Meadows, A. J. (1979). *Communications in science*. London, Butterworths.

Shapero, A. (1985). *Managing professional people: understanding creative performance*. New York, Theatre Press.

Other References

Allen, T. J. (1977). *Managing the flow of technology*. Cambridge, MA, MIT Press.

AnCo (1984). *Study of the training needs of small companies in Ireland*. AnCo, The Industrial Training Authority.

Åsell, P. (1984). 'Excerpts from the evaluation report concerning the Swedish micro-electronics campaign "The Little Giant"'. Six Countries Workshop, Limerick.

Blackburn, M. (1981). 'Backing small business to get winners', *Management Today*, May, 93 ff.

Bouvier, F. (1984). Setting-up of technological networks—theory and practice. Six Countries Workshop, Limerick.

Capital Planning Information (1982). *Information and the small manufacturing firm*. Edinburgh.

Communication Studies and Planning Ltd (1978). *Services for small business: potential for business support systems using telecommunications and computing*. PO2/78120/EB.

Donckels, R. and Degadt, J. (1985). 'SMEs and public authorities: on the information and communication gap'. *Intl Small Business Jnl*, 3(3), 11–30.

ENEA. (1984). Documentation on the Prato case study. Rome.

Eriksson, A. (1984). 'Regional policy in Sweden—from job creation to regional development'. Six Countries Workshop, Limerick.

Freeman, C. *et al*. (1971). The role of small firms in innovation in the UK since 1945. HMSO Committee of Enquiry on Small firms. Research Report No. 6.

Garber, S. (1984). The Small Business Development Centre Program: a unique resource for small business. 14th European Small Business Seminar, Lisbon.

Germon, C. (Chairman) (1985). *Proposition pour la mise en valeur de l'offre française de biens et de services et le dévelopment d'un secteur de l'information industrielle et commerciale*. November, Paris, Mission Parliamentaire de M. le Deputé Claude Germon. 2 volumes.

Glass, B. and Norwood, S. H. (1959). 'How scientists actually learn of work important to them' in *Proc. Intl Conf. on Scientific Information*. Washington, Nat. Acad. Sciences, vol. 1, 195–7.

Hawthorne, E. P. (1971). *The transfer of technology*. Paris, OECD.

Hemer, J. (1984). *Information networks designed to support innovation in less-favoured regions of the European Community: case study in Baden-Württemberg*. Karlsruhe, Fraunhofer Institut für Systemtechnik und Innovationsforschung, October.

Herner, S. (1954). 'Information gathering habits of workers in pure and applied science', *Ind. Engng chem.*, 46(1), January, 228–36.

Herner, S. (1959). 'Information gathering habits of American medical students' in *Proc. Intl Conf. on Scientific Information*. Washington, Nat. Acad. Sciences, vol. 1, 227–85.

ITU and OECD (1983). Telecommunications for development. Paris.

Lamberton, D. McL. (1986). 'Information, economic analysis and public policy', *Prometheus* 2, 4(1), June, 174–80.

Langrish, J. *et al*. (1971). Wealth from knowledge. London, Macmillan.

Leonard-Barton, D. (1983). 'Interpersonal communication patterns and Swedish and Boston-area entrepreneurs' in Hornaday, J. L. *et al*. (eds), *Frontiers of entrepreneurship research*. Wellesley, MA, Babson College.

Martyn, J. (1964). *Report on an investigation of literature searching by research students*. London, Aslib.

MITI (1984). White Paper on small and medium enterprises in Japan.

Murray, F., O'Brolchain, D. and Sweeney, G. P. (1973). *A survey of scientific and technical information in Ireland*. Dublin, IIRS, 2 vols.

Nielsen, L. D. (1979). *Government barriers to innovation by small firms in Denmark*: report prepared for the CEC. Tåstrup, Teknologisk Institut.

Parkinson, S. T. (1982). 'The role of the user in successful new product development', *R & D Management*, 12(3), 123–31.

Piatier, A. (1981). Barriers to innovation in European Community Countries. Brussels, Commission of the European Communities.

Piatier, A. (1984). *L'innovation dans l'industrie: les enseignements des quelques enquetes*. Paris, Centre de prospective et d'évaluation, Ministère de l'industrie et de la recherche (CEP study no. 32).

PIPIN (Project Promotion of Information Provision for Industry) (1983). *External information provision for small and medium-size industry*. The Hague, NOBIN.

Roberts, E. B. (1983). 'Business planning in the start-up high technology enterprise' in Hornaday, J. L. *et al*. (eds), *Frontiers of entrepreneurship research*. Wellesley, MA, Babson College.

Rosenberg, V. (1967). 'Factors affecting the preferences of industrial personnel and information gathering methods', *Inf. Storage and retrieval*, 3(3), 119–27.

Rothwell, R. (1975). 'Patterns of information flow during the innovation process', *Aslib Proc.*, 27(5), May, 217–26.

Rothwell, R. and Zegveld, W. (1985). Reindustrialisation and technology. Harlow, Longman.

Rothwell, R. *et al.* (1974). 'SAPPHO updated project SAPPHO phase II', *Res. Policy*, 3, 258–91.

Scase, R. and Goffee, R. (1980). The real world of the small business owner. London, Croom Helm.

Scott, C. (1959). 'The use of technical literature by industrial technologists', in *Proc. Intl Conf. on Scientific Information*. Washington, Nat. Acad. Sciences, vol. 1, 245–6.

Scottish Development Agency (1975). Small manufacturing firms in Scotland: a survey of their problems and needs. Edinburgh.

Shapero, A. (1984). Notes for summing up. Six Countries Workshop, Limerick.

Shapero, A. (1973). *Management of innovation: the role of communication*. Milan, Intl Inst. of Technology.

Smith, N. R. (1967). *The entrepreneur and his firm: the relationship between type of man and type of company*. East Lansing, Michigan State University.

Sofres (1983). Le développement industriel et la réorganisation des services régionaux de ministère du l'industrie et de la recherche.

SPRINT (1984). The impact of new technologies on mature industries: a case study in Prato. Prato, October.

SPRU (Science Policy Research Unit) (1972). *Success and failure in industrial innovation: report on project SAPPHO*. London, Centre for the Study of Industrial Innovation.

Sweeney, G. P. (1978). The sociology of information. Lecture to School of Information and Library Studies, University College of Dublin.

Sweeney, G. P. (1977). 'The use of national resources to encourage the more effective use of information by industry', *Aslib Proc*., 29(2), February, 91–103.

Thwaites, A. T. *et al*. (1981). Industrial innovation and regional development: final report to the Department of the Environment. Centre for Urban and Regional Development Studies, University of Newcastle-upon-Tyne.

Wickman, J. (1983). *Young growth in Danish trade and industry—entrepreneurs and their enterprises*. Copenhagen, Danish Fed. of Crafts and Smaller Industries.

X (1983). Profile of the successful SME-Manager. Brussels, Inst. for the Permanent Education of the Middle Class.

CHAPTER 6

Small Firms in European LFRs

Introduction

In April and May 1984, a survey, part of a larger contract funded by DG XVI of the Commission of the European Communities (Sweeney 1985) was carried out of small firms in four member states of the European Communities. The objective of the survey was to examine the information behaviour and needs of small firms in less-favoured regions (LFRs) of the Community, three peripheral and one declining, and therefore test in the field points made about information behaviour set out in the previous chapter and expose differences between prosperous and less-favoured regions. The regions surveyed were Salerno in Italy; Tyne and Wear in the United Kingdom; Magnesia and Pthiotis in Greece; and the Mid-West and West regions in Ireland.* A total of 241 firms were interviewed. An analysis of data gathered in other surveys from firms in the Neckar region of Baden-Württemberg was provided as a comparison with a prosperous region,† and has been presented for the most part in Chapter 5.

The data were analysed *inter alia* by separating the firms into those founded during 1979–84 (new firms) and those founded before 1979 (established firms). A further analysis separated out the 'progressive firms' from those designated established. These were identified by an arbitrary selection of all firms which stated that they carried out R & D, had undertaken a new venture in the previous five years, and had been successful in this new venture. This chapter presents the data under these three types of firm.

Sectoral Distribution

The sectoral distribution of the sample is shown in Table 6.1, together with the breakdown for each of the regions. There were regional biases in the new firms and progressive categories. Mid-West Ireland had more new firms. Salerno and Tyne and Wear had more engineering firms.

* The field surveys were carried out respectively by CNOS-Servizi, Rome; CURDS, Univ. of Newcastle; IEME, Athens and IIRS, Dublin.

† This analysis was provided by Fraunhofer-Gesellschaft ISI, Karlsruhe (Hemer 1984).

Table 6.1 Sectoral distribution of LFR sample (per cent)

Sector	Aggregate	Established firms	New firms	Progressive	Italy Salerno	UK Tyne and Wear	Greece Magnesia Pthiotis	Mid-West Ireland	West Ireland
N =	241	196	44	45	50	50	38	50	53
Mech.	23	21	27	20	32	29	13	20	17
Chemical	4	4	4.5	11	8	2	5	4	2
Food	18	19	11	22	16	10	29	18	19
Electrical	4	4	4.5	2	0	8	3	4	6
Clothing	12	11	15.9	7	10	10	16	10	15
Furniture	12	9.7	20	2	10	10	5	22	9
Packaging	7	8	2	7	6	8	0	8	11
Plastics	6	5.6	6.8	4	6	4	8	6	6
Other	14	15.8	6.8	22	10	18	21	8	15

Interestingly, Tyne and Wear, which, in its former prosperity, had a strong heavy engineering sector, had retained a strength in engineering relative to the Greek and Irish regions, but in itself was still at a weaker level than one would find in a prosperous West German region like the Neckar or in Copenhagen.

Not surprisingly, in less-favoured regions there was a strong representation of food firms. The new firms were well represented in two other traditional sectors, clothing and furniture, but relatively badly in food. Progressive firms were strongly present in the more technological mechanical and chemical sectors taken together, but most heavily represented in food processing.

The sectoral distribution of firms in the Neckar region was biased to the engineering sector (Table 6.2), even accounting for the fact that Baden-Württemberg has a high proportion of manufacturing employment in engineering and a large part of this is concentrated in the Neckar region.

Table 6.2 Baden-Württemberg: industrial employment by sector

Sector	Percentage employment	
Basic products, including chemicals	11	
Capital goods, including	78.6	
Machine engineering		38% of total
Electrical engineering		22% of total
Vehicles		2.4% of total
Consumer goods	7.9	
Food, drink and tobacco	2	
Others	1	

The sample firms in both the LFRs and Baden-Württemberg were drawn from firms employing under 200. Most of the firms in the LFRs, 81 per cent, had less than 50 employees, 11.8 per cent had 50–99 and 6.7 per cent had 100–199. Salerno had the highest number of larger firms. West Ireland had none in the 100–199 range. Mechanical engineering firms tended to be younger than those in other sectors, 23 per cent were in the new firm category whilst only 17 per cent of the rest were in this age group. In Baden-Württemberg, 50 per cent of the firms had under 50 employees, 21.4 per cent were in the 50–99 range and 28.6 per cent were in the 100–199 range.

An attempt was made to obtain some idea of the 'technological progressiveness' of the firms sampled by enquiring as to engagement in

R & D, whether a new venture had been undertaken in the previous five years, how successful this was and what impact it had had. The results are given in Table 6.3. Progressive firms register 100 per cent against the main questions since these were the selection criteria. One objective, dealt with later, was to explore whether there was any relationship between 'progressiveness' and information behaviour.

Table 6.3 Indicators of technical progressiveness

	New	Established	Progressive	Aggregate
Engaged in R & D	45	44	100	44
of which				
Design office	35	23	24	25
Laboratories	20	24	36	24
Quality control	30	58	78	53
Staff FTE (mean)	1.5	1.9	2.1	1.9
Process licence	0	3	0.5	2.5
Product licence	11	5	3.7	6.2
Innovative venture	88.6	66.8	100	71
of which				
New product	38	50	58	48
New process	18	44	47	38
Expanded market	28	34	42	40
New firm	74	8	18	24
Successful innovative venture	89.7	85.5	100	86
of which				
Increased turnover	48.6	71	80	66
Extended market	31	43.7	47	41
Reduced cost	20	32	31	29
Expanded product range	43	45	51	45

New firms were in fact as likely to be engaged in R & D as established firms. A higher percentage had a design office but this may have been related to the higher percentages in mechanical engineering, clothing and furniture. Relatively fewer had laboratories, but again the higher number of food firms in particular amongst the progressives may have influenced this. In other words, taking sectoral distribution into account, there may be little difference between new and progressive firms. However, there are distinct differences in levels of quality control, new firms scoring poorly in this regard. There were regional biases.

The percentage of firms in Ireland with quality control systems was much lower than elsewhere (15 per cent in the Mid-West, 45 per cent in the West, as against 68, 59 and 71 per cent in the other countries) and this, given the bias towards Ireland of the new-firm sample, gives some explanation of this particular figure. Firms in Salerno had larger percentages of firms with design offices, laboratories and/or quality control, but more firms in Tyne and Wear had design offices.

The number which saw themselves as having undertaken a new venture was very high, 71 per cent, as also was the rate of success, 86 per cent. It is possible that failure of new ventures led to the failure of the firm in a few cases. More probably the level of new ventures relates to that high rate of incremental innovation in which Bannock (1983), for example, sees small firms as being constantly engaged but in a generally unobserved fashion. Certainly, nearly all of this R & D and innovative activity was below the threshold of the science administrators who compile data on R & D and innovation. The high figure gives credence to Piatier's view that the life of a small firm is really a succession of new projects. Entrepreneurial and innovative drive is high in order to survive.

Greek firms had a lower rate of both new ventures, 34 per cent, and success in these, 62 per cent, reflecting what seems to be a major difficulty of expansion by Greek firms. Firms in Baden-Württemberg did not differ from the overall pattern—87 per cent had introduced a new product, of which 67 per cent were claimed to be genuine innovations. There was a high rate of market success.

That new firms had fewer staff resources devoted to R & D is not surprising. Although new firms are under a financial pressure which restricts R & D, they were shown to be as likely to be carrying out R & D as other firms. The mean number of staff engaged in R & D was 1.9. In Baden-Württemberg the number of staff was an average 2.9 in 1983, with a high of 4.5 in the electrical engineering sector. New firms had more product licences than established or progressive firms. The number of licences among progressive firms was very low. Overall the low number of product licences indicates a difference between less favoured and prosperous regions. Studies of small firms in other countries have shown a much higher percentage. Piatier (Table 5.12), reported 29 per cent of firms as having licences. The higher percentage of product licences amongst new firms possibly indicates a greater awareness amongst younger entrepreneurs (see Table 6.17) of the opportunity offered by product licensing especially as a basis for start-up. The figure was also influenced by the high number of licences amongst mechanical engineering firms in the West of Ireland.

The number of firms which perceive themselves as having undertaken a new venture is quite high, 71 per cent for the total sample. 11.2 per cent of all firms had in fact a subsidiary, and 7 per cent of the new firms had founded one. New firms were lowest in number of new product ventures, new process and market expansions, and progressive firms highest. This is as one would probably expect. The foundation of the firm saw new products as the basis of the start-up. The ones reported here were additional ventures. They were also more concerned, at a lower level, to expand their markets than introduce a new process. As new firms, they would probably tend to have more up-to-date technology and hence be in considerably less need of process improvement.

The New Venture

Looking at the prime reason why the new venture was undertaken (Table 6.4), meeting a market need was the most common and it had the highest rating amongst new firms, who were also keenest to diversify and to broaden their market. The established firms have a higher rating on the apparently conservative 'expand business'. Interpretations of the behaviour of new firms from the data in Table 6.3 seem to be confirmed here. They are much more orientated to diversification, and broadening the market and little to cost factors such as competitiveness or profit.

Table 6.4 Prime reason why venture was undertaken (per cent)

Reason	New	Established	Progressive	Aggregate
Meet market need	26	21	20	23
Expand business	10	15	9	14
Legal requirement	3	4	7	3
Diversification	13	7	9	8.7
Improve competitiveness	5	16	16	13.6
Improve quality	0	4	2	3
Cost of labour	0	2	0	1
Market depression	0	4	2	3
Increase profit	0	3	4	2
Broaden market	15	11	13	12
Need to change machinery	0	5	9	3
Others	21	7	4	10
No reply	7	1	5	5

New firms seem to be more market-conscious, which may stem from their younger managers and/or the pressure for survival. The low interest in improving quality does not seem to indicate the lower awareness of quality which exists in the less-favoured peripheral regions of Europe even though more than half of all firms had quality control systems.

Each firm was asked the number of its products in 1979, 1981 and 1983 (Table 6.5). Not surprisingly, new firms had the lower number in 1979, a mean of 2 each in a year in which only some were founded. From the figures, it would seem that most small firms have a range of products, and it takes time obviously to develop the range. In the year of foundation

Table 6.5 Mean number of products

	New	Established	Progressive	Aggregate
1979	2	7	7	7
1981	4	7	6	7
1883	5	9	11	8

Table 6.6 Source of venture idea (per cent)

	New	Established	Progressive	Aggregate
In firm	62	56	60	59
Import substitution	3	0	0	0.6
Customer	8	11	9	10
Competition	3	6	2	5
Law	3	2	2	2
New staff	0	1	0	0.6
Quality problems	0	2	4	1
Conference/exhibition	3	8	9	6
Publication	3	2	4	2
Supplier	0	5	4	4
Other	13	5	2	6
No reply	2	2	4	4

they may have 2 but rapidly increase this number to possibly around 7. However, between 1981 and 1983 there was a marked increase in the mean number of products of each firm from what appeared as a stable 7 in 1979 and 1981, but increased in 1983, substantially so in the case of progressive firms.

The source of the new ventures, Table 6.6, was predominantly internal, with new and progressive firms having a higher score. Customers were a more important source than suppliers, except that suppliers had not been a source of ideas at all for new firms. There was otherwise a wide distribution of sources. Suppliers were more important in Italy, 15 per cent, than customers, 7 per cent. The high focus on internal sources is one which would be expected for new firms, given that entrepreneurs tend to set up their new business around their own skills and ideas. As a general pattern it probably indicates the poorer environment in contrast to Baden-Württemberg and other countries reported in Chapter 5 (e.g. Table 5.15).

The strong pull by customers in more prosperous regions seems to indicate that a major difference between prosperous and non-prosperous regions is the role of the progressive, and particuarly engineering, customer as a source of innovative ideas as well as information. Less-favoured regions do not have such firms with local-decision making who will exert a technology pull through their purchases and purchasing specifications and a continuing interaction. In the LFRs the entrepreneur is very much dependent on his own resources. Less than half of firms who had had a successful new venture admitted to having had outside help. Most of this help was through the provision of information (Table 6.7).

Most problems met with in new ventures for new firms (Table 6.8) were finance-related, very much more so than for other firms which were conscious of more problems with government bureaucracy and information. New firms had a more conscious need for training than other firms. However, market-related problems received a low scoring from all categories but particularly new firms. Judging by the importance otherwise given to market information (Table 6.9) this problem of finance for new ventures in new firms weighs heavily.

Table 6.7 Outside help in the successful new venture

Received outside help	47
of which	
by information	84
by referral	12
other help	27

Table 6.8 High-priority problems in relation to innovation ventures (per cent)

Problem area	New	Established	Progressive	Aggregate
Finance-related	56	27	13	34
Government/bureaucracy	13	21	16	19
Information-related	18	25	24	24
Infrastructural	5	13	7	10
Market-related	3	11	7	9
Training	10	8	4	9
Other	0	5	7	3
Consider that the above problems can be helped by improved information supply	51	52	36	

Table 6.9 Information requirements of firms (per cent)

Type of information	Ranking											
	New			Established			Progressive			Aggregate		
	1	2	3	1	2	3	1	2	3	1	2	3
Finance	39	18	4	33	22	15	24	27	15	31	21	14
Markets	34	36	9	37	30	10	40	18	11	37	27	9
Legislation	0	2	9	3	3	7	2	4	9	3	3	7
Government policies	2	7	23	4	11	11	9	11	9	3	9	11
Information technology	0	2	2	5	8	10	7	15	11	4	7	9
Production/process development	5	9	20	3	14	23	4	11	15	3	13	21
New products	7	7	2	9	8	12	4	4	11	8	8	10
Other	0	0	0	1	0	0	2	0	0	1	0	0
No reply	13	19	31	5	5	12	8	9	18	15	12	19

Information Priorities

If we turn to consideration of the information priorities of the sample we find further confirmation of the financial difficulties faced by new firms. They were asked to rank a series of topics on which they required information (Table 6.9). Finance predominates as the first priority for new firms, and market information for other firms, very much so for progressive new firms. When we look at second and third priorities we find that new firms drop sharply their focus on finance and switch to markets. These results confirm results from other surveys, reported in Chapter 5, such as those carried out by Sofres and AnCo. The high ranking given to market information confirms the impression given by the high number of new ventures. Small firms are continuously in search of new products or new markets or both. Their business is change, if not innovation, to ensure survival of the business.

Other topics do not rate highly, including two aspects of technical information—for new product- and production-process development—except as the third priority. But new firms still give a higher score to another problem area, government policies, and it is only production-process information, not new product information, which concerns them. 'Government policies' represents the various actions and programmes which may affect a firm but especially assistance programmes. Established and progressive firms also give this a higher rating. All firms, especially new firms, seem confident that one way or another they have the technical skills to develop the product, and only down the line, having sorted out finance, markets, and for new firms what the government is doing, do they want to start looking at their production system. This is probably a result again of the fact that most firms are established around the product ideas and technical skills of the founder.

Sources of Information

Where did the firms go for their information? There was an interesting distribution of sources ranked first for information on finance (Table 6.10). New firms made considerably more use of persons outside and were relatively more heavily dependent on these persons, in that they were less self reliant. Progressive firms were heavily self-reliant. Information on markets was for all three types of firm a matter primarily of self-reliance to which new firms added market research. New firms seem to have a quite strong reliance on market research; perhaps younger entrepreneurs are more conscious of the need for the more systematic approach to gathering data on the market which they wish to service.

Not surprisingly, organisations and documentation, more formal sources, are ranked first for information on legislation and government

Table 6.10 Sources of information—finance and markets (per cent)

Source of information	Topic							
	Finance				Markets			
	N	E	P	Ag	N	E	P	Ag
Persons inside firm	39	51	67	48	45	45	42	45
Persons outside firm	43	26	16	29	9	12	9	12
Organisations	14	11	9	11	2	8	9	7
Exhibitions/conferences	0	1	2	1	5	8	9	7
Competitors' products	0	0	0	0	2	4	9	4
Direct market research	0	0	0	0	25	11	16	14
Training courses	0	0	0	0	1	0	0	0.8
Documentary sources	0	1	0	1	0	1	2	1.6
Mass media	0	1	0	0.8	0	1	2	0.8
Other	0	0	0	0	5	2	0	2
No reply	4	8	6	8	5	6	2	6

Table 6.11 Sources of information—government and legislation (per cent)

Source of information	Government policies				Legislation			
	N	E	P	Ag	N	E	P	Ag
Persons inside firm	9	19	27	17	23	20	24	21
Persons outside firm	14	11	11	12	11	14	9	14
Organisations	57	24	22	30	20	20	22	20
Exhibitions/conferences	0	2	0	2	2	1	2	0.8
Competitors' products	0	0	0	0	0	0	0	0
Direct market research	0	0	0	0	0	0	0	0
Training courses	0	0	0	0	0	1	2	0.4
Documentary sources	9	20	22	18	9	21	20	19
Mass media	0	6	2	5	2	6	4	5
Other	0	1	0	0.8	0	1	2	0.8
No reply	11	17	16	15	33	16	15	19

policy (Table 6.11). Documentary sources, also important for information technology, are much less used by new firms. New entrepreneurs seem to read less, perhaps because they are under greater pressure.

Exhibitions and conferences are much more important as sources on production processes and information technology (Table 6.12). The competition is important as a source for new product information. For

Table 6.12 Sources of information—technical (per cent)

Source of information	Topic											
	Production/ process development				New products				Information technology			
	N	E	P	Ag	N	E	P	Ag	N	E	P	Ag
Persons inside firm	41	39	44	39	45	31	47	33	11	19	27	18
Persons outside firm	14	11	9	12	7	9	0	8	23	16	2	17
Organisations	7	5	4	5	5	6	7	6	16	7	9	8
Exhibitions/conferences	16	11	16	12	5	10	4	9	20	17	20	17
Competitors' products	2	3	7	2	11	8	16	9	0	0	0	0
Direct market research	2	2	2	2	5	5	7	5	2	1	0	1
Training courses	0	2	0	1	0	0	0	0	0	0	0	0
Documentary sources	0	9	4	7	2	4	2	3	9	14	20	13
Mass media	0	0	0	0	2	0	0	0.4	0	2	2	2
Other	5	1	0	2	2	1	0	1	2	1	0	1
No reply	13	17	14	18	16	27	17	25	17	23	20	24

technical information on products and process there is a high dependence on internal sources.

Overall the pattern of information needs and behaviour which emerged was that

- for all small firms information on markets and finance were the highest priorities;
- new firms put the first priority on finance, and progressive firms, by a wide margin, on markets;
- as second priorities new and progressive firms reversed their first priorities;
- as a third priority new firms put highest emphasis on information on government policies followed closely by information for production process development;
- established firms put production process development as the highest third priority;
- people inside the firm dominated as the first source of information for all firms on finance, markets, production process development, new products, and information technology;
- new firms placed people outside the firm as the first source of information on finance and information technology;
- the widest range of sources were used for the three technical information topics;
- as the firm gets older and if it becomes a progressive firm it tends to become more self-reliant.

Let us look further at these sources of information used by small firms in European LFRs. Table 6.13 shows the people inside and outside the firms. Respondents were allowed to nominate three people in each category. The Chief Executive, in other words the entrepreneur, emerges as the main information source, especially in the new firm. The central role of the entrepreneur as the main information processor is thus highlighted, and he continues through the years to retain this role. The firm is built around his technical skills, but above all he is the main information processor and decision-maker.

At a lower level, the production manager in the new firm and the sales manager in the progressive firm were the next most important sources. This may also illustrate the evolution from new to progressive in which the priority need for information becomes strongly focused on markets.

Not unexpectedly, the informal network of business and professional friends of the entrepreneur is significant in its high ranking. They are of equal importance as himself or herself within the new firm with a lesser score in established and progressive firms. The new firm was also much more dependent on two other personal sources, suppliers and customers. Suppliers were more important than customers, a characteristic of less-

Table 6.13 People as information sources (per cent)

Information sources	New	Established	Progressive	Aggregate
In firm				
Chief Executive	82	77.5	76	78
Production Manager	34	31.6	26	32
Sales Manager	29	30.6	40	30
Others	22	25	24	24
People outside				
Professional/business friends	82	70	60	72
Personal friends	18	20	11	20
Supplier	59	40	36	43
Customer	45	30	29	32
Liaison officer	6.8	3	6.7	13
Others	2	5.6	11	9

favoured as against progressive regions. It is also an interesting difference from the sources of new venture ideas, where customers were at a very minor level.

As set out in Chapter 5, the literature on information sources clearly indicates that, except in one or two fields of pure science, informal sources are more important than formal and the personal informal source grows in importance as one travels across the spectrum from pure science to applied technology and within this from large science-based industry to small traditional industry. The latter becomes almost wholly dependent on personal networks.

The sources of information ranked first in Tables 6.10 and 6.12 showed formal information sources having importance only in topics which had low priorities except for market research. Table 6.14 gives the level of use of formal sources of information. Again, respondents were asked to nominate three organisations. Banks, trade associations and chambers of commerce inevitably become, in the passage of time, personal sources and entry points to other personal networks, as is shown by the table. New entrepreneurs are weakly linked to these. Progressive firms were less dependent on banks than established firms, perhaps reflecting their greater self-reliance for information on finance (Table 6.10). New firms made more use of agencies set up by government such as technical advisory or innovation centres and they made a particularly heavy use of business advisory bodies such as the small business advisory centres in the North-East of England or those provided by Shannon Development in the Mid-West of Ireland. New entrepreneurs obviously find these either useful or, as PIPIN, noted they are used because they are local.

Table 6.14 Formal information sources

Information source	New	Established	Progressive	Aggregate
Business organisations	48	86	69	78
of which				
Banks	6.8	19	11	17
Trade associations	6.8	25	29	22
Chambers of commerce	2.3	11	2.2	22
Scientific/technical organisations	38.6	13	18	19.5
of which				
advisory	13.6	5.6	6.7	7
innovation centre	13.6	1	2	3
Public Business Centres Development Body	36	11	13	16
Other				
Educational	9	10	13	10
Libraries	6.8	2.6	4.4	3.3
Conferences	2.3	7.7	4.4	6.7
Market research	2.3	1.0	0	1.3
Training	11	2.6	2.2	4.2
Published sources	9.1	7.1	8.9	7.5
Mass media	0	0.51	0	0.42

Other formal sources do not score particularly highly. It was noted earlier that new firms focused on training more than others as a problem in developing a new venture. Training is generally much more used by new firms. Market research by the firm seems to have a lower score than one would have expected from Table 6.10.

Overall, the sources used show that new firms are more heavily dependent on the Chief Executive, business and professional friends and suppliers and customers than other firms. The entrepreneurs' skills and his personal network are critically important, and he leans fairly heavily on his suppliers and customers. Compared to more prosperous regions, customers are a relatively weak source. He is also dependent on the local agencies set up by government to help small business. But reliance on the internal skills seems to increase over time.

Use of Information Technology

Given that a purpose of the study was to see if and how information technology and telecommunications-based services could be used to support new and existing entrepreneurs in less-favoured regions of the European Community, the field survey looked into the present use of

Table 6.15 Use of information technology (per cent)

	New	Established	Progressive	Aggregate
Phone	100	99	100	99
Telex	27	37	60	35
Word processor	11	14	24	13
TTY terminal	7	5	9	5
Modem	5	3	4	3
Videotex	0	2	0	2
Computer	20	37	56	34
Bureaux	14	11	11	12
On-line	2	0	0	0.4
Document transmission	0	2	2	2

these, begining of course with the phone (Table 6.15). One firm did not have a phone and at the other end of the scale one new firm made use of on-line databases (such as the Dialog service). It was a firm producing speciality chemicals set up by former staff of a technology institute.

A remarkably high percentage had acquired a microcomputer, 34 per cent, and a further 9 per cent made use of a bureau with 3 per cent making use of both an in-house computer and an external bureau. Clearly, a large number perceived that there was a need to improve their internal practices and management control.

New firms generally made use of the various possibilities than did established or progressive firms (Table 6.16). Progressive firms had a clearly higher use of most. The payroll was the most common application except in new firms, but in all applications the number of applications rose with established firms and again with progressive firms. This

Table 6.16 Purpose for which data-processing machinery is used (per cent)

	New		Established		Progressive		Aggregate	
	Int. DP	Ext. DP	Int. DP	Ext. DP	Int. DP	Ext. DP	Int. DP	Ext. DP
Wages/salaries	33	83	82	100	96	80	76	100
Production	55	17	60	4	76	0	59	7
Sales	66	50	78	27	92	40	76	32
Distribution	22	33	37	18	40	20	36	21
General/admin.	44	17	71	36	84	20	68	32
Other	0	0	28	18	24	0	25	14

matches the indications in Table 6.12 that new firms are more dependent for information technology information on outside sources whilst established firms and especially progressive firms have acquired more internal skills. Again, as with finance for example, it takes time to acquire skills outside the core skill around which the firm was founded. Unfortunately no data were collected but it appeared from the observations of interviewers that there were a number of firms which had bought a microcomputer but were not using it. The major problem seemed to be simple changes in a software package but neither servicing nor internal skills were available.

Most small and new firms fail for financial reasons and that usually is because of poor information systems. Some training of would-be start-ups in use of microcomputers for management information might therefore prove a very effective support to new firms. An Australian study has shown that small firms which have an in-house microcomputer have higher profitability and growth in employment, i.e. expansion in business, than do firms which have not (Macdonald *et al.* 1980).

Progressive firms had a greater use of information technology and over a larger number of applications than other firms, the one 'progressive' characteristic other than the selection criteria which could be associated with these firms.

Performance

The new firm is owned (for the most part) by a young entrepreneur, most likely to be under 40. Progressive firms interestingly show a more even age distribution than established firms, most of whose chief executives are over 50 (Table 6.17). In general, chief executives are major shareholders—they are owners/managers.

Table 6.17 Average age bands and equity holdings of chief executives (per cent)

	New	Established	Progressive	Aggregate
Less than 30 years	9	3	2	4
30–35 years	25	8	11	11
36–40 years	34	15	20	18
41–50 years	27	29	20	29
51–60 years	2	26	22	22
Over 60 years	0	7	4	5
Equity holdings (mean)	67	61	55	62

There is also an apparent correlation between new and young firms and growth in employment which is shown in Table 6.18. Each firm was asked to give the employment figures for each of three years. Given that the new firms were founded in any of the years 1979–83, the growth is good. Progressive firms also showed a better growth rate. The growth in numbers of new products has been given earlier (Table 6.5).

An attempt was also made to elicit information on profitability (Table 6.19), share of home market and share of sales exported. The number of responses for the latter two was too small. A greater number gave information on their profitability. New firms, as well as having a higher growth rate in employment and in number of new products, also claimed higher profitability.

Table 6.18 Numbers employed

	New	Established	Progressive
1979	6	36	47
1981	14	37	50
1983	20	38	53

Table 6.19 Net profit as a percentage of annual turnover (no. of responses)

	New	Established	Progressive	Aggregate
Total sample no.	44	196	45	241
1979	17 (11)	10 (113)	7 (25)	10 (124)
1981	15 (22)	10 (118)	8 (23)	10 (140)
1983	15 (31)	9 (123)	7 (26)	10 (156)

Conclusions

With regard to the information needs and sources of these firms in less-favoured regions, the main conclusions are as follows.

- There was virtually no difference between new and established firms in the proportion carrying out R & D, but established firms and progressive firms at a yet higher level were more conscious of quality control. The number of R & D staff increased with age and again with 'progressiveness'.

- New ventures were, for new firms, largely the founding of the firm. Otherwise there was a progressive increase from new to established to progressive in new products (highest score), new processes, and expanded market (lowest score). There was a high rate of success.
- The major source of the new venture idea was in-house in all types with customers at a much lower instance as the next source.
- New firms had the greatest problems with finance in relation to the new venture.
- The major information need was on finance for new firms with market information a strong second priority, market information closely followed by finance for established firms and market information the major priority for progressive firms.
- The major sources of information for finance, marketing production/ process development and new products were persons inside and outside the firm, with progressive firms more dependent on in-house sources. New firms made considerably more use of market research. For information on legislation, government policies, and information technology, more formal sources of information were used.
- Of the sources of information within firms, the chief executive dominated, more for new firms, with the production manager next for new firms and the sales manager for progressive firms.
- New firms were more dependent on business and professional friends, the next highest source of information for all firms. They were also more dependent on suppliers and customers. Established and progressive firms made more use of business organisations (banks, Chambers of Commerce, etc.) but new firms made more use of technical and small business advisory services funded by the state.
- A relatively large number of established firms (37 per cent) and of progressive firms (56 per cent) had purchased a microcomputer but there were indicators of difficulty in its use.
- Progressive firms were more self-reliant, had greater use of information technology and appeared to have less financial problems than other firms.

The perceived needs of these LFR firms did not show any significant difference from those reported in Chapter 5. Entrepreneurs see themselves as having much the same needs wherever they are located. The main differences lay in the non-perceived needs—for a technology pull and for awareness and adoption of the best practice. These needs can be seen in the one major difference in information behaviour, that is, in the role of the customer as a source of ideas and as the major stimulus to innovation. This role of the progressive customer is undoubtedly a major cause of the gap between the respective poverty or richness of regions in information. There are other factors, but this one of the progressive customer does appear to be crucial in most self-generating regions in providing the entrepreneurial potential with an enhanced innovative potential and with innovative opportunity.

References

Bannock, G. (1983). *The economics of small firms: return from the wilderness*. Oxford, Blackwell.

Hemer, J. (1984). *Information networks designed to support innovation in less favoured regions of the European Community: case study in Baden-Württemberg*. Karlsruhe, Fraunhofer-Institut für Systemtechnik und Innovationsforchung, October.

Macdonald, S. *et al*. (1980). *Computers in small business in Australia*. University of Newcastle, Australia. Discussion paper no. 14.

Sweeney, G. P. (1985). *A study on information networks designed to support technological innovation in less favoured regions of the Community*. Dublin, IIRS, 6 vols.

CHAPTER 7

Characterising Regions

Earlier chapters have examined a line of thought according to which

- some regions have an innovative potential;
- other regions have an entrepreneurial potential;
- yet other regions have brought these together to give self-generated prosperity;
- this self-generation occurred because of the technical progressiveness of firms in the region, and
- this technical progressiveness occurred because a rich stock of knowledge was accumulated and disseminated to new entrepreneurs and to new ventures by the educational system and/or the traditional technical culture, existing entrepreneurs, older ventures and in particular customers in the region through an open flow of nutrient information and short cycle time in logistic information.

The larger technically progressive firm would seem to have a critical role in entrepreneurial vitality but, if one takes an economy like Denmark and even more Prato, not an absolutely essential role. On the other hand if one turns to the regions without self-generated growth, the large firms have a major influence on the lack of vitality in these regions. It is clear that, one way or another, because of its role in Western economies, the large firm is perhaps not merely an influence but a determining influence equal to entrepreneurial vitality in regional development.

The influence of the multi-divisional large national or international corporation is multiple and stems from the way in which different stages of the innovation/product cycle of a large corporation are located in different kinds of region. Large corporations indulge in a spatial division of labour which reinforces the prosperity of the centre and diminishes that of the periphery. Profit, investment in information-intensive activities and in further self-sustained growth are appropriated to the centre.

Malecki's (1981) analysis of the literature on science, technology and regional development indicates that there are three types of region. Each is the location for a different phase of the innovation/production cycle of a high-technology or science-based firm, that is, a firm which has a high dependence on its research and on being at the forefront of knowledge. These regions are the core central, the intermediate and the peripheral region.

Core Central Region

The primary characteristic is that these are the regions in which the large investment in the research results in major innovative products and in which first production of these products is carried out. They are large conurbations, often cultural centres with an attractive physical surrounding environment.

The headquarters of large high-technology industries are located in these regions with the centralised information-intensive functions of R & D, finance, marketing, corporate planning and decision-making located in the corporate headquarters or in close proximity to headquarters. The research laboratories are the centralised laboratories and carry out the higher-level research of the organisation. These may be located in the suburban (and more attractive) areas of the conurbation. The conurbation has a concentration of high-quality universities with advanced research laboratories and institutes and also tends to have a concentration of government laboratories. Located in the area are information-intensive activities in consultancy, libraries and information centres, financial institutions, government services (research, industrial development incentives, tax, regulations, tenders, and so on). Such regions have a major administrative responsibility for the management of their own economy. A large percentage of radical innovations therefore emanate from them. Production plants where first production is carried out tend to be located in the vicinity, initiating production to test market volumes and meet initial orders and these have a lower percentage of low-skilled workers than later production stages.

As a result, the conurbation becomes an attractive centre for highly-qualified staff and skilled staff including skilled production personnel. There are a wide range of job opportunities giving satisfying and well-paid work at all levels. The conurbation has a high proportion of workers in the quaternary or information sector.

The region tends to have a large number of small firms and entrepreneurs breaking off and setting up in this rich environment, new dynamic firms, a vibrant fermenting mass of ideas, innovations and firms. This dynamism may occur in relation to a single sector or to several sectors.

Malecki identifies eight regions in the United States which have these characteristics of highly innovative regions, including Los Angeles, San Francisco, Boston and New York. In only two of these is the mix of industries such that three sectors are strongly present, Los Angeles and New York.

Intermediate Regions

Multi-divisional corporations in high-technology industries dependent on major innovations both in the development of the core original corporation and in the process of takeover and conglomeration, tend to centralise the higher level of R & D and leave short-term and highly-orientated product and process development at manufacturing sites in intermediate regions. The innovation has been brought from the idea through laboratory and pilot plant phases. The final phases of product and process development take place at these intermediate sites where there is also responsibility for specific marketing of the product. There is therefore still a strong mix of information-intensive functions in the pre- and post production phases and some degree of autonomy in these functions.

These intermediate 'manufacturing' sites are also the location for corporations based in other technologies and sectors such as food and textiles and most engineering-based technologies. For these the full cycle of new product development takes place in the one location or in close proximity, from the original idea through to the finalisation of product and process development and manufacturing. Such manufacturing areas or regions tend to have a more technological orientation in universities and research institutes, of which there is a considerable concentration. These 'manufacturing' sites may in fact be distinguishable in concentrations of information-intensive functions and self-administration from core regions only in the type of industry and type of research.

Peripheral Region

Peripheral regions represent the last phase of the product cycle, the mature to declining to declined phase. In the multi-divisional corporation model they are the regions in which are located plants for the production of mature standardised products which are well established in the market place. They may, in terms of a multinational, be established in the region in order to overcome tariff or other barriers and to enter a new market, that is to gain a wider market for an established product. The production system is well proven. The dominant factor in location is cost-efficiency, maintenance of a relatively low price, lower than that which could be achieved in the central core region or intermediate region. The motivation for location are a relatively low-cost unskilled and semi-skilled labour force and lower costs of establishment. Government and local incentives provide the latter.

Purchase of components and other sub-supply tends to be that established in the earlier phases of production either in the intermediate or core regions. The low level of technology of the indigenous industry, particularly small industry, remains uninfluenced by the entry of the new production plant. Del Monte (1980) has shown that the multiplier effects of new branch plants of large firms in pheripheral areas like Campania were considerably less than more balanced areas like Scotland. Even here it is still restricted. The region may fit between peripheral and intermediate, but the more important information-intensive functions including those of the second phase are located elsewhere.

Best Technical Practice

The above description of three types of region based on Malecki does not, however, embrace all regions, and does not directly confront all the issues in self-generated growth of a self-generating region. It does not embrace industrially declining regions such as the North-East of England or the North of France which were once prosperous. Equally it does not fit a country such as Denmark or a region such as Prato which have been relatively little influenced by major science-based enterprises or large-scale mass production and the operations of multi-divisional corporations.

The missing factor is that of 'technical progress', the major determinant in creation of economic wealth (Kennedy and Thirlwall 1972). Technical progress consists of all the changes in technology and techniques which lead to new processes, new goods and new methods in industrial and distributive organisation. It is a widely embracing phrase. 'It includes of course what may be termed technological knowledge. It also includes what I call "managerial knowledge", that is knowledge of techniques of management, construed in the broadest sense, and of business organisation' (Dennison 1967). Technical progress includes innovation, the first introduction of a radical development, but it also includes the diffusion of innovation, the adoption of new technology and techniques as the best current technical practice. And it is this latter, adoption of the best practice, which is the key component. Whilst innovation is the stimulus, it is the diffusion of the innovation as the best practice which creates economic wealth.

There seem to be two modes of technical progress in its role as the most significant determinant of growth:

- The speed with which the best technical practices, once known, are adopted into production—the diffusion of innovation process. This speed creates a significant gap between those with the best practice available and those with average practice. The gap can be further widened by patents, level of current investment or inertia.
- Early identification of advances in knowledge and effective innovative utilisation of this knowledge, that is, the first use of the knowledge with commercial success.

The Japanese have made a pre-eminent practice of both modes. In doing so, they

> have by and large been able to avoid the costly and unrewarding missteps associated with the R & D effort by buying in further downstream in the innovation process, and this they have done by using and adapting knowledge that is available for anybody (Park quoted in Holm 1983).

Firms and regions which are slow in adoption inevitably lose competitive advantage.

Identification and translation of knowledge and information, together with speed of decision-making, would appear to have more impact on economic prosperity than investment in science and research as such. The world of innovation, entrepreneurial activity and of creation of economic wealth is the world of business. This is a world full of uncertainty. Policies are formed and decisions made on the basis of knowledge which is always inadequate, profit is then made on the degree to which rejected or unexpected alternatives are not encountered. One economist, Shackle, has said that

> the business of living, and within that larger whole, the business of producing and exchanging goods, essentially and inescapably involves and requires the continuous and endless gaining of knowledge. To say that there is always potential new knowledge to be gained is to say that possessed knowledge is always incomplete, unsure and potentially wrong.

Hence, as discussed in Chapter 2, Carter and Williams, in their investigation of technically progressive firms, found that what distinguished them were not characteristics associated with research or sophistication of technology but characteristics concerning information and knowledge which pervaded all sections and departments of the company. They had a strong technological orientation and a good stock of knowledge from which they gave openly to others. They nourished this with a continuing inflow of new information from anywhere and had good internal information and decision-making. They were at the centre of spatial and professional information networks. These firms were more actively in pursuit of information and knowledge than the rest. Thus they were in continuous search for the best practice, ready to adopt or buy it in order to be at the forefront of commercial success. Through the best practice they achieved and maintained their growth and prosperity.

The analogy between the information behaviour of technically progressive companies and regions with high and continuing entrepreneurial vitality, referred to earlier, is related to this factor—the search for and willingness to adopt the best practice and all the other characteristics which go with it—technological orientation, open information flow, good internal logistic information and decision-making. The technically progressive firm in which decision-making is delegated, that is decentralised, to its most relevant level, has autonomy in its various parts.

'Technical progressiveness' is virtually a cultural characteristic, a way of doing things, an attitude of mind which permeates all activity. The propensity of a region to adopt the best technical practice and to have the information identification and communication characteristics which lead to this is not immediately identifiable from economic and industrial data. The Stuttgart region within Baden-Württemberg presents a very different picture to Prato. Yet both have this propensity.

In identifying why a particular region, given certain other characteristics, has a continuing prosperity, one is left with the 'residual' method employed by Dennison (1967) and others to identify the contribution of knowledge to economic progress. That is, the contribution of knowledge to economic growth is presumed to be equivalent to what is left after the other readily identifiable causes of growth (increases in the capital stock, transfer of labour from low-productivity agriculture to higher-productivity industry, and so on) have been taken into account. This residual is massive. Depending on the period and the economy surveyed, the contribution of 'knowledge' can range from 86 to 96 per cent of growth. This contribution of knowledge is provided by the technical progressiveness of a region which results in the adoption of the best practice.

Using technical progressiveness as the key characteristic in classifying regions, let us look at regions in the terms normally used—prosperous, industrially declining and peripheral—beginning with industrially declining because these raise the most questions.

The industrially declining regions present a complex picture. Why have they declined? Most have not only been prosperous but have had strong concentrations of industry and of information-intensive functions such as in the Manchester or Lille areas. Their prosperity was built around specialisation in one sector and even though other strong sectors developed in engineering, chemicals and specialist products and services these specialised in supply to the dominant sector. In the growth phase, there was a strong level of entrepreneurial vitality and innovative development. As the region matured in its production and marketing, concentration took place, entrepreneurial vitality declined and with it innovation. The major factor was that as concentration began, possibly even preceding and leading to it, the level of best practice declined. The dominant industry and its satellites become more inward-looking, less searching and aware of what was happening elsewhere, less communicative in passing on information. The region declined not because its technologies could not be replaced or renewed. Textiles, steel products, ships, cars are still made. It was because the industries of the region became incapable of renewing their technologies and creating new economic activities.

In such regions there is a multiplicity of skills in the labour force left behind by the declining industries. Many emigrate, but others are available for employment in branch plants. These may have some higher-order functions in the assembly operations as compared to a branch plant in a Third World country. Some innovative potential is retained whilst skills are retained, but the entrepreneurial potential is a spent force. However there are currently prosperous regions dominated by one or two sectors and/or a few large firms which in fact are the industrially declining regions of the future. They behave like company towns and mirror exactly a company which is founded, grows great and then declines. Manchester, Tyne and Wear, Lille, all have passed through a cycle, a technology rather than a product cycle. Their best practice may appear to be currently good but may be seen to be declining in their centralisation of decision-making and the use of takeover for growth rather than growing by self-generated innovation. They may have lost their decision-making autonomy in this process to a more central region.

Malecki's core central and intermediate regions may be such regions or they may be self-generating regions. Where they have self-generating prosperity, they have a strong technological orientation stemming from the education system and their large engineering industry. As a result there is a wide use of the best technical practice, the larger firms, the engineering ones in particular, searching out the best practice, obtaining it through the regional research system or from outside the region. The progressiveness of these firms means that there are good linkages to smaller firms and new entrepreneurs who are 'pulled' into adopting the best practice. These also are progressive in their behaviour, and create that vibrant fermenting activity where there is higher innovativeness.

Core central regions which have all the characteristics described earlier will inevitably pass through a technology cycle if there is not the mix of technologies, sectors and information-intensive activities, and/or a strong entrepreneurial vitality and small-firm sector. Concentration and loss of autonomy in these concentrated industries will otherwise bring decline.

As regards peripheral regions, these tend to have a dominance of employment in low-technology agriculture, low-skilled branch plants and low-skilled personal services. The adoption of the best practice is low. Awareness is low. Without a technological orientation in the educational system and leadership in adoption of the best practice in customers and in the engineering industry, these regions on the periphery of Europe are technically isolated. They do not have autonomy in information-supply and even though they may have autonomy in decision-making their decisions are based on a long cycle time of information supply. That peripherality can be overcome, as Denmark and Prato have demonstrated.

Industrially declining regions include regions whose prosperity was based on the extraction of coal and the extraction and primary processing of iron ores. Such regions should probably be considered in the same category as peripheral agricultural regions. They depended on a primary resource which is now exhausted, and the primary production did not lead to a range of other industries. There has been no best practice to disseminate into other industries.

In all such regions, peripheral agricultural, industrially declining, resource-exhausted, the introduction of a branch plant to produce established and/or mature products brings about a temporary relative prosperity through job-creation but there is no impact on the technological environment and technical culture of the population. Flows of information to and from the branch plant are independent of the region. The plant is not part of a technological or sectoral mix in the region, a point which highlights aspects of the problems in carrying out analyses of statistical data. There may appear to be a mix which in practice does not produce a diversity of information flow. Furthermore, the entrepreneurial potential of the region, if such existed, is further depressed.

Any interaction with research, universities or other organisations regionally by the branch plant is at a lower level of consultancy or testing. It does not involve the mainline technology of the firm.

Information-Rich or -Poor

One thesis of this book is that the ability of a region to create new economic activities in a continuous way is directly related to its

- stock of knowledge whether to make major innovative breakthroughs or to stay at the front of the best practice;
- nutrient flow of information to create awareness of new knowledge and identify new knowledge and best practices;
- autonomy in logistic information so that knowledge of the best practice or resources to implement new ideas can be speedily obtained;
- and its entrepreneurial potential.

Various aspects of these have been discussed in this and previous chapters, often in what appears as a disjointed and repetitive manner. It has been a cumulative process, like economic growth, going around in a circular fashion but gradually building up to an identification of the factors which give a region self-generating growth or prevent such growth. From them one can construct a classification of regions which uses four headings: innovative and entrepreneurial; progressive and entrepreneurial; technology-cyclic; and, technically isolated.

Innovative and Entrepreneurial

Regions characterised as being 'innovative and entrepreneurial are Malecki's core central regions but correspond more to Los Angeles than San Francisco. They are regions with science-based and high-technology industries which produce major innovations and best practices. They tend to be large conurbations and have a concentration and dominance, compared to other regions, in decision-making in finance, business and manufacturing and often of national or regional government. As a result, they also exhibit a concentration of the information-intensive functions required to support major decision-making, in higher-level research and development, marketing, finance and information services. This concentration of information services includes internal services of an organisation as well as external ones such as consultancy in all fields, information-brokers and intermediaries, publishers, libraries, and on-line services. They tend to have a concentration of these activities in science-based but also in technology-based industries. Together with the concentration of headquarters of large organisations, there is also a high level of entrepreneurial activity in a significantly large number of smaller independent firms. As a result of the concentration of higher-level functions there is a higher level of innovative activity in new products and management/business systems. These and the consequential impact of these tend to a higher diffusion of innovations and of best technical practice in the region. They have a strong SME engineering sector but good representation of other sectors in their industrial structure. Such regions are prosperous and have a continuing and self-sustained prosperity, arising from both their innovative and entrepreneurial potentials.

In information terms, such a region is information-rich and is characterised by

- a high-level stock of knowledge which is continuously refreshed and enlarged through the research and development of products, processes and techniques in science, technology and business organisation and management and through experience.
- a rich nutrient information flow through a variety of social and professional networks which have their pivotal points within the region—scientific, technological, business/management, financial, entrepreneurial;
- a high awareness of and access to the best current technical practice with the larger firms in particular being technically progressive as well as major innovators;
- strong potential for information-intensive contact and networks based within a relatively small geographical area within which the half-hour contact potential is maintained;

- a short cycle time between demand and supply of logistic information and an autonomy of decision-making in customers and suppliers of resources;
- an entrepreneurial vitality and small-firm sector which is not dominated by large firms in any sector;
- entrepreneurial networks interconnecting entrepreneurial ventures between themselves and with customers and suppliers;
- buy rather than make policies in the larger firms which provide opportunity for new ventures and exert a strong technology pull;
- a strong flow from the stock of knowledge of the larger firms to the smaller supplier and subcontracting firms leading to a combined market-technology pull on entrepreneurial activity.

Technically Progressive and Entrepreneurial

These regions are strongly manufacturing- and technology-orientated and have a mix of sectors and sizes of firms. There is a strong SME sector within which there is a strong engineering sector. For the most part, that is in business, manufacturing and administration, there is autonomy or near-autonomy in local decision-making and information-intensive functions. These information-intensive functions operate at the level of adoption of the best technical practice and of incremental innovations and improvement of products and processes. They improve the best practice in production technology, in which many of their products lie. Research activity is shorter-term and technology- and design-based rather than science-based.

Products tend to be differentiated by the quality of their design, performance in use and in matching customer needs, and in incorporating technological excellence, and to have science-based technology incorporated in them or their production processes rather than being science-based themselves. There is a strong tradition in crafts and in design. The larger firms tend to have interaction with consultancy expertise in the higher education sector and research sector, particularly the industry or technological research institutes. Such regions tend to have more consultancy, information and technological institutes and organisations than regions other than the core regions within their countries or are themselves a central but not over-dominating region, as for example Copenhagen in Denmark.

Such regions are also information-rich. They have the same characteristics as innovative regions with some change of emphasis:

- the stock of knowledge and technical culture are of high level but more concentrated within technology-based and design-based manufacturing sectors; but it is continuously enriched through the search for the best practice and new knowledge;

- there are strong external linkages, hence the nutrient information flow is rich, creating an awareness of new technical developments and techniques and opportunities for new products;
- the larger firms are technically progressive and there is a high awareness of the best current practice and pressure to adopt it;
- the cycle time of the logistic information supply is good and there is autonomy in decision-making;
- the information-intensive contact potential is within a short time period, the half-hour contact potential;
- the entrepreneurial networks are intense and closely connected to the larger-firm customer and supplier networks;
- buy rather than make policies exist in the larger firms and the progressiveness of other customers leads to creation of opportunities, a strong technology pull on smaller suppliers and a flow of information to these suppliers.

Technology-Cyclic Regions

These are regions dominated by one or two sectors within a relatively weak engineering sector tied to the dominant sector or sectors. These regions may be at varying points on a long product or technology-type cycle corresponding to that of the dominant firms or sectors. They may therefore be on a curve of increasing or declining prosperity. Depending on the point of the curve, they may be innovative, progressive and entrepreneurial within the dominant sector or not. The small-firms sector may be larger in the earlier phase of growth, have high vitality but be strongly orientated to the dominant sector. As this dominant sector reaches maturity there is a trend to integration and concentration, causing decline in the small-firm sector. With concentration the level of best practice also declines and with it the open information characteristic of progressive firms. Entrepreneurial vitality declines through lack of nourishment.

Some regions which are technology-cyclic are dominated at an early stage by large companies and large establishments. These large companies and establishments tend to be either largely self-sufficient, that is, vertically integrated, or to deal with other large plants or companies. They may be controlled from within the region or may be externally controlled from a core region or another country. They are not technically progressive. There is a relatively small SME sector and this tends to supply local markets other than the large dominant companies. The engineering sector amongst the SMEs tends to be smaller than in technically progressive and entrepreneurial regions, but higher than in technically isolated regions. These regions tend to be two-tiered—the large firms for the most part on one level with the smaller firms on another, with little interconnection between them.

Such regions, when they reach maturity and start to decline, lack the elements necessary to generate new economic activities through the foundation of new firms. They do not have a diverse and rich flow of information and have limited opportunity for entrepreneurial innovative venture. The entrepreneurial potential is weak in technology-cyclic regions which have become industrially declining:

- The stock of knowledge may be good in terms of the technical educational system and the research carried out within this system but the linkages are to centres outside the region; there may also be a residual traditional technical culture which is frustrated in finding a local outlet.
- Larger firms tend to have closed rather than open information networks or to have their decision-making located elsewhere and there is therefore little technology pull or diffusion of the best technical practice from large to small or customer to supplier.
- The SME sector tends to be relatively small; there is not the mass of small firms and particularly small engineering firms to create dynamism from within the sector itself through nutrient information flows.
- Larger firms tend to be controlled from outside the region or are large centralised firms with a dominance of employment in the region; they do not act as customers, neither creating new economic activities themselves nor stimulating their creation by others.
- For smaller indigenous firms the logistic information supply is long or is difficult to obtain from large organisations accustomed to dealing with large organisations.

This is the region in the decline phase. In the growth phase, it might appear to be an innovative or progressive region, but the concentration of activity in and around one or two sectors is the seed of its future weakness. As the process of concentration in a few firms in the sector proceeds, openness and therefore entrepreneurial vitality decline. Silicon Valley may well be a declining region in the twenty-first century or earlier, if the larger firms grow and take over others to maintain competitiveness or protectionism grows.

Introduction of branch plants controlled from elsewhere and without virtual autonomy in information-intensive functions into such declining or declined regions adds nothing to their entrepreneurial potential, nor does it create opportunity for new entrepreneurs. Lacking information-intensive functions, they do not interact with the local industrial and other infrastructure, and thus do not provide a market and technology pull on manufacturing and service SMEs in the locality. At the best they provide low-technology subcontracting. The picture of sectoral mix or apparent engagement in more advanced technology is superficial. The nutrient information flow remains weak and the region continues to lack information autonomy.

Technically Isolated

Technically isolated regions are those in which agriculture tends to be the largest sector in employment or those formerly dependent on extractive industries. They correspond chiefly to peripheral regions but not entirely.

The overall technical culture in these regions is heavily influenced by the low technology, efficiency and quality of the agricultural sector. Indigenous industrial employment is largely in more traditional industries but at a lower level of technical practice and quality. Other industrial employment is in branch plants, including possibly large capital-intensive plants, and since these lack information-intensive functions and employ largely unskilled and semi-skilled labour, there is little diffusion of the best current technical practice into the region. There is no market or technology pull which creates a strong entrepreneurial engineering sector. The orientation of the higher-education sector and of the population in seeking education is towards the humanities and classical disciplines. The region is isolated from the best technical practice and has not within itself the technical progressiveness to search for the best practice and new knowledge and speedily adopt it. It is cut off from nutrient information flows.

There may, however, be a strong entrepreneurial potential in that the population has a large proportion of independent or self-employed people in farming, small industry and local services. Some of this entrepreneurial potential, however, is fulfilled through emigration to more prosperous areas.

The former coal- and ore-mining regions have many of the same problems. They were isolated from other technologies by the particular nature of mining and ore-processing industries, and gradually by the concentration of these industries in large corporations with remote decision-making. The skills developed were not transferable to other industries. They were introverted regions. Therefore for these several reasons they lacked technical progressiveness, innovation and entrepreneurial potential. One can see similar problems of regaining growth in Third World countries which have been led into large-scale commodity agriculture and in the process have lost their traditional skills and technical culture.

Essentially the problems of these regions stem from their being technically isolated:

- the stock of knowledge and technical culture is low;
- there are virtually no large local customers or local customers strongly linked to other and progressive regions; nutrient information flow is weak, with a lower level of awareness and opportunity and little technology and market pull;
- the logistic information cycle time tends to be long which with the lower level of skills to implement new activity reduces such potential as exists;
- the indigenous industrial sector is very largely in small firms and a strong entrepreneurial potential exists in the agricultural regions but this potential is frustrated by the low innovative potential;
- networks in these agricultural regions between entrepreneurs tend to be good but are not linked effectively to sources of information which are very largely located outside the region.

References

Del Monte, A. (1980). 'Dipendenza, proprietà e struttura organizzativa dell' imprese; il caso dell'industria elettronica Campania', *L'Industria—Rivista Economia e Politica Industriale*, 2, 275–300.

Dennison, E. F. (1967). *Why growth rates differ: post-war experience in nine Western countries*. Washington, DC, The Brookings Institution.

Holm, K. (1973). *Innovation*. Milan, International Institute for the Management of Technology.

Kennedy, C. and Thirlwall, A. P. (1972). 'Surveys in applied economics: technical progress', *Econ. Jnl*, 82(325), March, 11–82.

Malecki, E. J. (1981). 'Science, technology and regional economic development: review and prospects', *Res. Policy*, 10, 312–334.

O'Brien, R. (1985). 'Technology and industrial development: the Irish electronics industry in an international context' in Fitzpatrick, J. and Kelly, J., *Perspectives on Irish industry*. Dublin, Irish Management Institute.

Shackle, G. L. S. (1970). Expectation, enterprise and profit. London, Allen and Unwin.

CHAPTER 8

Regional Programmes

Implanting Growth Potential

Implanting in regions a growth potential which is at the moment inadequate or missing must concentrate in the long term on enhancing the technical culture through the technological orientation of the education and training system and encouraging decentralisation of decision-making in government and large corporations. Change in government is difficult, but France has been demonstrating that it can be done where there is the political will. However, to large business and manufacturing organisations, the transition from being non-progressive to being progressive is a much more difficult question in capitalist societies. Banning of takeovers to force decline or self-generated growth might be one way—if only all nations would agree. Undoubtedly, prosperity in a region or locality can only be obtained by shifting to a democratic free enterprise system away from a bureaucratic capitalist system.

In the short term but with long-term accumulation of benefit there is one major step—the adoption of a systemic innovation policy and within that as a priority measure the development of information networks within regions—which will

- extend and update the stock of knowledge;
- provide diversity in the nutrient information flow;
- shorten the cycle time of logistic information;
- and seek modes of substituting in the short term for the lack of technology pull from progressive customers

In the last two decades, and more particularly in the last decade, there have been a number of new approaches to improving the environment in which the entrepreneur exists and to increasing his ability and propensity to innovate. These have been local, because as Hull (1984) has remarked, 'national programmes of assistance to small firms can never be other than more or less schematic, and directed at particular segments of the small-firms sector'. In West Germany there are said to be 10,000 programmes of assistance offered by national and regional governments and agencies to a small-firm sector which has a bewildering heterogeneity and is a most difficult group to target. The 'metal basher' in his garage and the jet-setting cosmopolitan entrepreneur are equally members of the target group for the assistance programmes. It is only at a local level that chaos gives way to order

> The heterogeneity is still there but the number of firms is often sufficiently small to allow them to be individually known. The importance of local networks for helping small firms is precisely due to the greater scope at the local level for appreciating the specific needs of individual, not to say, idiosyncratic, firms and for matching these needs to the public programmes and indeed private resources (e.g. business services) in principle available to small firms but which they often fail to utilise.

Many of the regional services being developed are based on placing liaison officers, extension agents or liaison-animateurs in regions and localities with the function of acting as personal and informal switching centres. They develop and maintain personal contact with small firms, becoming part of the network of business and professional friends, and linking the small firms into the more formal networks of administration, research and consultancy. They often provide consultancy and advice directly but their main function is as the local centre linking the local entrepreneur networks to other local, regional and national networks. The rest of this chapter provides a brief glimpse at some of the measures being undertaken in a number of European countries. Whilst development of local networks is common to most, the context varies somewhat. In France, policy has been directed to creating a truly regional administrative and technological environment for entrepreneurial and innovative growth. In Denmark, the focus has been on a responsive servicing of the needs of small firms within a decentralised administrative structure. In other countries, the focus is on providing an interface at a local level without change to the overall national structure.

France

France has had a most wide-ranging policy of decentralisation and regionalisation aimed at creating more favourable conditions for innovation and entrepreneurial activity within the regions. This has been based on a perception of the role of information in innovation and in economic development and of the need to have stronger and more qualitative flows of information from its sources in the research and information infrastructure to smaller firms.

Although there is a complexity of agencies involved in the process of regionalisation, a central part is played by DATAR (Délégation à l'Aménagement du Territoire et à l'Action Regional). This was created in 1963. It prepares the work of the inter-ministerial committee on regional development, CIAT, the overall co-ordinating committee. In the last ten years, the focus has been increasingly on decentralisation with funds being channelled through the *contrats du Plan*, under which regional authorities receive the funds to carry out actions and implement programmes.

In practice, the ratio of funds, state to regional, being used is still very heavily biased to the state, although regional funds are increasing. However, the *contrat du Plan* and the very general provision of a law of 1982 under which 'the region is authorised to promote economic, social, health, cultural, and scientific development together with regional development' have given regions considerable power. They control the direct aids and subsidies in many areas of activity (Gaudemar 1984). A considerable range of decision-making is thus in the hands of the regional authorities, so that implementation of programmes can be carried out within the requirements and infrastructure of the regions. The process of devolution has been gradual, with central authorities and agencies taking initiatives to decentralise and set up pilot or demonstration projects and the regions gradually incorporating the various initiatives in their *contrats du Plan*.

The organisation which played a key role in stimulation and funding of initiatives for information transfer and dissemination to SMEs in the regions was ANVAR (Agence Nationale de Valorisation de la Recherche). Originally set up to provide for the dissemination and transfer of research results to industry largely through financial aid, ANVAR was decentralised in 1979 and given greater responsibility for SMEs. It now has 22 regional offices which have local decision-making on financial aid to SMEs. This action reversed the two to one ratio of its 'innovation aids' (grants) going to large and small firms. By 1982, two-thirds of the total fund went to SMEs. ANVAR provides direct aid to industry, and funds and coordinates indirect aid in support of regional information and technological services. It provides finance to all steps in the innovation process as a unitary process and gives a premium to SMEs where they use external research or consultants. It also provides finance to ARIST offices, to technological consultants of the CTI (technical centres) in regions and to other activities.

A major policy step being encouraged by DATAR and ANVAR and which is a major influence on a number of the organisations described below is the designation of 'technological poles' for particular regions, and further 'poles' which are pervasive of all sectors such as electronics and materials. For example Alsace has 'poles' for biotechnology and fine chemicals, Burgundy for food, biological and medical engineering and the Midi-Pyrénées for biotechnology and mechanical engineering.

CNRS (Centre National de la Recherche Scientifique), with its heavy concentration in the Île de France is carrying out a process of decentralisation and redistribution of its resources under plans developed in conjunction with DATAR. The decentralisation has four major objectives:

- the territorial redistribution of its facilities;
- the organisation and structuring of R & D potential;
- the support of regional development through support of industry in the regions;
- co-operation with higher-education institutions and other research organisations in the regions.

To avoid excessive dispersion of scientific resources, a structural theme is given to particular decentralisation where possible. For example, CNRS is regrouping its teams in the framework of the regional technological poles and other regional actions. Clubs have been set up on scientific themes through its Industrial Relations Committee, linking CNRS, universities and industry. GIS (groups of scientific interest) and GRECE (groups for co-operative research) have also been set up. Industrial relations officers have been placed in the regions and CNRS is giving strong encouragement to research workers to accept secondment to industry. To improve identification of expertise in its staff and laboratories and access to this, CNRS has, in association with ANVAR, created a databank 'Bank of Knowledge and Techniques'.

The Centres Techniques Industriels have traditionally provided a variety of information services with an emphasis on providing a response to enquiries which give direct immediately usable information. The CTI, traditionally national sectoral centres, have been increasingly involved in networks based on the 'technological poles' development. They are therefore placing an increasing number of technological consultants in the regions with a particular focus on providing assistance to SMEs.

From 1984, following a number of initiatives set up in different regions and of a more or less experimental nature, distribution of these initiatives in all regions is developing under CRITT (Centres for Regional Innovation and Technology Transfer). CRITT groups bring together the diverse competence of organisations in a region, public and private on either:

- themes connected to the economic and cultural charactersitics of the region or to the need for industrial reconversion; or
- technological themes in which the region has particular strength.

The objectives are to:

- raise the awareness of industry and to orientate it towards new technologies;

- to make available materials, products, procedures and workshops for innovation;
- to contribute to training and to raise the level of technical culture of industry;
- to assure the transfer of technological know-how through an inter-regional network of CRITT.

Amongst the initiatives which are being developed through CRITT in which both DATAR and ANVAR have played a role is the setting up of regional networks of technology advisors to encourage the use of research and other centres and services:

- two regional networks of technological advisors in Pays de Loire and Lorraine in microelectronics, materials and energy;
- creation and development of local offices, 'antennae', for CTI and other technology organisations;
- extension of the network of technological advisors and 'antennae' in the Grand Sud Ouest and Auvergne;
- Groups of Scientific Interest (GIS) and Groups of Economic Interest (GIE), which are encouraged by favourable tax treatment.

A central role in information services to SMEs is played by ARIST (Agences Regionales d'Information Scientifique et Technique) set up in 1973, now with 19 regional offices in Regional Chambers of Commerce who partly fund them, and co-ordinated by ANVAR. They are typically staffed by a director, one or two engineers, a documentalist and one or two secretaries, and their physical information resources consist of a basic reference library, reproduction equipment, a terminal for interrogation of databanks and databases, and lists of specialists and experts.

Another action similar in principle to the innovation clubs and other groups is the setting up of Regional Innovation Workshops to support new entrepreneurs by providing workshop facilities to develop prototypes and by providing resident engineers to give advice and information. Since their creation, these have adapted to the very diverse demands encountered and increasingly work as intermediaries for specialised information and technological consultancy services.

CFCE (Centre Française du Commerce Exterieur) has several offices in each region to provide information and advice on export procedures, legal and financial matters, market studies and support in promotions and seeking new business. It has three databases—ULYSEE, a register of exporters and their products; Telematique, aimed at the rapid dissemination of export opportunities; and MENTOR, information on world markets.

INPI (Institut National de la Propriété Industrielle) is the French patent office. It has some 15 regional centres, with which some of the original ARIST offices had close collaboration, and has created a number of on-line databases on French and European Patents.

RIO (Réseau Inter-Opportunités) is a network set up under the auspices of the Ministry for Industry to bring requests and offers in a variety of intercompany transactions—financial (e.g. sale or investment of new enterprises), commercial (requests or offers of a distribution network) and technological (product and know-how licensing). Available on-line, there are also a number of regional offices.

Overall, organisations like DATAR and ANVAR have been attempting to remove barriers to innovation by SMEs by not only decentralising decision-making and making it more accessible and personalised but also by simplifying the procedures and bureaucracy.

The main focus of action and control of the action is now shifting to the regions, and 'innovation' has become a very considerable part of regional plans and funding. Of the 21 *contrats du Plan* agreed in the first half of 1984,

> all adopt professional training actions in the priority technological fields such as electronics, recourse to external consulting by small and medium firms, modernisation of cottage industries, regional centres for innovation and the transfer of technology, assistance with exports or scientific and technical culture (Gaudemar 1984)

The regions have all decided to set up or develop regional technological centres, intended to provide the closest possible link between the existing technological research and development potential and the region's economic and social development strategy: the actions falling within the *contrats du Plan* between state and region range from the support of fundamental research to the setting up of structures for transferring technology to business:

- agreements between the regions and the national research organisations (CNRS and INRA) jointly to define the outlines for the development of laboratories located in the region and to reinforce their resources;
- construction and fitting out of research laboratories;
- setting up of university analysis centres;
- creation of regional research grants;
- creation or development of institutes of applied research as a function of the specific capabilities of the region and in relation to the requirements of the regional industrial fabric.

But above all, it is in the field of the transfer of technology and of innovation that *contrats du Plan* have allowed the most novel actions and the most spectacular progress, since all the regions have made this a priority and have taken on one or more supplementary structures:

- CRITT: almost one hundred are to be set up over the entire country;
- networks of technological advisers, responsible for contacts with small and medium-sized industries.

The *contrats* also contain important sections devoted to modernisation of small and medium-sized firms, and therefore indirectly to innovation within them. The policy rests on two observations:

- the potential for job creation will be found more and more in the small and medium-sized firms;
- their 'light' structures, which are one of their assets, also give rise to weaknesses: difficulty in taking over the results of research and technical innovation; inability to make large investments in modernisation; insufficient control of their environment and insufficient knowledge of the development prospects of the market.

This diagnosis has led the state and the regions to undertake diversified actions, in order to help the small and medium-sized firms to overcome their own handicaps:

- scientific and technical information networks;
- encouragement of *productique* investments through actions involving information, demonstration and expertise, and through assistance with investment in automation;
- partial financial assistance for recourse by the firm to external consultants;
- creation of community services such as making available advanced equipment (CAD/CAM) (Champagne-Ardenne) or databanks accessible by Minitel (Rhône-Alpes);
- development of new financial mechanisms such as regional shareholding institutions;
- support in the search for new outlets for subcontracting firms and financing of projects to develop exports.

Innovation will not automatically result from these measures, but its development may be somewhat facilitated.

In the Midi-Pyrénées (Bouvier 1984), the strategy is to set up three superimposed networks:

- a network of technological advisors;
- a network of technological support centres;
- a network of scientific and technical information and training.

There are 16 technological advisors based in the three main urban areas of the region but with a central co-ordinating office. Between them they cover specialisations in vertical sectors such as mechanical engineering and biotechnologies, and horizontal sectors such as energy, value analysis and patents. Their function is to respond to requests from firms, to visit and establish contacts with them and to link them to expertise in research laboratories.

The technological support centres being developed are a series of centres being established in the main towns of the region, each specialising in the dominant technology of the area but also 'being open to spreading technologies'. They vary between 'transfer centres' based in university faculties in Toulouse and acting as contact points for mechanical engineering and biotechnology, and a 'heavy centre' with its own laboratories in Mazamet based on the Centre Technique du Textile (ITF Sud), but with close links to laboratories in Toulouse. This is also closely linked with the two textile industry associations of Mazamet. Others are being set up in conjunction with technical high schools. The technological advisor network will work closely with this network. The two networks are aimed to overcome the relative isolation of firms and entrepreneurs outside the Greater Toulouse area.

Supporting these is the scientific and technical information network which will create awareness of new technological developments through decentralised activities based in the various industry centres. Other actions will be the formation of clubs, scientific and technical culture centres, resource centres, and so on.

A technology centre or 'technopolis' is also proposed close to Toulouse and various research centres, and which would house firms and the state administrations and agencies concerned with the activities of the technopolis.

Overall, the objectives are to overcome the 'spectacular' contrast between the research potential of the centre and the state of technology in most of the small and medium enterprises 'by a network of men and meeting places connected by modern telematic relays and psychologically linked by a sense of belonging to the same structure'.

Federal Republic of Germany

Germany, in contrast, is a federal and therefore much more decentralised state with a variety of old and more recent federal and *Land* institutions and initiatives. They are also more mixed in sponsorship: government, federal and state; semi-private, government, industry and unions; private, industry, unions and other private associations; and commercial for profit organisations. Inevitably, there are considerable variations between *Länder* in the provision of information services. The description provided here is based largely on Baden-Württemberg (Hemer 1984).

Hemer draws a distinction between 'points of contact' at which information is offered about the innovation process and aids available and at which arrangements for consultancy can be made, and 'points of consultancy' which provide information to solve technical problems.

Chambers of Industry and Commerce (Industrie- und Handelskammern—IHK), primarily contact points, are established throughout West Germany and membership is compulsory. There are 73 IHK, many with branch offices. The chambers assist firms in need of consultancy and information through meetings and seminars, contacts with research and consultancy organisations, provision of technical information and assistance in applications for financing. The IHK have three databases one of which is now on-line.

- IHK Technologiebörse (Technology exchange): This lists offers and requests for technological know-how. Traditionally available in printed catalogue form, it is also now available on-line.
- DIHT-Ko-operationsbörse (Co-operation exchange) provides a listing of domestic business contacts with a list of foreign chambers of commerce.
- Lizenzspiegel is a printed list of licence opportunities and requirements published by IHK, RKW (see below), VDI (Verein Deutscher Ingenieure) and VDMA (Verein Deutscher Maschinen- und Anlagenbau).

39 of the IHK have Innovation Consultancy Bureaux. The Rhine-Neckar IHK bureau has a staff of three, one acting as consultant, the second as information intermediary, and a secretary. In 1983, 130 firms were offered advice, of which 70 were first consultations, and 60 follow-up. A first consultation describes the services offered and firms are informed about new technologies, databanks, financing problems, possibilities of external contract research, and how to set up co-operative and licensing schemes. Analysis of the special problems of firms identifies needs and modes of fulfilling these.

RKW (Rationalisierungskuratorium der Deutchen Wirtschaft) is a non-profit membership institution sponsored by industry, scientific institutions, unions and government to provide consultancy and information services to industry, mainly SMEs, on productivity (or rationalisation) problems in the areas of engineering, business administration and labour and social management. The services to SMEs comprise referral or contact-making for consultancy, information and maintenance of contact and assistance through a consultancy project:

- state of the art surveys through literature, licence and patent searches, information about new technologies, market trends etc.;
- idea search and planning diversification;
- operation of a Co-operation Exchange, establishing contacts among firms willing to co-operate;

- assistance in organisation, management techniques, etc., through consultants (research and industrial);
- problem-solving through referral and contact-making—know-how, consultancy by specialists, R & D co-operation;
- organisation of workshops, in-plant courses and group discussions.

There are six professional staff in the Baden-Württemberg RKW, who make some 1,100 contact-making visits and 200–300 consultancy maintenance visits per year. The consultancies are arranged with research and private organisations, for which grant-in-aid may be payable.

The RKW has an intensive promotional awareness activity through daily newspapers, specialised journals, the bulletins of chambers of commerce and industrial assocations working with RKW. It has a monthly bulletin and is a publisher of monographs, textbooks and specialist periodicals.

The LGA (Landesgewerbeamt Baden-Württemberg) is a *Land* administrative organisation established to support manufacturing SMEs in the *Land* and has a Technology Consultancy and Technology Transfer Centre. The Centre acts essentially as a referral centre to research institutions and other organisations and either provides funding directly or advises on sources of funding particularly funding for research and development. In addition it has a specialist Energy Information Centre providing similar services in energy conservation, a Patent Documentation Centre, a Documentation Centre in business economics and two libraries, the larger in Karlsruhe. The two documentation centres are provided with computer terminals for on-line search.

The SfW (Steinbeis Stiftung fur Wirtschaftsförderung) is a foundation with its head office in Stuttgart. In 1982, the Baden-Württemberg State Cabinet established a Government Commissioner for Technology Transfer who became chairman of SfW, amalgamating the function of SfW to make the findings of research available to industry in the state with those of the Government Commissioner to act as a clearing-house for technology transfer and co-ordination centre for the institutions involved. The functions are broadly grouped as follows:

- transfer of information on the state of the art and on market trends;
- establishing contacts with research and development institutions;
- providing information about government funding measures.

There is a full time staff of 28 but the resources of polytechnical schools are used on a part-time basis, some 561 in all. Most are teachers acting directly as consultants but technicians and students are used for R & D work in support of the consultancy projects.

The SfW makes use of a network of sources:

- Chambers and industrial associations:
- the universities which have established contact offices for industrial firms seeking advice;
- national research centres, Fraunhofer and Max-Planck institutes, and industrial co-operative research associations.

In 1983, 1,700 research contracts and 1,400 special consultancies were carried out under the auspices of the SfW.

The information services are referral. It is indicative that, even so, 50 per cent of enquiries relate to funding programmes. The one area in which SfW appears to play a direct role is the search for potential business partners. It finds information about such partners, establishes contacts, organises joint discussions and otherwise assists in development of new entrepreneurial activities. It also uses its authority to organise discussions with banks, productivity centres and new entrepreneurs interested in setting up new businesses.

There has been a particular focus in West Germany on encouraging new technology based firm foundations, in all phases of their development. One major part of the programme which began in 1983 was the establishment of 'incubator, innovation and technology centres'. Krist (1984) describes one of these, Aachen, as an example of many different types of centre, but all with more or less the same objective.

> The technology centre in Aachen relies on a much more complicated legal and institutional organisation, than that in Berlin established in the Technical University of Berlin. A kind of regional association was established which includes as members: chamber of industry and commerce, chamber of handicrafts, university, a research institute, town and county Aachen, banks, an insurance company, and private enterprises. The association is, together with the chamber of industry and commerce, town and county Aachen, shareholder in a limited company, which is managing the center. The center is financed mainly by the shareholders and receives a subsidy of 50 per cent of the running deficit in the first three years from the state of North Rhine-Westphalia.

A short evaluation overview covering the first centres in the Federal Republic showed that the institutional and organisational arrangements are manifold and represent institutional and political innovations.

- For a long time economic policy at local and regional levels has concentrated on established and larger firms. The firm founder was left to the organisations of the private sector like chambers of industry and commerce and of handicrafts or to financial institutions. Only in the last two years have firm foundations become a topic of interest to the public administration.

- Because of the orientation of these activities towards new technologies, local and regional initiatives in the field of technology and innovation policy start to develop from the bottom. Regionally orientated institutions and activities in innovation policies had already been in existence for some time, but they were mainly started as pilot projects within the framework of federal and state programmes.
- The example of Aachen shows that many different institutions which are relevant for the economic development of the local or regional economy can work together with one objective.
- In this process many of these institutions have to take up new activities which were not before part of their remit.

If co-operation within the framework of an initiative of this type can be established, this might be an important success at local and regional level even if the direct objectives cannot be reached. It can be assumed that the possible indirect effects on the local economic climate will be of much wider importance.

> 60 centers are in some stage of action, construction and planning. If such a large number develops in a rather short time period the question of the potential for these centres becomes very important. Even if we reduce the level on which we define technology orientation, we arrive at a figure of 1 to 2% of all firm foundations in manufacturing industries which are innovative, 250 to 500 cases per annum. From this estimate it is quite clear that the objective of many of the initiatives will have to be reduced and that many centers will have to define themselves as incubator or enterprise centers in general.
>
> Taking into consideration the limited potential of technology based firms the probability that we run into a race of subsidies becomes very high (Krist 1984).

Denmark

The Technological Council, established by the state in 1973 and totally state-funded, lies at the core of the service network available to industry. A number of private, independent institutes, supported by this Council, comprise the Technological Service Network. These include the Danish Technical Information Service (DTO), the 19 ATV (Akademiet for de Tekniske Videnskaber) Institutes, the Technological Institute at Tåstrup near Copenhagen and the Jutland Technological Institute located at Århus. The latter two technological institutes each have several regional Technological Information Centres.

The ATV institutes are independent, non-profit research and development institutes affiliated to the Danish Technical Academy of Sciences. Each institute specialises in a particular technical field and carries out commissioned applied research and some basic research.

The Danish Technical Information Service (DTO) provides information services to Danish industry on a contract basis. It makes extensive use of on-line services and analyses information for clients. Having originally concentrated on technological information, DTO now finds that commercial and market information is much more in demand.

Links between universities and industry in Denmark have traditionally been poor and, despite attempts to address this problem in recent years, no concerted programme of co-operation is in existence.

The first two Technical Information Centres were established in 1971 as a pilot experiment, and the last in 1983. There are now 14, one in each county outside Copenhagen. They provide direct advice and assistance to small companies and craft industries. Each centre is staffed typically by an engineer, an economist, an artisan/crafts person and a secretary. In 1983, an evaluatory analysis (Colding 1983) was carried out of the centres, taking March as a typical month, with about 8–9 per cent of the annual total of activity. In this month there were about 1,000 individual contacts with firms, 50 per cent of which were visits to companies and half of these on the initiative of the TIC. Two-thirds of the visits were to firms of less than 10 employees. Of the visits from 'old' TICs, 56 per cent were at the request of firms whereas only 41 per cent were so from 'new' TICs. Thirty visits took place as part of a survey collecting information for the register of sub-suppliers of the Danish Association of Master Smiths. Ten per cent of the visits were to entrepreneurs in some phase of start-up. There were 21 information meetings attended by more than 800 participants. Of the 265 self-initiated visits, 40 per cent led to further work either in delivery service or by referral elsewhere. Almost all, 96 per cent, of the 213 visits resulted in further work. Seven hundred problems or opportunities were dealt with. Of these, 400 were dealt with directly by the TICs, 393 through the free advisory service and 11 through the paid service. In the other 289 cases, the TICs acted as mediators between the firms and relevant experts. About half the referrals were to the technological network as follows:

Technological Institute Copenhagen	30%
Jutland Technological Institute	18%
ATV Institutes	3%
Local centres	9%
Business concerns	15%
Private consultants outside the local area	5%
Others	20%

The Netherlands

A very small country in area, The Netherlands does not have the decentralisation developing in France or the distinct regions of Belgium. Most regional activities tend to be central or national ones and where appropriate they have regional offices.

A number of organisations play prominent roles in advising industry, including the government-funded Industrial Consulting Service (RND), the applied scientific research organisation (TNO), the three regional microelectronics centres, the Federation of Netherlands Industry (VNO), and the 'Kleinnood' Foundation. The Netherlands Organisation for the Promotion of Information Procurement (NOBIN) advises the government on information policy. In 1983 NOBIN identified 300 government-financed services delivering information products to industry and some 12,000 services which could be called information-transfer agencies, ranging from market research companies to engineering consultancy firms. Although none of the services was essentially regional in character, the smaller agencies tended to operate on a local basis.

RND offers a consultancy service—essentially techno-economic information and advice—principally to small and medium-sized firms. It operates through regional offices spread throughout The Netherlands and has developed links with the universities and with the main Dutch applied scientific research organisation, TNO. Government policy aims to improve TNO's links with industry by greater interaction between TNO and RND and by increasing its direct interaction with small industry.

Improved interaction between universities and industry is also a feature of government policy. Traditionally the universities' links with industry have been mainly with large companies. Mechanisms introduced to improve links with smaller firms include a regional system of transfer points at the major technical universities. These act as contract research liaison offices and as information centres. Some offices of RND and TNO are also designated as transfer points.

The three regional microelectronics centres in Delft, Twente and Eindhoven, in collaboration with the technical universities there, aim to improve awareness in SMEs concerning changes and threats of microelectronics, and to supply information and advice on the application of microelectronics in such firms.

Government funds have been provided for innovation-orientated background research programmes to increase expertise and knowledge in areas regarded as important to the development of Dutch industry.

It is believed that a wide variety of local initiatives by local authorities, chambers of commerce, and so on, have been initiated but it is extremely difficult to identify them. One such initiative was taken in 1982 when the Federation of Netherlands Industry (VNO)—the main Dutch industry confederation—made available an information and advisory service to young people wishing to start a business. This was started in Groningen and later spread to South Holland.

In the late 1970s some 25 firms in the Netherlands established the 'Kleinnood' Foundation to give free assistance from large firms to small entrepreneurs. Retired executives provide an advisory service to small firms. Firms benefiting are mainly rural-based and tend to be existing rather than start-up operations. Developments akin to the local enterprise agencies in the United Kingdom have not yet emerged.

A project proposed by NOBIN is to provide small firms with a computer and information package for a six-month period, to include software for accountancy and general business organisation plus a videotex facility which could access information in government departments.

Belgium: Flanders

In Belgium, the three regional governments of Flanders, Wallonia and Brussels are each responsible for regional economic expansion. In Flanders, each of the five provinces has a Regional Development Authority which has promotion of innovation as a specific responsibility (Neeson 1984).

The Flemish regional government policies are aimed primarily at the diffusion of new technology in microelectronics, biotechnology and new materials throughout all individual sectors. To promote these new technologies, technology days and technology exhibitions are held, a microelectronics centre has been established to help SMEs incorporate microelectronics in their products, and five 'technology groups' of firms have been set up in the fields of aerospace, medical technology, robotics and office automation, agricultural industry and energy. These attempt to promote co-operation including through joint research projects, and are similar to the French CRITT.

The Regional Development Authorities have set up a joint technological prospecting service, the Technological Innovation Cell Flanders. This has the function of surveying new technological developments in metal, textile, food and chemical industries and analysing this information for its potential to Flemish industry. TIF also undertakes specific information analysis for enterprises and acts as a referral centre to university and other expertise.

The Limburg RDA concentrates on a 'business proposal' service, mainly of licensing opportunities, on the one hand disseminating offers of licences and so on, and on the other searching for opportunities for individual firms.

United Kingdom

Information for industry is provided by the Research Associations, by a variety of schemes under the auspices of the Department of Trade and Industry, by the Chambers of Commerce, by Enterprise Agencies and by COSIRA, the Council for Small Industries in Rural Areas. There are no specific regional programmes.

The Research Associations carry out co-operative industrial research in different sectors and offer a range of information services, from enquiry answering and referral to information analysis, document delivery, current awareness and consultancy. These services are mainly used by larger firms and by both large and small firms in geographical proximity. For local smaller firms, research associations provide referral for a wider-than-sectoral range of commercial, technical and market information. Some Research Associations operate schemes for industry under contract to the Department of Trade and Industry. The most pertinent are the various schemes operated by PERA, the Production Engineering Research Association:

- The Manufacturing Advisory Service (MAS) provides free up to 15 man-days' work by specialist advisers to help large firms improve their manufacturing efficiency. A second advisory project of up to 15 man-days' work is provided at half-cost. Specialists are selected from 300 consultants, technical centres and research associations which are registered with MAS.
- The Technical Enquiry Service (TES) is a scaled-down version of MAS designed especially for small firms, whereby a firm can have up to four technical enquiries answered within an overall limit of 5 man-days' work for any one firm.
- The Quality Assurance Advisory Service is offered as an extension to MAS and again a scaled-down version is available to help small firms improve their product quality.

The Department of Trade and Industry in addition promotes schemes through the Design Council (the Design Advisory Service); the British Overseas Trade Board; and the Small Firms Service. The British Overseas Trade Board provides computerised export intelligence services through its ten regional offices, covering export opportunities, guidance on selling particular goods and services in particular markets, and information about specific overseas companies. The Small Firms Service provides information and advice for owners and managers of small businesses. Simple enquiries are referred to appropriate information sources and complex problems are passed to a Small Firms Counsellor—

an experienced businessman likely to have faced a similar situation himself. The information service and first explanatory counselling sessions are free but a modest fee is charged for subsequent counselling. The 11 Small Firms Centres and 50 Area Counselling Offices are spread throughout the United Kingdom.

The Chambers of Commerce function as an information point on local industry to overseas enquirers and provide enquiry answering, referral, and some degree of statistical searching and document supply. Their importance is due to strong links with local firms, a relatively extensive network and expanding international linkages.

In recent years there has been a significant increase in information intermediary services provided by university libraries and university departments, mainly in the specialist areas of the particular university with no particular regional dimension. Many polytechnics provide an industrial information centre for local industry with a full range of services, including liaison in some cases. A number of institutions (at least 35 universities, many polytechnics and a smaller number of further education colleges) finance their own Industrial Liaison Bureaux, but mainly operating on a relatively small scale.

Many lcoal authorities and local initiatives include an element of information, mostly aimed at assisting the start-up of new firms.

There are some 160 Enterprise Agencies throughout the United Kingdom, funded and staffed mainly by the private sector. They owe their origin to the initiative of large firms willing to spare resources such as land and managerial staff. Their activities typically include: counselling and training in management skills using high-calibre, seconded staff from larger private firms; an investment marriage bureau to link small firms with potential private sources of finance and skills; an action programme to extend the availability of small, cheap business premises; marketing advisory services; and information about government aid schemes. Small Business Clubs are common in most regions, offering information through monthly magazines, buyer's guides, and monthly meetings, exhibitions and seminars.

COSIRA is government-funded and provides information, advice, counselling, training, loans and factory units to any manufacturing and service industry employing less than 20 in rural areas. Great emphasis is placed on local knowledge and assistance, with a representative in every county in England and over 100 professional experts in the field. This service is usually provided directly on the small firm's premises and is highly regarded by its users.

Ireland

The dominant sources of information for industry are the Institute for Industrial Research and Standards (IIRS) and, in export marketing, Coras Trachtala Teoranta (the Irish Export Board). The Industrial Development Authority is the funding agency and has a coordinating role in industrial development. SFADCo (otherwise known as Shannon Development) is responsible for industrial and tourist development in the Mid-West Region. All the universities, except the two Dublin ones, and the two National Institutes for Higher Education have industrial liaison officers. Trinity College, Dublin, is building an Innovation Centre, and University College, Dublin has just completed a University-Industry Centre.

IIRS is the national industrial technology institute and provides services in product development, technical consultancy, laboratory investigation and testing and analysis. It offers expert advisory services in a number of fields, and is also the national standards organisation. It is probably unique in Europe in providing a full coordinated range of information and consultancy services from one organisation. Its activities comprise:

- techno and techno-commercial enquiry and document delivery services;
- on-line intermediary and intermediary training services;
- database development (an industrial database, a pilot project in Videotex);
- programme of courses and workshops in technologies and techniques;
- *Technology Ireland*, the national technological magazine;
- liaison advisory service with offices in each region;
- product search and product licensing;
- inventions evaluation and patent support.

Mechanisms developed in recent years to support small firms (under 50 employees) include:

- Small Firms Development Fund: up to five-days free consultancy by IIRS experts, particularly to initiate new product development; this fund has been extended in the Mid-West and Gaeltacht (Irish-Speaking) localities in cooperation with SFADCo and Údarás na Gaeltachta.
- Graduate Placement Programme: initially started in the Mid-West in conjunction with SFADCo, this programme is now funded on a national basis by the Youth Employment Agency. The objective is to place each year some 60 science and engineering graduates in small firms which had not previously employed a graduate for engagement in non-routine activities.

More recently, following the White Paper on Industrial Policy, one-stop shops have been set up in each region. In these, the Industrial Development Authority provides a referral service to the appropriate state agencies. The regional liaison advisors of IIRS operate out from these, carrying out the technological animateur and direct information service roles to smaller firms. Coras Trachtala Teoranta is also to provide services from these centres. It has a large number of offices abroad and three regional offices in Ireland and is the major source of information on export markets.

The Industrial Development Authority has a range of funding programmes to assist in start-up and development of small firms, including feasibility study grants and product and process development grants. It is in process of decentralising decision-making and administration of its funding programmes for small firms to its regional managers and regional committees.

SFADCo is the only autonomous regional development authority, carrying out functions for small firms in the Mid-West region similar to those of IDA in other regions. It has, however, undertaken a number of initiatives unique to the region. Its involvement with IIRS in the Small Firms Development Fund activity and the Graduate Placement programme has already been referred to. It has a Business Advisory Service, providing business management and marketing advice directly or by referral to other services. The Microelectronics Applications Centre helps firms to be in a position to take maximum advantage of microelectronics developments, in particular assisting in the development of new products embodying microelectronics. It aims to become self-funding. The Innovation Centre was set up as a 'one-stop shop' particularly to help new entrepreneurs to identify new products and develop their business. Incubator factory and workshop facilities have been provided with common services.

An example of links between universities and small firms is provided by University College, Galway, which has established eight 'incubator' units. A university 'tutor', who may have an interest in the company, introduces the potential entrepreneur to relevant services, such as library, computer, marketing expertise, and laboratories. Office accomodation, complete with telephone, telex, microcomputer facilities and secreterial staff, is provided. After a maximum of two years, successful projects will move to commercial premises.

Austria

Although small, Austria is a federal country with nine provinces, and a regionalised structure for many institutions. An exception was the Industrial Research Promotion Fund (Ratz 1984). However, when an analysis was carried out of the geographical distribution of its grants, there was a clear bias towards Vienna, and outlying provinces were distinctly disadvantaged.

As a result, more intensive promotion campaigns were undertaken in the provinces and some provincial governments entered into agreements with the central fund to the effect that firms located in a region could receive a supplementary grant from the provincial government. Many more grants are now paid to provincial firms.

The most important step to overcome the disadvantages of provincial location was the creation of the post of 'Innovation Agent' at nearly every provincial Chamber of Commerce. Their function is one of consultancy in relation to R & D projects and their commercialisation. *Inter alia*, they assist firms to draw up their applications for funding, source expertise for firms and develop the information network for firms in their province. Ratz (1984) is of the opinion, based on the experience of the development of this provincial network, that

> the demand for a regional approach may be nearly as important as in any big country, because the gaps to be bridged are rather psychological than geographical. To solve this dilemma cooperation with bodies already regionalised must be sought—regional governments, chambers of commerce, banks etc. The only important thing is to become integrated in a network that already functions.

Sweden

The Royal Commission on regional policy expressed the view in 1984 (Eriksson 1984) that competitiveness rather than jobs created will be the key concept in the future. Whilst regional policy must establish an overall reduction in production costs where there is severe regional unemployment, two further actions are crucial in order to stimulate innovation:

- SMEs in these regions must be given the same access to venture capital as firms in other regions;
- they must have ease of access to professional advice in matters such as marketing, management, product development and so on.

The Regional Development Funds of the northern part of the country are therefore to be increased. Each county has a fund financed previously in equal parts by the state and the county. They work with manufacturing firms of less than 200 employees which were profitable or expected to be so. Entrepreneurs with a business idea can be helped to start up or with marketing, patents, licensing and so on.

The county boards, in a further decentralisation move, will also be able to establish 'competence centres' in the regions and to strengthen the northern universities of Umeå and Luleå. The centres will have a twofold mission:

- to act as intermediaries between small firms, on the one hand, and, on the other, universities, research laboratories, research institutions, big firms and other small firms;
- to provide consultancy from their own expertise in the process of adapting and/or adopting new technologies according to each firm's needs.

The purpose is to develop a counter-competence in the regions as against the present concentration of information-intensive activities in the bigger cities.

Sweden, like many other countries, has carried out a campaign to alert small and medium engineering firms to the possibilties of incorporating microelectronics in their products. It began with a publicity campaign followed by technical presentations at local groups funded by the county regional development funds. Visits were then made to firms which expressed an interest and companies could then apply for a small grant to investigate the potential of introducing microelectronics into their products. Of 200 companies visited, 66 firms used the grants in 1981–2. In an evaluation of the project, 44 firms were visited:

- nine had competence before the campaign but three had undertaken further development work as a result;
- 11 had obtained technical benefit;
- six had got new important contacts;
- 14 had been stimulated into working with electronics as a possibility for their product development;
- three had increased employment and turnover in Sweden (and one in West Germany).

The evaluation showed that better identification of 'target' companies before the campaign would have improved the rate of success. On the other hand, the campaign might have alerted other firms where the results were not yet tangible.

The evaluation of the Swedish microelectronics awareness programme is of a national programme, although it was funded from regional development funds. It is a type of activity which in countries like France is carried out within a more regional framework.

Evaluation of Networking

Little evaluation of the effectiveness of regional information network systems or extension liaison systems working with small and medium enterprises has been carried out. There has been some evaluation of agricultural extension systems, the US Agricultural Extension Service being the first and the 'role' model for all agricultural and industrial extension services.

At the Six Countries Programme Workshop in Limerick, in 1984, a project was described which in effect gave an evaluation of a local liaison-animateur, a maker and a user of networks. Hull (1984) reported on research in West Germany 'on how local institutional arrangements affect the delivery of assistance, both material and immaterial, to small independent firms to help them tackle impediments to their growth'. The research project is founded on the 'best case' approach, the best case in four localities studied. It is not *per se* concerned with innovation but with 'how do you get through to firms with advice and assistance'. Problems come in 'constellations of several dimensions' so that an innovation problem for example may manifest itself as a capital-finance, skilled labour shortage and management problem. The four regions selected were:

- the county of Borken, a rural periphery on the Dutch border, with a population of almost 300,000 and 210 inhabitants per square kilometre;
- the city of Paderborn, a medium-sized town with central place functions, population 100,000 and 610 inhabitants per square kilometre;
- Oberhausen, an old industrial agglomeration economy in the Ruhr, population 230,000 and 3,000 inhabitants per square kilometre;
- Hamburg, a major regional centre with high levels of public and private service provision, a population of 1.6 million and a density of 2,610 per square kilometre.

In each area, all firms of 10–200 employees were surveyed by postal questionnaire and a total of 105 interviewed face-to-face. The interviews were to specify the kinds of problems met with and to identify the 'actors' contacted by the firms. The principal actors mentioned were then interviewed together with further ones brought in to assist the firm by the first-named actors.

Table 8.1 shows the percentage change in employment among the firms at the four sites during 1974–80. Borken's firms and to a lesser extent Paderborn's performed better, and Oberhausen and Hamburg were consistently worse. Locality seemed to be the dominant factor in these differences, but further analysis using the percentage of firms who contacted a single actor showed that the differences were due to certain actors.

Why did Borken, the 'best case', perform so well? It is a peripheral rural county with a 100-km border with The Netherlands and long an object of regional aid, and with 30 per cent manufacturing employment

Table 8.1 Surveyed firms' employment change 1974–80

	1974–6		1976–8		1978–80	
	(%)*	No. of	(%)*	No. of	(%)*	No. of
Borken	14.7	(97)	21.8	(103)	18.8	(108)
Paderborn	11.8	(36)	13.1	(37)	8.2	(38)
Oberhausen	5.7	(35)	−0.8	(37)	3.8	(37)
Hamburg	5.7	(211)	4.6	(217)	0.7	(234)
All sites	8.6	(379)	9.4	(394)	6.4	(417)

* Percentage change in total employment among surveyed firms extant throughout each sub-period.
Source: Hull (1984).

Table 8.2 Cumulative percentage of interviewed firms with at least one contact

Number of contacts	Borken	Paderborn	Oberhausen	Hamburg
At least				
1	100	83	88	78
2	81	67	55	51
3	56	46	33	19
4	49	36	22	17
5	28	15	11	12
6	21	10	—	—
7	14	—	—	—
(Firms with no contacts (%))	—	16	11	22
Average number of contacts	3.49	0.58	2.11	1.77

in clothing and textiles. The striking difference between Borken and the rest was the frequency with which firms contacted external actors, as Table 8.2 shows. Forty-three per cent of the firms in Borken had contacted the County Development Agency, 36 per cent the County Savings Bank and the same percent the local Labour Office; 25 per cent contacted both the Agency and the Bank and 11 per cent both the Agency and the Labour Office. These three actors appeared to be at the core of a wider network spanning both public and private institutions in the county and beyond, national and regional government ministries and agencies and specialised consultancies and other organisations. The County Development Agency has been the principal actor but none of the three has any formal characteristics which would set them off from others.

There are similar banks and labour offices in other regions. The Borken Development Agency has been run in the last ten years by a single professional with more recently two junior assistants and two secretaries. Hull, in giving a description of the agency director and his mode of operation, provides a description of what is probably a model intermediary or liaison-animateur.

> Borken currently has some 235 industrial establishments, of which roughly 140 fall into our category of small independent manufacturing firms; there are less than a dozen establishments employing 500 or more persons. The agency's director of the past ten years recognised very early on that there was little practical purpose in relying on a policy of external acquisition: ever more localities were pursuing a shrinking number of major mobile investment projects, and the comparatively modest financial and other advantages which Borken might be able to offer could easily be exceeded by other contenders. What Borken had was an industrial economy dominated by small, typically family-owned industrial firms, and it was upon these firms that he chose to place his bets. Today, his strategy would be called 'mobilising indigenous potential'; at the time, it had no particular name—it simply seemed the obvious and only thing to do.
>
> When he arrived in the early 1970s, he was new to the locality (but not to the wider region; understanding and accepting the local 'mentality' undoubtedly counts for much in these things). He set about the systematic cultivation of a relationship with as many industrial firms as possible, particularly the small- and medium-sized independents. His notion was that he would be able to do little for 'his' firms until he had won their trust and confidence. It became his aim to contact every one of his firms at least once a year. Typically he would go out to visit the firm, to see for himself how the firm was operating in practice; he would often visit firms with no other ostensible reason than to pass the time of day. As a relationship developed with each firm, it would be the firm which spontaneously contacted him for advice.
>
> He seems never to have sought to impose his services on firms, but always to have insisted on his availability if they felt he might be useful. He has never thought to tell firms what to do, but tries to have them talk through their problems with him until the appropriate solution emerges. He has tried to be not so much a 'father figure' as an understanding, competent and neutral friend and discussion partner. When necessary, he will help firms identify what their problems are,

help them to tackle their problems and help them to identify and mobilise the external resources or finance which they are lacking.

His role is best described as that of an 'intermediary', for much of what he does is to bring together firms needing solutions to problems and the institutions, be they public or private, local or national, which seem likely to be able to supply solutions. It is in this role of intermediary that he has built up a network encompassing firms and problem-solving institutions, a network in which he is largely the hub holding the whole together.

The role of intermediary implies not only building and maintaining a relationship of trust with firms; in many instances it implies the same with respect to the institutions upon which his firms need to draw for resolving their problems. Thus he cultivates specific, whenever possible personal, relationships with local governments, banks, regional and national ministries, trade associations and various commercial firms supplying specialised business services (e.g., engineering consultancies). Since much of the work involves helping a firm identify and mobilise financial resources of one kind or another, his contacts with departments and agencies of local, regional and national government as well as with banks (both local branches and regional headquarters) are probably his chief preoccupation.

It is important to stress that, unlike many of his contemporaries, both inside Germany and without, he is no mere 'sign-post' for his firms; he does more than simply send out leaflets describing this or that public programme of assistance or provide addresses of relevant institutions. His style is more 'hands-on', but consciously with 'kid-gloves'. When the case allows and warrants it, he will actively help the firm define its problem and then help identify ways of tackling it. When it comes to actually mobilising external resources, he will directly assist the firm in formulating applications and submissions, even to the point of accompanying and representing the firm in difficult negotiations with other parties. Similarly, where a firm's mobilisation strategy risks falling foul of conflict between external contacts whose joint efforts are necessary for success, he will try to mediate an amenable solution.

It should be apparent from this that the role of intermediary is a delicate one at times. As much of the objective may be to act as firms' 'advocate', the need not to jeopardise relations with external actors who will continue to be important to him and other firms in the future requires diplomatic skills and an acute sense of realistic room for manoeuvre. In its turn, this bids caution against assisting any and every firm with any and every problem; here, too, a 'nose' for what is good and worthwhile is important in order not to endanger future relations with external actors.

It is difficult to give more than a taste of how and why the Borken network to assist small firms appears to work so relatively well. Much has been left unsaid, and no doubt too much attention has been accorded the County Development Agency and its long-standing managing director; yet all of the evidence which we have been able to assemble and sift thus far points to the role of this institution and actor as a central ingredient in the explanation for why Borken's independent manufacturing firms have achieved such an enviable job-generation record in recent years.

Conclusion

In many of the programmes there is a common theme—that creation of self-generated growth in regions is highly dependent on informal and local networks of people. If the quality of the nutrient information is to be enhanced, then there must be a local personal influence from the research or technological or other organisation whether this is regional or national. If the response is to be such as to provide an efficient supply of logistic information then decision-making on provision of resources and inputs must be local or apparently local. The local interface or agent who animates the entrepreneur to develop and the infrastructure to respond to his needs is not, however, any man or woman. He/she is a very social person who becomes the star communicator or gatekeeper, known to everyone, easily accessible and very well connected into other networks. He/she is the referral to the formal sources and networks. These formal sources to be used however must adapt to the real needs of the entrepreneur and small and medium enterprises, and be aware of the specificity and urgency of these needs.

References

Åsell, P. (1984). 'Excerpts from the evaluation report concerning the Swedish micro-electronic campaign "The Little Giant"'. Six Countries Workshop, Limerick.

Bouvier, F. (1984). 'Setting up of technological networks: theory and practice'. Six Countries Workshop, Limerick.

Colding, T. (1983). *Analysis of the activities and results of the Technological Information Centres: one month's collected activities*. Copenhagen, The TIC Coordination Commmittee.

Eriksson, A. (1984). 'Regional policies in Sweden—from job creation in regional development'. Six Countries Workshop, Limerick.

Guademar, J. P. de (1984). 'Regional measures backing up innovation in France: some food for thought'. Six Countries Workshop, Limerick.

Hemer, J. (1984). *Information networks designed to support innovation in the less-favoured regions of the European Community: a case study in Baden-Württemberg*. Karlsruhe, Fraunhofer Institut fur Systemtechnik und Innovationsforschung, October.

Hull, C. J. (1984). 'Local assistance networks and small firms growth'. Six Countries Workshop, Limerick.

Krist, H. (1984). 'The promotion of new technology based firm foundations as part of regional innovation policies'. Six Countries Workshop, Limerick.

Neeson, V. (1984). 'Transfer mechanisms for stimulating technological innovation in the Flemish region'. Six Countries Workshop, Limerick.

Ratz, K. (1984). 'How to link up central and regional policies on research promotion and information networks'. Six Countries Workshop, Limerick.

CHAPTER 9

A Systemic Innovation Programme and Network

Local regions rather than nations are the environments in which entrepreneurs actually exist and try to set up their new firms. In Chapters 5 and 6, the nature of information flows and information behaviour was set out with the results of empirical studies on small firms and their information needs and sources. If there is to be self-generated growth in regions presently without it, then it is the entrepreneur and his peers who are going to make the decisions which will create growth. Government and its agencies can create the environment in which entrepreneurs will prosper, but they cannot make the decisions to invest, to innovate, to start or to expand. Only the entrepreneur does this. He is the central figure. Innovation is entrepreneur-led.

In developing the concept of a systematic innovation policy after a decade of workshops and studies, the Six Countries Programme has recognised this central role of the entrepreneur. Direct support to the entrepreneur is one of the principles which should underlie an innovation policy. Another is that it should create or contribute to the creation of a technical culture. The task of creating a technical culture must necessarily be part of the education programme, and is not dealt with in this book. Nevertheless, any programmes undertaken should have a strong technological orientation so that the awareness of the need to adopt the best technical practice is heightened through a nutrient information flow. The third principle is the removal of barriers to entrepreneurial investment and expansion. In the context of this particular book, the main barriers are the long cycle time in obtaining information, or decisions, for decision-making by the entrepreneur and lack of diversity and current awareness in the information flows.

To be systemic, each action in an innovation programme should be undertaken in the context of the entrepreneur's need and mode of behaviour and the context of the total environment in which he lives. Each action should complement and reinforce other actions rather than being a unique or unilateral action. An innovation programme should be multifunctional and multidisciplinary crossing traditional boundaries by adopting a total system approach and taking account of the way in which innovative creativity and information and technology transfer actually occur.

An information network designed as a first stage but also as a major part of an innovation programme should take account of the characteristics of the entrepreneur and of the regions within which he naturally gives and receives information.

Entrepreneurs have a heavy reliance on personal and informal channels of communication. They make strong use of personal, business or professional friends. The personal channels are heavily localised, that is they are people in the same locality or region as people who contact them, such as representatives of suppliers. They use these as a final source. They browse more, especially through informal literature such as trade journals and suppliers and competitors literature. In particular, they browse through conversations and meetings, deliberately sought meetings or chance meetings.

Overall, they make relatively little use of formal sources of information, whether higher-quality publications, libraries, on-line systems, or research institutions. Nevertheless, the use of the formal infrastructure does increase where such use is made easier and more local in access. A major obstacle is that information from the formal infrastructure tends to be too costly and too slow in delivery. However, use of more formal sources tends to increase with the level of education and as the firm is more orientated to the higher technological and science-based sectors.

In innovative and progressive regions, the client or customer is a stronger source of information than in other types of region, and provides a major, even crucial, input to innovation and adoption of the best technical and managerial practice. In these regions, needs for technical information are largely fulfilled by these sources and to a lesser extent by suppliers. In other regions, particularly technically isolated, the supplier is a more frequently used source.

The information needs of the entrepreneur as perceived by him have two dominant characteristics. They cover all aspects of manufacturing business and they are biased towards specific and immediately usable information—that is, they concentrate on logistic information relevant to the decision-making problem.

Finance, both access to it and management of it, and market information are the dominant perceived needs of entrepreneurs in all types of region. Management of finance is an aspect of the lack of management skills in most entrepreneurs. Access to finance and identification of all appropriate sources are major needs of entrepreneurs in all types of regions, but the entrepreneurs in the more technically isolated regions have greater difficulty in identifying the source and in obtaining access. Management of finance and of the financial aspects of the business is a major need of most entrepreneurs due to their lack of management expertise. It tends to be at a lower level in technically isolated regions due to the lower level of technical practice pervading these regions. The need for better practice is, however, perceived fairly widely.

Market information is the other dominant need, and is reinforced by the focus on new ventures. Indeed, the lower perceived need for technical information is in essence lost in the dominant need to find new products and new markets. Technology *per se* is not a perceived need. In more progressive regions, much of the need for market, new product and technical information is largely filled by clients and customers. The urgency of the need is seen in the continuing demand for more specific information.

Non-perceived information needs are, however, much more significant. In them lie the differences between innovative and progressive regions and other regions. The dominant influences lie in the overall environment and technical culture of regions, the levels and extent of the technological mix and the pervasiveness of the best technical practice. Clients and customers are a major innovation pull in more progressive regions because they are more demanding in technical, performance and delivery specification. The entrepreneurial drive, as evidenced by the number undertaking new ventures and the success achieved in these, is an expression of the need for a mix of information which will result in further new ventures. Innovation could be at a much higher level. The major non-perceived needs are for a richer nutrient information flow, a technology pull and a logistic information provision all of which will in a cumulative manner result in a higher-level adoption of the best technical practice.

Most information passes from firm to firm, from client to entrepreneur, from entrepreneur to entrepreneur and a programme for self-generated growth must recognise this.

Government policies and programmes are inevitably confined to the government-funded infrastructure of research, education, information-providing services and financial grant or loan services. Their impact on local services is indirect, through attitudinal change and stimulating contact and support from private organisations. For the direct services to have their intended effect, the structures and modes of operation of government-funded activities need to adopt characteristics analogous to those of a technically progressive firm:

- responsiveness and openness in information provision;
- decentralisation of decision-making in such a manner as to shorten the cycle-time;
- localisation of the interface, on a person-to-person basis between information-providing services and the decision-making of the entrepreneur so that, whether national or regional, the service operates as though it were locally based.

In other words, each service should be geared to serve the entrepreneur and be anxious to overcome barriers between it and the entrepreneur.

The one known programme which had such a systemic approach was that of the US Department of Agriculture. Although this had the appearance of operating within one sector, it in fact had characteristics of a service to small business operating within a wide product area, with a wide spread of climatological and other conditions and directed to a diversified target population widely scattered across geographical distances. This service integrated the various elements of information provision.

- the creation of a technical culture amongst farmers through an education and training system which provided skills and a wide appreciation of technologies relevant to agricultural development;
- dissemination of new technical developments and practical research results through the extension agent or county agricultural officer—the local men—specialist field experts and leaflets and handbooks which gave the specific data and information;
- creation of informal networks between farmers at a local level through courses, clubs and informal meetings;
- fast response to problem-solving through the extension agent from the laboratory and research infrastructure;
- from feedback through the extension agent and problem-solving activities, identification of needs for longer-term applied and basic research.

The system reversed the more common approach to research as starting with basic or fundamental research and progressing through applied research to development of new products or techniques. It commenced with the actual problems and needs of the farmer and proceeded from these through development to applied to fundamental research. It had another significant characteristic in that there was virtually equal funding given to the information-dissemination/interface activity and to the research activity. Most important of all, it operated at a local level through the personal informal contact of the extension agent with the individual farmer. The economic justification has been seen in the results. A similar approach to information provision to SMEs in Europe could achieve a similar economic result. The information, expertise and best practice is available in Europe, the problem lies in its transfer to the entrepreneur and his SME.

A Model Information Network

A model information system which can be flexibly adapted to meet the needs of differing structures and political systems is set out below. It is a social network system, dependent on personal and social contact, but is also very dependent on the conclusion of Hull, having seen an effective intermediary in operation: 'Our basic proposition is that how resources are harnessed contributes independently of their form and volume to their effectiveness.' Good people can make even a bad structure and inadequate resources work well. The model network is put forward as a model but also as an aid to people working in regions who would like to tune up their systems and structures rather than attempt the impossible immediate restructuring for long-established institutions. It is based not only on the various indicators and evidence presented in earlier chapters but also on initiatives and programmes described in Chapter 8 which seem to fit this evidence optimally and harmoniously.

The Network

The overall layout of the network is shown in Figure 9.1. Each of the points can be considered as a node or intelligent switching centre, carrying out processing itself and providing a direct service, but also switching messages to other nodes and for further processing. The function and operation of each of these nodes is described in the following sections.

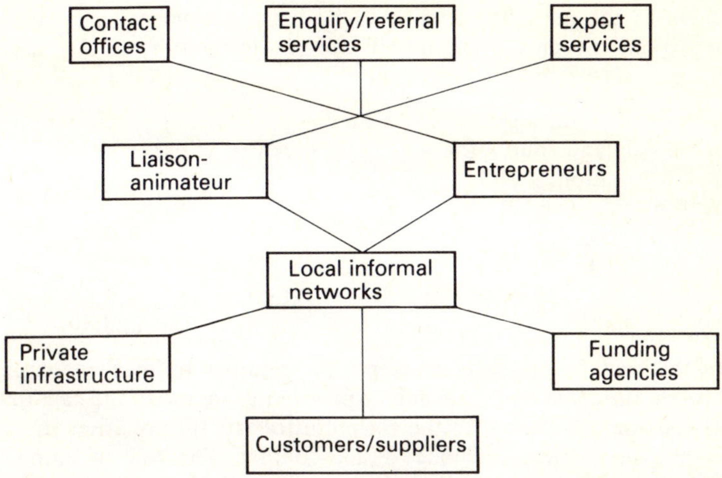

Figure 9.1 The innovation support network.

At the centre is the local network of entrepreneurs and the liaison-animateur, who is the main interface or switching centre between the government-funded infrastructure and the entrepreneur. Through him or animated by him, the individual entrepreneur is switched to the contact offices of universities and research institutes, to the experts of technological and sectoral institutes, to funding agencies and to the enquiry services. Other activities lead to interaction with the private infrastructure of consultants, banks, and so on, and to technology transfer between customers and suppliers on the one hand and the entrepreneur on the other.

The Liaison-Animateur

The first priority of an innovation programme is to establish a local or regional interface with the entrepreneur—a liaison-animateur. This activity is essential to the effective operation of the total network and to a system designed to deal with the actual needs of the entrepreneur. From this interface comes the feedback to the rest of the network indicating areas of need for expertise, applied or basic research.

The primary objective of the liaison-animateur is to animate the entrepreneur owner/manager of the smaller firm in order to encourage and assist him to adopt the best technical practice and to create innovative products. The chief means used in this process of animation is an active programme of visits to firms in the locality or region, seeking out the firms and establishing personal contact with the entrepreneurs. This personal contact is then maintained through further visits and other contacts to the point that, when faced with a problem or in need of information, the entrepreneur will automatically turn to the liaison-animateur.

- to assist the entrepreneur to define his problems or specific information needs and source the appropriate centre of expertise to provide the information;
- to respond directly with specific data or information to meet immediate needs;
- to encourage the use of expertise in consultancy and product development and investment in innovation by indicating sources of funding and possibly assisting in application for this funding.

As the visit programme develops, the number of specific enquiries increases. Time spent on these and on processing enquiries and calls for in-depth assistance referred to the formal infrastructure restricts the time available for visiting and face-to-face contact. The role of animation suffers. A solution is to have an information officer also working in the same office or to have a still wider operation which includes advice on business management and funding sources. Advice on funding can be a function of liaison-animateurs, in particular funding to support innovation-orientated activities. The ability directly to provide financial support for such activities can be a considerable stimulant in the work of the liaison-animateur. Such work can also be time consuming. The concept of the 'one-stop shop' has therefore been devised to provide a full co-ordinated service at a local level.

One-Stop Shops

The concept of the one-stop shop is to provide within one centre in a region or locality the full range of information and referral to information sources required by the entrepreneur. Within this concept, the liaison-animateur is one component, but the dynamic animating component. The one-stop shop provides him with full back-up in handling the day-to-day enquiries of entrepreneurs but also in providing a total service, looking after enquiries regarding funding and business management. Entrepreneurs have several overlapping needs for information.

- specific data and information to meet immediate decision-making needs;
- sourcing, and assistance in applying for, financial aids;
- internal business management information and financial control systems;
- in-depth technical inputs to raise the level of practice and to innovate at a more internationally competitive level, for which financial assistance may be required.

The one-stop shop should therefore have the following components:

- the liaison-animateur as the dynamic component;
- a fast response service to provide immediate data and information to meet urgent technical and techno-commercial problems on production, product development, sales, marketing and supply of materials, equipment and components;
- advice on business and financial management information systems, their design and installation;
- advice on sourcing of the appropriate financial aid in support of activities concerned with the adoption of the best technical practice and with development and marketing of innovative products.

The one-stop shop centre would therefore be staffed as follows:

- Liaison-animateur: function as previously described.
- Information specialist: his first function is to provide fast response to immediate data and information enquiries, either directly or by obtaining information from a more central enquiry service or source of expertise or by referring to such services and sources; the information specialist should also be concerned in processing other projects for entrepreneurs in research and other organisations as an assistance to the liaison-animateur; he would be responsible for interaction and use of national and international databases including videotex systems.

- Business management information system specialist to advise and assist entrepreneurs in the selection or design of management information and financial control systems and to advise on the selection of computer equipment and programmes.
- Secretarial staff of high calibre since they handle many enquiries and are first to handle all enquiries at the switchboard.

The business management specialist and the liaison-animateur would share the functioning of identifying the most appropriate source of funding and in assisting firms to apply for it. Where funding for innovative activities is decentralised, which ideally it should be, this funding should be under the direction of the liaison-animateur with business evaluation from the business specialist and final approval by a local committee which includes a representative of the central funding agency.

Enquiry Service

Whether a one-stop shop is provided or not, an essential service in support of the entrepreneur, the liaison-animateur and the information specialist in either the liaison office or the one-stop shop is an adequately staffed and resourced enquiry centre. The investment in such a centre is considerable in library, documentation, information technology and staff resources and can be justified only on the basis of a larger region of 3–5 million population and with between ten and twenty liaison-animateur or one-stop centres. Its functions are as follows:

- To provide specific data and directly usable information obtained or compiled from resources of the library and/or experts in other organisations in response to enquiries received directly from entrepreneurs or through local liaison-animateurs or information specialists. Enquiries are usually by phone. Urgent responses may need to be made by phone or by telex (which can be more exact) or other message-sending systems. The enquiries may be wide ranging covering technical data as such, sources of materials or equipment, standards, technical regulations, solutions to relatively straight forward problems. They will also cover all the technologies and industry sectors present and needed in the region.
- To provide documentation directly requested by an entrepreneur or by an intermediary, or documentation which may contain the response to an enquiry. Documentation contains the exact statement of a technical subject and is usually the only means of transferring this technical exactness.
- To provide state-of-the-art or in-depth surveys of a specific scientific, technological and competitive/commercial product area, including techno-commercial surveys and patent surveys. These and the following items are an essential support to innovation development and

to support of the commercial success of such developments through identification of the best technical practice to be adopted.

- To provide on-line literature and information searches. The centre is the main regional point to national and international databases and databanks which require intermediaries for efficient use. The output might go directly to the entrepreneur or as input to an information analyst compiling a state-of-the-art survey.
- To provide referral to specialists for advice and information to incorporate in a response or referral by placing the enquirer in contact with the source of expertise when the enquiry is highly specialised or requires consultancy, research or other detailed work.

Expert Services

Expert services provide the interface between applied research and technology centres, on the one hand, and industry especially smaller firms, on the other. They are consultants expert in a particular sectoral or pervasive technology. Their function is essentially communication and translation of the best current technical practice into practice within a firm and to ensure that the results of research, scientific investigation and laboratory testing are assimilated by the firm. The best current technical practice may be as identified and acquired from elsewhere by the research or technology centre or as developed through the applied research of the centre. This latter may have been carried out as a result of problems identified in industry. Other research or investigation may have been specific to the firms.

Such experts work mainly out of industrial research and technology centres but may also work from technology-orientated government laboratories. In the network presented here they have two roles:

- firstly, as interfaces between the liaison-animateur and his client entrepreneur, on the one hand, and the research centre, on the other, providing to the small firm the expertise of the research centre which might otherwise not be available to it;
- secondly, as liaison-animateurs themselves working with firms in the particular sector, animating them to adopt new or better practices, or working across sectors in pervasive technologies such as microelectronics.

In the first instance there is co-operation with the local liaison-animateur. In the second there should be. There are advantages in an expert from a research or technology centre adopting the role of an animateur. He has the ability to communicate new practices and to identify and define problems in the mainline technology of the firm. He is able to give on-the-spot advice and information and provide some immediate consultancy.

He can introduce new ideas and techniques. On the other hand, because he is a specialist in the mainline technology of the firm, he may not identify other problems or refer these to centres or sources other than the one out of which he is working. It is important therefore that in each locality, expert-animateurs work in close conjunction with liaison-animateurs. They have complementary roles.

Expert interfaces are best provided from national rather than regional resources or centres, due to the wide range of technologies on which information may be required and the need for in-depth research and other back-up to the transfer of expert know-how and current or new technical practice. On the other hand, in technologies which may pervade several or all industrial sectors such as information technology expert services are more optimally provided at the level of a region.

A major factor in the credibility of such experts and their parent centre or institutes in the eyes of the entrepreneur is their responsiveness and their willingness to provide service within a time frame which is realistic to the entrepreneur. This demands flexibility and an orientation to service rather than research.

Contact Offices

Universities and national research laboratories have traditionally tended to work only for large industrial organisations which also have their own research laboratories. Need for use by small firms is highly intermittent because university and national laboratory research is highly specialised. The needs therefore tend to be restricted to specialist areas of product development or consultancy or to specialist areas of higher technology. Polytechnics and technological universities tend to have more to offer small firms and to want a closer interaction with small but innovative or progressive industry. Nevertheless, it is very rare for there to be a continuing relationship between a small firm and a higher level research or education institution. Their primary task is not provision of service to small firms and entrepreneurs. They can also be very complex organisations.

Hence if they are to be part of the network of support to entrepreneurs and small firms, it is essential that there be a contact point or office within universities or national laboratories, a point to which the liaison-animateur or entrepreneur can refer. This contact office acts as a switching centre itself, identifying the expertise needed and establishing contact between the expertise and the entrepreneur. It can also act as a translator, assisting the entrepreneur to communicate with the university's researchers and to understand their communications.

Some contact offices may have other roles in the stimulation of closer university-industry relations. They may have a dynamic role, seeking out firms with whom to carry out research or seeking placement opportunities for their graduates. Such dynamic activity is beneficial if it is concentrated in the region of the university. It helps thereby to provide a more entrepreneurial and technological orientation to the university and helps in enriching the nutrient information flows in the region.

The Sub-Networks

Figure 9.2 illustrates the linkages between the liaison-animateur or one-stop shops and the wide range of institutions and activities of the formal infrastructure through the enquiry and information analysis centres, expert interfaces and contact offices. This is an ideal network which working ideally would best support the needs of the entrepreneur.

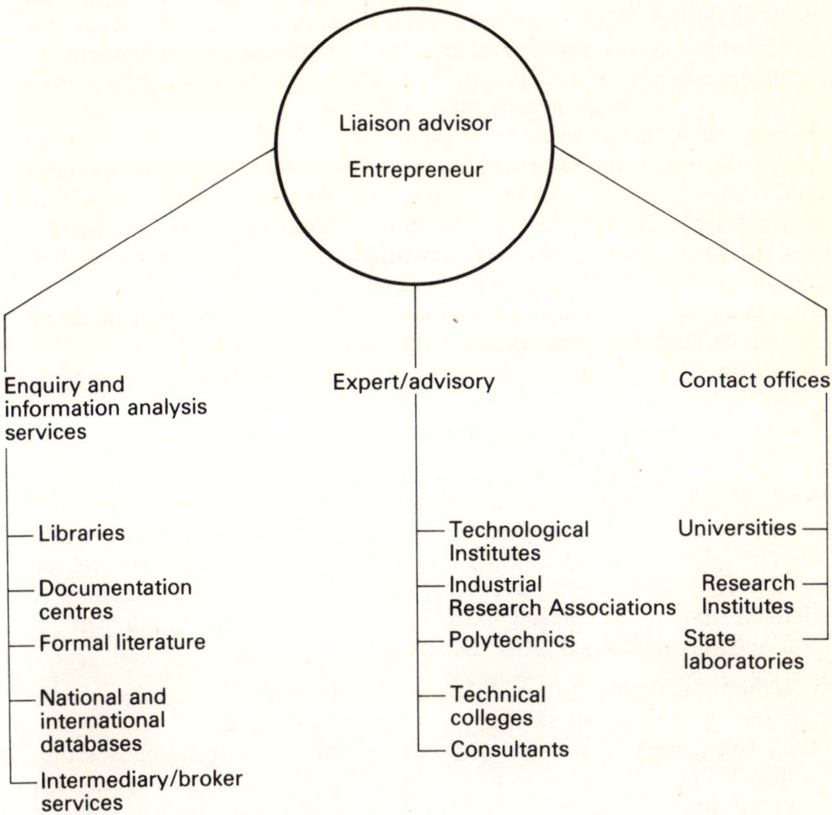

Figure 9.2 Access to formal services.

The greatest demand for service in numbers of demands is that placed on the enquiry centres even where an information desk has been established in a liaison office or one-stop shop. The most frequent and continuing need for the entrepreneur is for specific data and information for day-to-day decision-making and problem-solving. At a lower level of frequency is the demand for more in-depth but specific information, which may be the basis for an entrepreneur carrying out his own innovative development work or improvement in his processes and products. Much of the credibility of the local network lies within the enquiry services—it is day-to-day, immediate, urgent. Their responsiveness, efficiency and good service are very visible to the entrepreneur.

The next level of frequency of demand is for expert advice. This may in fact be provided on some occasions through the enquiry service. On other occasions, it may be direct to the enquirer but take the same format—advice over the telephone or by letter perhaps supplemented with documentation. More in-depth advice will require a visit and consultancy or research and development. Time will be required for implementation of the results. Use of such in-depth consultancy is therefore infrequent.

The enquiry service as illustrated in Figure 9.2 is the access point to a number of information and documentation activities and for the most part will remain the intermediary. Only rarely would an entrepreneur make direct contact with these. However, the enquiry service itself, in order to respond to the needs of the entrepreneur, must develop linkages and formal arrangements with major suppliers of documentation (such as the British Library Lending Divison), on-line host services (such as the European Space Agency or Lockheed Dialog USA), and with national resources, such as university libraries, where these exist.

Implementation of a Programme: the First Steps

As stated earlier the first priority of an innovation programme is to establish the interface and interaction with the entrepreneur. However, achieving credibility with the entrepreneur is of vital importance. If a first enquiry or contact fails to elicit an efficient and effective response, the total programme may fail. It is therefore important to have a number of elements in place at the start of the programme, even though they might not be highly developed or sophisticated:

- some central point to which enquiries for specific information can be referred—that is, the skeleton of an enquiry service;
- contact points in research institutes or universities informally established; that is professors or researchers have been identified who are committed to support of entrepreneurial ventures and to acting as contact points;

- decentralisation of funding for consultancy, research, prototype development, information search and other projects related to new ventures of entrepreneurs.

The key to success is the selection and training of the staff—good people can make even a poor structure work well. They will overcome institutional barriers and bureaucratic procedures.

Whether to set up liaison-animateur offices or full one-stop shops as from the beginning will to a considerable extent depend on the existing structure. Are there already a number of organisations each carrying out a single function such as information, funding, or research services? Are these decentralised, do they have local offices? Where there are separate functional organisations, each with local offices, then establishing a one-stop shop *ab initio* may be difficult. The function of the liaison-animateur in this case becomes more critical in directing the entrepreneur to the various sources of support. Where the various functional organisations exist only at a national level and where some may not exist at all, it is more feasible to commence with the objectives of establishing a 'one-stop shop'.

The core network interfacing directly with the entrepreneur, animating his entrepreneurial enterprise and meeting his day-to-day needs is the network of liaison-animateur offices or one-stop shops and the enquiry centres. The enquiry centres are very closely linked to the one-stop shops or liaison-animateur offices staffed with an information specialist (see below). This network ideally should be under one central management—it is critical that the local office can demand a fast response from the central facility and not have to negotiate or cajole.

This organisation can be a restructured or reformed existing organisation or a new one. It should be new in spirit since it has to have a dynamic animating role and a service-orientated role. Its mode of operation must be a highly decentralised one, the central management providing policy guidelines, stimulating the dynamism and providing central support activities such as database management.

The central organisation has also the very important functions of determining the needs in technological support services and in negotiating with government and other organisations to provide these. These needs are determined both by analysis of the enquiries received and projects undertaken as recorded in the main data file or database (see below) and by special surveys of needs of entrepreneurs by the liaison-animateurs.

The role of the central office in maintaining the animation role of liaison-animateurs can only be undertaken by having close and frequent contact and by having an interaction between the liaison-animateurs in which the centre is closely involved. They should be a network of interchange between themselves and not merely on behalf of the entrepreneur. They are lonely people. They can easily become isolated. It is important, therefore, that they have regular but short meetings at the central office, say one day every two months.

However, in a larger country many of the central office functions are better decentralised to the level of a major region or province. Numbers otherwise become too large and inhibiting bureaucratic procedures inevitably develop within a larger organisation.

Selection of Locations

The optimum population of SMEs to be served by a liaison-animateur is of the order of 400–500. Selection of a centre from which a liaison-animateur will operate is dependent first in the number of SMEs in a natural catchement area. A natural catchement area often reflects also the natural hub of informal spatial information networks. It may therefore be more effective to have two liaison-animateurs working from one office than arbitrarily to create two centres.

The actual office can be located as an independent unit in the 'high street' of the urban centre of the locality. Consideration should be given to location in a chamber of commerce, regional polytechnic or other centre but the decision must be influenced by the need to create the image as well as the reality of a new approach—location in an existing organisation might be self-defeating in this regard.

Selection of Staff

In any particular and in each locality selected as a centre for a liaison-animateur office, the innovation programme as a whole will depend for its effectiveness on the quality of the person selected. Selection criteria should emphasise the personal characteristics—easy to approach and talk to, good communicator, maturity—as well as including technological qualifications. Whilst industrial experience, particularly in smaller firms, is highly desirable, an academic with commitment to the personal skills may be an equally good liaison-animateur. The authority of qualifications and/or past experience is important to his role as the point to which entrepreneurs should automatically turn when in need.

Budget

The budget for a liaison office should err on the side of generosity. The salary should be such as to attract people of calibre, and the expense allowance should provide for an intensive visit programme to be maintained together with visits to information and research centres. Telecommunication, postage and photocopying costs will also be high.

Programme of Contact

Experience indicates that a liaison-animateur can maintain effective contact with about 200 firms in any one year. This number includes one group with whom there is relatively intensive contact. They tend to be more dynamic or progressive firms undergoing a period of change and requiring in-depth inputs. Such firms may be visited three or four times with phone contact between visits initiated by either the liaison-animateur or the entrepreneur. For such firms, the liaison-animateur is also in contact with sources of inputs—information, advice, testing, product development—first to establish the contact between the source and the entrepreneur and then in follow-up to ensure efficient and responsive processing of the problems. He also contacts the entrepreneur to ensure that there is effective understanding of the inputs, that is that there has been good communication and that there are no barriers to implementation.

An intermediate group requires less contact, two visits per year with occasional phone contact initiated by either the liaison-animateur or the entrepreneur. Such a group may consist of firms which are entering a period of change or emerging from it into a period of implementation. Their need for in-depth input has been satisfied or they are working towards such an input. The phone contact in particular is usually concerned with specific data and information required by the entrepreneur for day-to-day decision-making. Provision of such an enquiry service is a critical part of the function of a liaison-animateur, helping him to maintain contact but also demonstrating his credibility in meeting the actual problems of entrepreneurs.

A third group of firms will have a low-level of contact of one visit in a year with some subsequent phone contact. Some are firms with whom a first contact is being established. With others it is a matter of maintaining or refreshing a contact to explore the possibility of problems or to stimulate the development of new thinking.

There is a fourth group of entrepreneurs—those considering starting a new business. They are the element which provides the self-renewing vitality of a locality. They are, however, obviously unknown to the liaison-animateur, they are not listed in any directory and have no name or address. They must therefore initiate contact with the liaison-animateur. Reliance must be placed, therefore, on publicity through local events, newspapers and radio and most importantly on the local informal network so that start-up entrepreneurs will initiate the contact. They may require intensive help and counselling through to actual start-up and in the period following start-up. They can be a troublesome and demanding group and they may fail. In fact they probably will fail, most do. But theirs is a learning process, another time they will succeed. Support to them is an essential element in generating a conducive environment and in maintaining the vitality of a locality.

Through the visit programme and phone contacts, the liaison-animateur begins to enter the local informal network, but to enter it fully he must himself become a member of local business, golf or other clubs, social informal networks which overlap and reinforce the business and professional informal networks. Thus he reinforces his contact-making and extends the range of contacts, increasing the probability that he will be automatically turned to when there is a problem or information is required. And generating more opportunity for entrepreneur browsing.

Information Resources

To carry out an effective and efficient operation the basic requirements of the liaison-animateur's office are as follows:

- a good secretary who can not only manage the routines of the office itself and maintain records but can also handle enquiries coming in or check on progress of work passed to enquiry or other centres;
- telephone and telematics equipment such as computer and videotex terminals with which to access external databases, telefacsimile equipment mainly to receive urgently needed documentation and possibly a personal computer on which to compile local databases;
- a small library of directories and handbooks with which to make some immediate response to enquiries for specific data and information urgently required;
- databases, particularly of local industry.

The main data or file of the office is a record of all known SMEs in the locality giving basic information—address, name(s) of owner(s) and senior personnel, sector, product range, special capability, trade names, numbers of employees, etc. Each visit and contact, with note of enquiries and note of contacts with research and technological institutes, etc., should be recorded under each firm. This builds up a picture of the needs of entrepreneurs in the locality as well as providing a measure of the performance of the liaison animateur.

Ideally this record should now be kept on a personal computer and its contents periodically transferred to the parent organisation for further processing and analysis. Firstly, this creates a database of manufacturing industry, which itself can be used to stimulate trading between SMEs and between them and larger companies. Secondly, it provides the essential feedback on the actual demands of entrepreneurs and thus a basis for 'market research' on facilities or expertise which should be developed to meet growing needs.

Another important file is that of local information sources and expertise which can be used especially to provide a fast response to an enquiry or problem. Such a database is a reflection of the process of stimulating a responsive local environment, and it is part of the network of referral between liaison-animateurs. An entrepreneur in one locality may be assisted by expertise in another. Again the local files help to build up a regional and then a national file.

The construction of such databases is the responsibility of the national or regional organisations to which the liaison-animateur is attached. The software and structure, together with overall maintenance of the database, are most efficiently handled at national level, leaving the local liaison-animateur office with responsibility for inputting new or updated data. Other possible databases are noted later.

As the interaction between the liaison-animateur and local industries develops, the demand for information increases and hence the need to provide an 'information desk' manned by an information specialist. The function of this information specialist is to act as an expert intermediary in accessing remote databases, in maintaining local databases, in providing response to specific enquiries and in progressing enquiries referred elsewhere.

Undoubtedly the efficiency and depth of operation of a liaison-animateur office can be very substantially increased by the addition of an information desk. It is a step towards a one-stop shop.

Business Management

A further step is the addition of a business information system/financial management specialist so that the full span of expertise can be handled. Most small firms fail because of lack of financial control and a management information system. They need guidance through the maze of funding from both the public and private sectors. Provision of advice and referral to expertise or the appropriate source of funds is in fact a critical element in the information process. Whilst entrepreneurial investment in industrial innovation is the engine of economic growth, this investment succeeds only where there is good management control of finances. It can therefore be argued that the 'one-stop shop' is the minimum level of operation, if support is to be provided to meet the actual needs of entrepreneurs.

Enquiry Centre

As stated earlier, an enquiry centre is required at the level of a major region or province and should be located in the main centre of that province. To carry out its functions, it requires a very well-stocked library, extensive ranges of directories, handbooks and monographs and a fairly large number of technological journals and technical magazines, between 600 and 1,200, the majority foreign in less-developed countries.

It requires all the facilities to carry out in-depth literature searches, state-of-the-art and techno-commercial surveys.

However, it must have a service orientation—to exploit its information resources on behalf of the entrepreneur and provide him with the information he requires in whatever format. Its function, in other words, is the opposite of the traditional library function of conservation.

It is important therefore, that careful attention be given to the location of the enquiry centre and to its staffing. Where resources are limited it might seem to be good sense to locate it in a university or technical college library. In the longer term this may well be disastrous, unless highly motivated. The environment would otherwise not be conducive to what in itself should be a reflection, mirror image, of entrepreneurial enterprise, dynamic in service to customers.

Staff should have information specialist training but be focused on information analysis and provision rather than on systems. They should also have technological qualifications but tending to breadth rather than specialisation. Most enquiries will come by phone, will have to be discussed, interpreted and accepted immediately. They will cover virtually every aspect of technology. They will involve referral to expert or other sources, perhaps 35 per cent, quick reference (data, sources of materials and equipment, test methodology, etc.) perhaps 40 per cent, and more extended and in-depth search and survey, perhaps 25 per cent. A broad capability, together with the personal ability to discuss with a client the exact nature of the problem or enquiry, are the main characteristics required.

Organisation and Stimulation of the Network

The network and sub-networks described above are ideal networks. In most regions, innovative, progressive, technically cyclic or isolated, it is only in recent years if at all that liaison-animateur activities have been established. In very few regions are there effective enquiry centres. These represent the network as such and the new initiatives to be taken. But in all regions or countries there is an established university system and a national research system, even if, in peripheral and isolated regions, these are at a less intensive stage of development and have a lower technological orientation. Less-prosperous regions tend to have only a weak technological infrastructure of industrial technology institutions and industrial sectoral research organisations, co-operative or state.

There are, therefore, three main problems to be tackled, once the core network of liaison-animateur offices has been established together with at least embryonic regional enquiry centres.

- how to stimulate an existing infrastructure into new modes of behaviour;

- how to provide expert and technological services;
- how to stimulate the entrepreneur.

These problems have to be seen against the background that in developed and prosperous regions most information passes from firm to firm and adoption of the best technical practice and innovation takes place because of the technology pull of the larger progressive firms on their smaller clients. This technology pull, together with a demand for good service and appreciation of quality which permeate the environment, are part of the cumulative process by which new techniques, technologies and industries build on and replace old techniques, technologies and industries. Less developed and declining regions lack such pull and a quality environment. The innovation programme must therefore operate in such a way as to stimulate the cumulative process of creation of new activities and wealth through a responsive and more nutrient and quality-rich environment.

Stimulation of the Infrastructure

Any network needs amplifiers. Any product needs marketing to stimulate greater sales. Whichever analogy is used, the network described earlier will require continuing actions to promote its use and promote responsiveness in the existing scientific and technological establishment. The entrepreneur needs stimulation and encouragement and so does the academic scientist and technologist. The liaison-animateur needs means to influence both.

Funding

Funding is the primary mechanism. In one country, a liaison-animateur who was attached to a technological institute which charged fees found a much warmer welcome in industrial firms when he changed jobs to a grant-giving development agency. Funding is the carrot which encourages the entrepreneur to take a step forward and animates him to take a risk. It is a means of motivating the scientist or engineer or technical school teacher to carry out development work or give advice or information. For the funding system to be an effective instrument of animating or motivating the academic it must be within the control of the liaison-animateur. The fund must therefore be decentralised, the decision-making as to allocation to specific projects being taken at a local level. The types of funding which in various countries have proved useful include the following:

- R & D or product and process development grants: payment of, say, 50 per cent of the cost of research, whether carried out within the firm or in a technological centre or university.

- Design grants: similar to above for industrial or graphic or similar design.
- Market research: payment of travel or other costs involved in carrying out market research for a new product.
- Free consultancy: payment of up to five days' consultancy for a small firm from mainly expert services including university or technical school experts.
- Graduate placement: subsidised salary of a graduate in a small firm which has not previously employed a graduate and has non-routine process or product development work for such a graduate. This is an effective way of raising the level of skills within a firm and of giving a stronger capability to communicate with the scientific and technological infrastructure—to identify, define, and articulate its problems and needs.
- Research graduate: subsidy to the salary of a postgraduate researcher in a university provided the research project is being carried out for a smaller firm.

Grants for research or product development are in some countries administered as loans repayable on advantageous terms if the product is successfully commercialised.

Motivation of universities or relatively academic research organisations can be further developed by earmarked funding for the establishment of contact or industrial liaison offices. The functions of these can include:

- placement of graduates in local industry;
- promotion of research projects by larger firms;
- point of contact for smaller firms and entrepreneurs;
- promotion of research, product development and consultancy for smaller firms.

All these tasks enhance the environment for and responsiveness to an entrepreneur seeking information and solutions to his problems.

Technological Support

A major problem in less developed prosperous countries or regions lies in the absence or weakness of industrial technology institutions whether national, sectoral or industrial co-operative organisations. Expert services and their back-up in testing, laboratory investigation and applied research cannot be developed overnight, yet they are critically necessary. Any industrial firm requires a range of inputs from several technologies and from different sources. A fish-processing and canning plant may require inputs on bacteriological quality control, energy utilisation (heating and freezing), effluent and waste treatment and disposal, plant layout, machinery adaptation and design, automation, electronic controls, pneumatics, in addition to product development—new types of presentation, sauces, and so on. Some products may have to be certified as conforming to technical regulations of the firm's home country or of countries to which it exports. These are some of the technical inputs it requires. If the firm is to become internationally competitive, that is, compete with products from progressive industrialised regions and countries, whether on domestic or foreign markets, then it requires these inputs to be at the level of the best technical practice. There are three main requirements:

- expert information, advice and consultancy;
- testing and laboratory investigation, including testing as to conformity to national and international standards;
- product development.

As the innovation programme begins, reliance must at first be placed on developing what is virtually an *ad hoc* group of experts, people in universities, polytechnics and technical schools who are willing and committed to giving advice and assistance. Government can help by allowing staff of such institutions to engage in such work and earn additional income. One method is for the fees earned to be shared between the institution and the staff member or to be tax-free. Governments can stimulate this activity further by giving special grants for equipment to be used for work for SMEs and in particular by having a scheme of approval of laboratories for testing to national and international standards.

In addition, the organisation responsible for the liaison-animateur offices can enter into agreements with sectoral and industrial research organisations of industrialised and developed countries. In this way, specialised information services and expert services become immediately available at a progressive and best technical practice level.

Clubs

Whilst much of the network and mechanisms described so far are concerned with raising the stock of knowledge within the firm and with shortening the cycle time between need and supply of logistic information, a major task of the liaison-animateur is the enrichment of the flow of nutrient information. Creating an awareness of the best technical practice and of new technological and other developments which might lead to innovative ideas will happen to some extent where an entrepreneur engages in a consultancy or product development project with a university or other institute, but there is need to increase the diversity and range of information flowing. Most information will continue to pass between entrepreneurs themselves and their professional friends. The enrichment of the flow depends on linking this informal network to external sources of information but in an informal and personal way through 'clubs'.

The term 'club' is used here for a variety of activities in which groups of people are brought together to stimulate personal contact and flow of information. For the most part, they are directed to stimulating awareness and ideas, the nutrient information flow, but they may also provide access to specific information for problem solving. Some may result in the creation of a further nodal point for access into the formal information infrastructure (as has happened in the innovation workshops in France).

Such group activities should involve not more than 20 people, the maximum for dynamic interchange. They are modes of increasing information-intensive contact between entrepreneurs, between entrepreneurs and larger firms, between entrepreneurs and experts and researchers in universities, government laboratories and technological centres:

- Innovation workshops: prototype development and start-up workshops or small start-up premises with common workshops and other facilities with a business manager or engineer-adviser who in practice becomes a node in the network.
- Research groups: groups or researchers from university, government and other research centres together with entrepreneurs or their technical managers. The objective is to promote interaction, communication of advanced activities and identification of problems, often apparently low-technology, to which more advanced technology can be applied.
- Technology groups: much the same as the above but with applied research and technological institutes.
- Dynamic groups: the above research and technology groups can be organised on an informal *ad hoc* basis between entrepreneurs in a locality and a specialist research group, perhaps of a seemingly unrelated high-technology nature. Such groups are based on the concepts of group dynamics and are led by someone experienced in group dynamics. The objective is to promote a clash of needs and expertise which will lead to innovative ideas and a more in-depth interaction between the researchers and the entrepreneurs.
- Inter-firm groups: these are organised to bring together the managers of larger and smaller firms; to promote group visits to firms and interaction between larger and smaller firms which will lead to transfer of techniques including through temporary loan of staff.
- Overseas study groups: visits to overseas industrial exhibitions led by the liaison-animateur with visits to more progressive firms in the same sector in the host country.

- Seminars and workshops presented by experts in a specific new technology or technique, providing at least sufficient information for a decision to adopt the technique and manage its introduction.

Technology Pull

Technology pull in innovative and progressive regions is exerted predominantly by larger but technically progressive firms, customers for the equipment, components and materials produced by the small firms. This is obviously difficult to develop within declining or technically isolated regions, which may have few or no such progressive companies. It is important, therefore, that opportunities be created to bring about some technology pull from inside and outside the region. An important area is that of public procurement. Two actions can be taken:

- to upgrade specifications and to make purchase conditional on a certified quality assurance system being in operation in the firm;
- decentralisation of decision-making so that regional requirements are supplied from regional sources and by smaller firms.

Another area is the encouragement of product licensing or know-how agreements with small firms in other regions but particularly in other and more advanced countries or regions. Product licensing is engaged in by a large proportion of smaller firms in progressive regions, between 25 and 30 per cent in some sectors, and can be an important mode of acquisition of technical practice as well as a new product. Arrangement of marriages between two firms is a lengthy and difficult process. It starts with the liaison-animateur identifying firms in his locality capable of entering into such an arrangement with success, and through formal and informal search in foreign countries identify potential products and small firms willing to enter into arrangements with firms in other countries. A process of marriage can then begin, aided by an intermediary, expert in such matters. The difficulties should not be underestimated but the benefits in technology transfer and in adoption of an improved level of technical practice can have a wider effect than the specific firms. This wider effect should also be nourished through clubs and other devices which enrich the flow of nutrient information.

Embassies and export promotion agencies can be brought in as active partners in a programme to generate a technology pull on small entrepreneurial and potentially innovative firms. Identification of high-calibre importing agents, wholesalers and retailers as well as of actual opportunities for specific products can give not only a good market orientation but lead to working to product specifications of a high standard. Marks and Spencer has set a pre-eminent example of the influence of a retailer which sets a high standard and thereby exerts a strong technology pull.

Databases

Some of the activities of the liaison-animateur and his information and business advisory colleagues in a one-stop shop can be supported by creating databases (or directories). Reference has already been made to databases of industrial firms and local expertise and that databases should be nationally rather than locally managed.

Any databases developed should reflect an activity initiated in the locality or between two or more localities. Interaction between firms and between firms and the infrastructure at a more local level stimulates further information flow and therefore develops technical practices and supports innovation. Such databases can include:

- Expertise: sources of expertise—names of specialists and contact points in universities, research centres, technological institutes and other organisations.
- Testing and analysis equipment: lists of specialist testing, analysis and other laboratory equipment available in industry, research or educational establishments in a locality or region together with a note of capability to test national or international standards and a note of terms under which available.
- Skill sharing: a listing of the skilled employees of firms who might be made available to other firms whose requirements for such skills are intermittent. Such skills can be both in management and production techniques, for example in design of a production-cost control system or software for this or in specialist welding skills.
- Product licences, joint venture opportunities: such databases, whilst useful, require expert intermediaries and a close relationship between the liaison-animateur and the prospective adopting firm.
- Export opportunities: compiled by export promotion agencies or embassy commercial sections, these also need an expert intermediary.
- Distribution opportunities: offers within a country for distribution—transport, wholesalers and retailers. Such a database can be useful in overcoming high costs of distribution for a new firm or new product.
- Financial aids: the various grants, loans, subsidies and tax or other concessions together with the local point of contact for further information.

The primary objective is to make matches between the entrepreneur, on the one hand, and, on the other, the solution to problems or opportunities for further development by promoting direct personal contact.

Postscript

With imagination, other actions and programmes can be developed which provide a social and technological environment conducive to entrepreneurial and innovative development in a region and which will enhance the cumulative process of information flow and creation of new economic activities. The ideal economic and industrial structure would seem to be a molecular one. It is a structure of small independent units linked and networking with decentralised autonomous units of large organisations, government and private. In such molecular societies, economic prosperity seems to be more maintained and renewed.

Large and centralised firms appear to have a limited life as innovating and entrepreneurial units creating new economic activities. When they become decentralised and progressive smaller units, they are able to stimulate innovation in others for their own advantage. Since it is virtually impossible in capitalist or even mixed economy systems to bring about such a change from outside in large and bureaucratic organisations, the optimum approach can only be to focus on the potential dynamism of the entrepreneur and the small-firms sector which is his seedbed in his own locality.

Nevertheless, there does remain that critical and crucial question of how to generate a technology pull from progressive customers in localities and regions where these do not at present exist. Other issues have also been raised. The role of the education and training system, together with the enhancement of traditional expertise, are key factors in developing a technical culture within which the best practice is more readily adopted and new products developed. The role of government and of decentralisation of government administrative decision-making is another key factor whether in relation to subsidies, specification and purchasing or in management of the quality of its many activities. These and other issues are being examined by others or need further explanation.

Index